STATISTICS FOR K-8 EDUCATORS

This book offers an introduction to descriptive and inferential statistics tailored to the teaching and research needs of K-8 educators. Using statistics to tell a story, veteran teacher educator Robert Rosenfeld pushes readers away from simply performing a calculation to truly understanding the statistical concepts themselves. In addition to helping educators develop this statistical habit of mind, Rosenfeld also focuses on developing an understanding of the statistics in published research and on interpreting school data, which can be applied in school assessment and educational research.

Features of this must-read resource include:

- Numerous exercises and activities throughout that are related specifically to the world of educators and are designed to foster conversation and small group discussion.
- Connections drawn between statistics and the regular mathematics curriculum to aid teachers who do classroom-based action research.
- A section covering the basic concepts of standardized tests, such as summative versus formative assessment, and standards-based versus norm-referenced tests.

Accessibly written and conversational in tone, *Statistics for K-8 Educators* provides the technical foundation to help teachers make good sense of quantitative information connected to their classrooms and to their schools.

Robert Rosenfeld is Co-Director for Statistics and School-Based Research at the Vermont Mathematics Initiative, University of Vermont, and Professor Emeritus of Mathematics and Statistics at Nassau Community College.

STATISTICS FOR K-8 EDUCATORS

Robert Rosenfeld

Routledge
Taylor & Francis Group

NEW YORK AND LONDON

First published 2013
by Routledge
711 Third Avenue, New York, NY 10017

Simultaneously published in the UK
by Routledge
2 Park Square, Milton Park, Abingdon, Oxon OX14 4RN

Routledge is an imprint of the Taylor & Francis Group, an informa business

Library of Congress Cataloging in Publication Data
  Rosenfeld, Robert.
  Statistics for K-8 educators / by Robert Rosenfeld.
  p. cm.
  Includes bibliographical references and index.
  1. Mathematical statistics—Study and teaching (Elementary)
  2. Mathematics—Graphic methods—Study and teaching (Elementary) I. Title.
  QA276.18.R67 2012
  372.79—dc23
  2011046364

ISBN: 978-0-415-89988-8 (hbk)
ISBN: 978-0-415-89989-5 (pbk)
ISBN: 978-0-203-15574-5 (ebk)

Typeset in Bembo
by Swales & Willis Ltd, Exeter, Devon

Certified Sourcing
www.sfiprogram.org
SFI-00453

Printed and bound in the United States of America
by Edwards Brothers, Inc.

For Bob Laird and Judi Laird

CONTENTS

PREFACE

This statistics text is based on class notes that were originally developed within the context of a larger professional development program intended to increase K-8 educators' content knowledge in mathematics. The overall program, the Vermont Mathematics Initiative (VMI), also aims to increase the number of teacher leaders in the state, with a long-term goal to make professional development in mathematics self-sustaining and teacher-based within districts.

Over a three-year period, in addition to receiving substantial support in pedagogy and leadership skills, VMI participating teachers take a total of 12 courses covering mathematics from arithmetic to calculus. Three of the courses focus on concepts of statistics and educational research, and these notes provide the relevant explanations and exercises. In addition to helping participants master the basic concepts of statistics in the K-8 curriculum we also provide opportunities for our participating teachers to present and interpret school data to administrators and to do small action research projects that bring a more critical eye to some aspect of their own teaching. As a result, these notes contain some topics not always found in an introductory statistics course, especially topics useful in reading published research articles and in interpreting the results of standardized tests. The over-arching goal is to develop a statistical habit of mind.

The title of the book refers to K-8 educators because teachers, math specialists, and curriculum experts at those grades have been our primary participants, but we have seen increasing numbers of secondary teachers as well as the occasional principal decide to join VMI. Increased confidence in statistical thinking has proved beneficial at all these levels.

The following three points sum up very quickly why we consider statistics to be an essential component of a teacher's knowledge of mathematics:

1. **Statistics is part of mathematics.**

   State and national mathematics standards include topics in statistics.
   It is empowering to see the connections of statistics to other areas of math, including arithmetic, geometry, algebra, and probability.

2. **Statistics plays an essential role in assessment.**

   Statistics is used to describe classroom performance.
   Statistics is used to describe the results of state-wide standardized tests.
   Statistics is used in the evaluation of effective teaching in so-called "value added" analyses.

3. **Statistics often is a significant component of educational research.**

   Statistics may be used to describe the results of action research projects.
   Familiarity with statistical tools helps a reader understand and interpret published formal research.

Organization of the Book

The topics of statistics may be divided into two broad sections, **descriptive statistics** and **inferential statistics**, as depicted below. This is an arbitrary but convenient way to think about the material for a sequence of topics in statistics, and it serves as the organizing principle of the book.

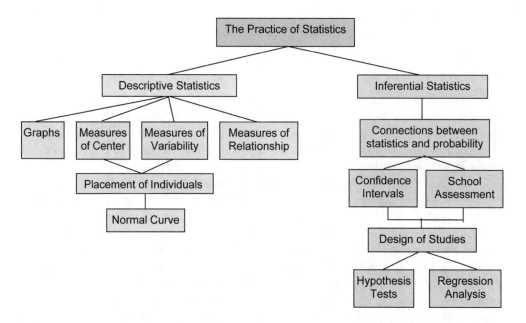

In descriptive statistics we emphasize how to summarize data using tables, graphs, and specific summary numbers such as means or percentages. We might determine, for example, that the mean test score is 72.4 for our 4th grade girls and 71.9 for our 4th grade boys. We conclude with certainty that the mean test score for *these* girls is higher than the mean for *these* boys.

In inferential statistics we generalize from the people in our study to some larger group they reasonably represent. Because this generalization involves people we have never seen and on whom we have no data, we must give up certainty and use probability. We might conclude from the data above that *district-wide* there is *probably* not very much difference between the mean scores for boys and girls on this test. The tools of inferential statistics are used to estimate the risk we take of being wrong when we generalize.

You can certainly read this book by yourself to learn the basic concepts of statistics. The experience, though, will be enhanced by working in a group situation with ample time to exchange opinions and shared insights. Most chapters start with an introductory activity or investigation to present the issues dealt with in the chapter. This offers the instructor and the students a chance to see what people already know and to focus the learning. Each basic topic then has explanatory material followed by an exercise set. Many of the exercise sets are followed by an extra exercise section called "Math extensions" or Math connections," which suggest connections to arithmetic, algebra, or geometry or involve higher-level math skills.

Chapters 1 through 8 include the topics you expect to see in a basic text on descriptive statistics. For some pre-service and in-service programs these chapters alone may provide sufficient material. The later chapters concern issues of inference, particularly in connection to assessment of students and schools. Overall, the earlier chapters of the book tend to have more exercises than the later ones do. The later topics on inference, assessment, and design of research studies provide more illustrations and commentary. Though there are fewer exercises in the later chapters they are designed to provide opportunities for discussion.

We have found that many of our participants go through a "mind shift" when they move from a familiar style of math course, such as algebra, to a statistics course. Typically, in the other professional development math courses, a given problem has one or more correct solutions, and you frequently discuss a variety of approaches to finding these solutions. You may discuss common student misconceptions related to the problem. In a so-called "story problem" the story is given in the problem. A desirable and practically guaranteed result of working in these math courses is that you become more flexible and confident in your approach to problem solving.

In the statistics courses, you are generally not given a story in the same way. Rather, the emphasis shifts to looking at data from which *you decide* what story they tell. You are not so much finding the solution of a mathematics problem as deciding what conclusions you can reasonably draw from a given set of data. The tools of statistics help you tell your story effectively and justify your conclusions. It is often the case that you cannot be certain of your interpretation, but that you can say why your interpretation makes sense and is very likely correct. A common result of studying statistics is that you become much more critical of published reports and much more aware of what is missing from the evidence.

ACKNOWLEDGMENTS

Many colleagues and students played a role in improving this work over the past ten years. How can it be that a paragraph or exercise that seemed so clear and brilliant was, in fact, incomprehensible? So my gratitude goes to all of you for your contributions to the clarity of the text—the remaining errors and murky bits are all mine. Thanks to Kate Morrow for checking almost all of the exercises, to Douglas Dickey, Sheila Weaver, John Tapper, and Kiran MacCormick for suggestions, as they have taught from the notes over the recent years, and to Beth Gambler, Jim Wright, and Julie Theoret for ideas they mentioned years ago and have no doubt forgotten by now.

Even though they had nothing at all to do directly with the words in this text, the support and encouragement of colleagues Susan Ojala, Wayne Harner, and Bill Jesdale were indispensable to my completing the project of turning the original notes into a book. A special thank-you goes to Ken Gross, who originally invited me to teach at the Vermont Mathematics Initiative soon after it was created under his guidance. Ken assembled a wonderful and supportive faculty and staff, whose friendship I have treasured all these years. For keeping my VMI head on straight in every way, and particularly for making sure that the correct notes got to the students and professors on time, I thank Kathy Lamphier.

This book and the courses for which it was developed would not exist without the work of Bob Laird and Judi Laird. They are master teachers and have both co-taught the courses with me and with other mathematicians many times. They are the colleagues who know best and show best the connections between this material and the lives of school teachers. Building on some original ideas of Regina Quinn, they have designed the courses and all the supplementary activities and assignments directed to developing teacher leaders who are comfortable with the language and tools of statistics. It has been a privilege to develop these notes as part of this enterprise.

1

SHAPES OF DISTRIBUTIONS

If real life worked like the artificial world of typical math problems we wouldn't need a course in statistics.

For example, a typical math problem may start something like this: "It takes an electrician two hours to do a job." Well, sure. Maybe once it did. But the next time she did it maybe it took two hours and ten minutes. There's a good chance that if she did this same job 20 times each one took a different amount of time. And what, really, does it even mean to do the "same" job again? When a statistician looks at the world he or she sees *variability*. A major function of statistics is to help us make sense of data that is variable. Is there some basic pattern or "truth" lurking within this variability? How can we say what it is?

The first task we take up is how to summarize and describe a set of variable data. That is the basic job of **descriptive statistics**.

We can divide descriptive statistics into tools for describing entire sets of numbers, and tools for describing the placement of individual values within a set.

To describe a whole set of numbers (in statistics also called a **distribution** of numbers) we usually do several things:

- We say something about the overall *shape* of the distribution. Mainly we describe whether or not it is symmetrical around a central value or if there is something peculiar about the shape. We try to make the shape apparent by using appropriate graphs.
- We give one value that is supposed to indicate what is *typical* or usual in this data set. Familiar examples of such statistics include the mean and the median, which give you a rough idea of the magnitude or typical "size" of the numbers in a data set.
- We describe the amount of *variability* in the list of numbers. Are the numbers pretty much the same or are they quite scattered? Statisticians quantify variability using measures such as the range and the standard deviation.

We may also describe how two sets of numbers, such as family wealth and SAT scores, are related. This is the topic of correlation and it is associated with graphs called scatter plots. A special statistic called the correlation coefficient is used to help measure such a relationship.

To describe the position of a single value within a set of numbers we often choose one of these approaches:

- We give its absolute position ("2nd out of 12").
- We give its relative position ("in the top quarter," "at the 90th percentile").
- We compare it to the average ("5 points above the average").

Organizing and Graphing Data to See the Shape of a Distribution

Using Tables to Organize Data

You may have already collected data in a few activities and have had to decide how to organize it. Here is a brief collection of typical organization schemes.

Simple Data Table

Table 1.1 is a simple listing of the times it took students in a certain class to learn Topic A. The data have been organized by putting the variable of interest (days) in numerical order. The student labels serve to make it easy to refer to specific children.

TABLE 1.1 Data in order from smallest to largest observed value

Days to achieve mastery of Topic A

Student ID	1	2	3	4	5	6	7	8	9	10	11	12	13	14	15	16	17
Days	5	6	6	7	7	7	8	8	8	8	9	9	9	9	9	10	10

Student ID	18	19	20	21	22	23	24	25	26	27	28	29	30
Days	10	10	10	11	11	11	11	12	12	12	13	13	14

Exercise on a Simple Data Table

1. What is the average of the numbers in the row labeled "Days"? Does this average have a useful interpretation? What about the average in the row labeled "Student ID"?

Frequency Table

Table 1.2 is called a **frequency table** because the entries are counts or frequencies. For example, the first line of values implies that three of the students took seven days to master Topic B.

TABLE 1.2 A frequency table

Days to achieve mastery of Topic B

Days	Number of students
7	3
8	7
9	3
13	2
15	1
17	1
21	1
23	1
24	1

Exercises for Frequency Tables

1. a. The second row of numbers in Table 1.2 consists of an 8 and a 7. What do these two numbers tell you?

    b. What is the sum of the numbers in the column labeled "Number of students"? Does this sum have a useful interpretation?

    c. What is the average of the numbers in the column labeled "Number of Students"? Does this average have a useful interpretation?

2. Convert the Topic A data in Table 1.1 into a frequency table. What information is gained or lost when you present the data this way?

Spreadsheet Table

Many computer programs that do statistical computations expect the data to be entered in spreadsheet format with *one row per person*. Figure 1.1 is a small example produced by the statistical program called Minitab©.

Exercise for Spreadsheet Tables

1. a. What might be the purpose of the entries in column C4?

    b. What system was used to create the student IDs?

    c. How many female students were there in teacher 2's class?

→	C1	C2-T	C3	C4
	Student ID	Gender	Test Score	Teacher Code
1	101	m	80	1
2	102	m	65	1
3	103	f	78	1
4	104	m	57	1
5	105	f	82	1
6	201	f	76	2
7	202	m	90	2
8	203	f	55	2
9	204	m	58	2
10	205	f	81	2
11				

FIGURE 1.1 A spreadsheet data table

Introductory Question about Shape

Starting Salaries for Lawyers

NALP, an organization devoted to the professional development of law students and lawyers, each year conducts a survey to find starting salaries for people just out of law school. For the graduating class of 2008, NALP collected data for 22,000 salaries. For this group they found that the median starting salary was $72,000. The minimum and maximum salaries were about $15,000 and $200,000 respectively.

Based on this information, describe how you think the salaries might be distributed among the lawyers. For example, name some salary ranges that might cover large percentages or small percentages of the lawyers. Then sketch a graph that you think might reasonably picture the distribution you described for these 22,000 salaries.

Figure 1.2 is the graph as shown on the NALP website, based on the salaries reported in their survey. Does it match pretty well to your guess? Can you explain why your guess was either excellent or poor?

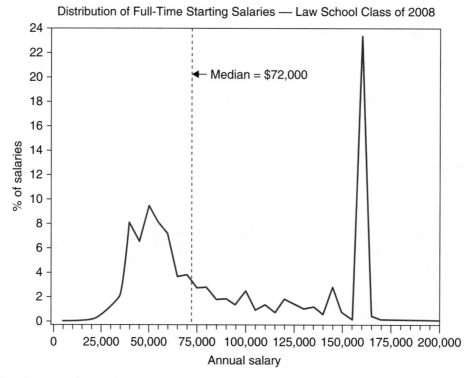

Distribution of Full-Time Starting Salaries — Law School Class of 2008

FIGURE 1.2 Salaries for lawyers

Source: www.nalp.org/apictureworth1000words. Graph reproduced with permission by NALP.

Note: n = 22,665 salaries.

The moral of this little exercise:

It is extremely risky to come to any conclusions about a set of data without first seeing a picture.

Using Graphs to Describe Data Sets

Statistical Variables

Roughly speaking, a **variable** is some characteristic of a group of subjects that may vary from one subject to another. In many statistical graphs the variable provides the label for the horizontal axis. In Figure 1.3 below, the variable is "Number of Days to Master Topic A." In this case, different people took different amounts of time to master the topic. We recorded these times as *numbers* that measure how long something took, so we say that "number of days to master Topic A" is a **numerical** or **quantitative variable**. If our variable had been eye color, we would have recorded labels such as "blue" or "brown" for each person, not a numerical measure of something. We say that eye color is a **categorical** or **qualitative variable**, because the labels describe some non-quantitative quality of a subject.

In spreadsheet format the column headings name the variables in the study. In Figure 1.1 above, there are ten subjects and four variables. Test Score is a quantitative variable, and Gender is clearly a categorical variable, but so are ID and Teacher Code. ID and Teacher Code are categorical because the numerals used do not have any quantitative meaning—they are just labels; they could just as easily have been names or initials.

The nature of a statistical variable, numerical or categorical, determines the types of calculations and graphs that are appropriate.

Dot Plot

The dot plot is perhaps the simplest graph appropriate for recording the frequency of *every possible individual value* of a numerical variable. A dot plot allows us to see the overall shape of the distribution of values for the variable.

Figure 1.3 is a dot plot for the data in Table 1.1 on time to learn Topic A, which was shown earlier.

FIGURE 1.3 Dot plot

The number of dots at each given number represents the frequency with which that number appears in the data set. Essentially, the dot plot is a visualization of a frequency table. In Figure 1.3, because these dots form a symmetric pattern, we say that these data have a **symmetric distribution**.

Note: The names given to various kinds of statistical graphs are not perfectly agreed on. You may find that someone uses a name for a graph that is different from the one you are familiar with. This lack of standardized terminology exists because statistics is a relatively new science, and contributors from various fields of work may make up different names for the same thing.

Histogram

The histogram is a kind of extension of a dot plot. Histograms are used *only* for numerical variables that can be put in increasing numerical order. In a histogram we often collect values into consecutive intervals (like 5–6, 7–8, 9–10, etc.). Almost always, the bars in a histogram are shown touching to remind you that the value axis is a continuously increasing numerical scale. Sometimes the internal vertical bar boundaries are not shown.

The vertical axis in a histogram refers to *frequency*, either direct counts or percentages. A histogram, like a dot plot, is a visualization of a frequency table, but geometrically a histogram allows us to see frequencies as *areas*. The area of a bar in a histogram is proportional to the count for that interval. A bar with twice the area represents twice as many data points.

When we look later at the connections between statistics and probability we will often represent probabilities as areas. In that context we may draw some histograms purely on the basis of probability calculations, rather than by collecting data.

Figure 1.4 is a histogram for the data in Table 1.1 on time to learn Topic A. The **interval width** for this histogram is 2, because the distance from the lowest value of one bar to the lowest value of the next bar is 2 units. In some software the individual intervals are called **bins**, and this distance is called the **bin width**. Usually, all the intervals in a histogram are the same width. (This simplifies the comparison of areas.)

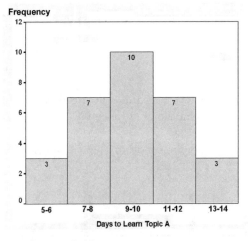

Frequency table for the data grouped into intervals of width 2

Interval	Frequency
5–6	3
7–8	7
9–10	10
11–12	7
13–14	3

FIGURE 1.4 Symmetric histogram

Figure 1.5 is a histogram for the Topic B data in Table 1.2. It is a histogram even though the values have not been grouped. The interval or bin width is 1 unit. This distribution is clearly not symmetrical. A distribution with a long tail on one side is called *skewed*.

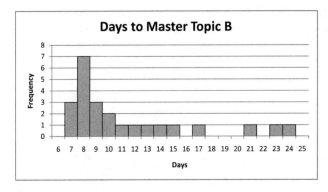

Figure 1.5 is a **skewed histogram**. It is skewed *to the right* because the long tail is on the right. Skewed to the right means *stretched* to the right. We also say that the distribution of the data values themselves is right-skewed or positive-skewed.

FIGURE 1.5 Skewed histogram

Because the variable represented in a histogram is a continuous numerical variable, such as time, theoretically we could measure it as precisely as we wish. In any actual research, precision is limited by the nature of the measuring instrument. In Figure 1.5, we recorded time to the nearest whole day, but the bar over 8 days can be interpreted to represent any time from 7.5 to 8.5 days.

Bar Chart

What is the difference between a histogram and a bar chart? This is a bit like asking what is the difference between an apple and a piece of fruit.

When you talk about the way a graph *looks*, both a bar graph and a histogram are made of bars. So you can say that a histogram is a particular kind of bar graph. But in terms of when they are used, there is a crucial difference.

In a histogram the variable on the **scale axis** (usually the horizontal axis) *must* be an increasing numerical variable whose values have a legitimate quantitative meaning. We call the axis then a **value axis**. The other axis (the frequency axis) gives you the count or the percentage corresponding to each interval.

In a bar graph, the scale axis is not restricted to numerical variables; the order in which the bars appear may be arbitrary. For instance, you can have the names of political parties or colors or cars on the horizontal axis, which is then called a **category axis**. The vertical axis counts the number or percentage of the data in the various categories. Figure 1.6 shows two different choices for ordering the bars in a bar graph. (What are those choices?)

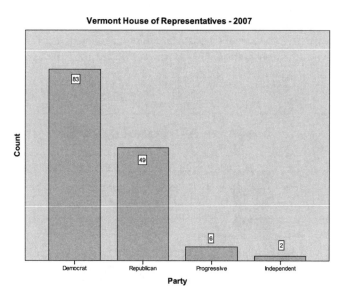

FIGURE 1.6a and b Two bar graphs for the same data. The second one is called a Pareto graph because the bars are in order by size

Note: In either a bar graph or a histogram the bars can touch or not touch. But, *usually,* in a bar graph they do not touch and in a histogram they do touch. Touching or not touching is *not* the important distinction for statisticians. The important distinction is the nature of the variable on the scale axis.

The final word: The name of the graph is not as important as the need for the graph to represent the data sensibly.

Pie Chart

Generally speaking, pie charts show the same information as bar charts. Like bar charts they are appropriate for categorical data. Figure 1.7 shows the same information as Figure 1.6. Note, too, that this information is easily given in a simple table.

Pie charts tend not to be used in formal research. One reason is that it can be difficult to compare slices that are similar in size. You see them mainly in the popular press. They communicate relative size nicely for large slices, but less so for small ones.

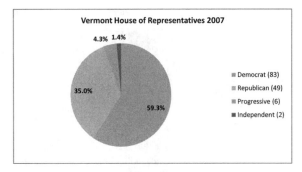

FIGURE 1.7 Pie chart with the same data as the bar graphs in Figure 1.6

Exercises about Graphs

1. Redraw Figure 1.5, using intervals of width 2, starting with the 7–8 interval. Can you still see the skewness? What happens if you use intervals of width 5? 10? 20? All the choices are "correct," but some convey a clearer story of what is going on.
2. Describe how we have changed the horizontal axis on this alteration of Figure 1.5. Do you think this change affects the story of the data in some way? Do you think this approach is a good idea?

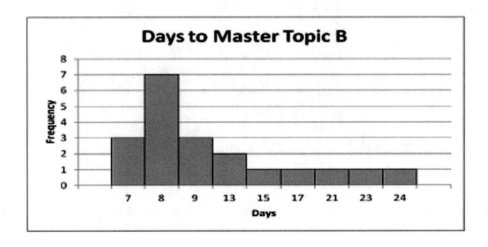

3. Complete this frequency table for the Topic A data in Table 1.1. Draw a histogram using the percentages column (instead of the frequency column), but keep the same intervals that were used in Figure 1.4. Compare the shape of this new histogram to the original one in Figure 1.4.

    Terminology: The number of people in a category is called the frequency for that category, and the percentage of people in a category is called the **relative frequency** for that category.

    Frequency table for Topic A data

Days to learn Topic A	Number of people (frequency)	Percentage of people (relative frequency)
5		
6		
7		
8		
9		
10		
11		
12		
13		
14		
Total		

4. Here are a pair of histograms which were adapted from a presentation about a formative assessment program called OGAP. (Thanks to Marge Petit and Bob Laird for permission to use their data.) The two graphs show data for the same group of students. What story do you think they tell? Read the titles carefully.

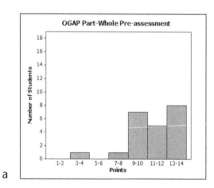

a

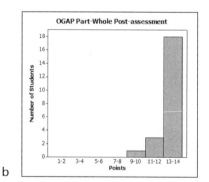

b

5. The given histogram shows the age distribution of all people convicted of driving drunk in Vermont in either one of the two years 1997 and 1998. (Data courtesy of the Vermont Justice Center.)

    a. In this histogram what is the width of each interval? Is this distribution symmetric or skewed? Does the vertical axis indicate frequencies or relative frequencies?

    b. According to the histogram, about

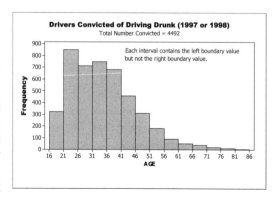

how many drivers under the age of 26 (young drivers) were convicted of drunk driving in 1997 and 1998? About how many were age 56 and older (old drivers)?

c. Why can't we use these data to determine the chance that a young driver is convicted of drunk driving?

Hint: Try to complete this table from the given data.

	Convicted	Not convicted	Total
Young drivers			
Other drivers			
Total			

d. Can we use the data to determine the chance that a driver convicted of driving drunk is young?

6. Here are a few graphs representing relative frequencies for some large collections of exam scores. *Note that the data are grouped into four intervals.* The first interval represents all exams with scores from 350 up to but not including 400; the next includes all scores from 400 up to but not including 450, etc. (*Geometry connection:* These questions are all equivalent to questions about area.)

a. This histogram is *flat.* Confirm that 100% of the exam scores are accounted for in this graph. What percentage of these exam scores were less than 400? Convince yourself that this is the same question as what percentage of the total area in this histogram is to the left of 400 on the horizontal axis.

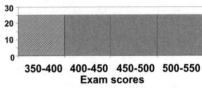

What percentage of the scores were 400 or higher? If a grand total of 200 people took this exam, how many of them scored less than 400?

b. This histogram is *not* flat. Note how this changes your responses. What percentage of these exam scores were less than 400? What percentage were 400 or higher? If a grand total of 200 people took this exam, how many of them scored less than 400?

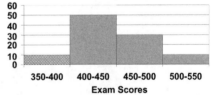

c. Construct two new histograms each with 60% of the exam scores less than 450. These two histograms should be different from each other, but they should both use the same four intervals from a. and b. above.

d. The entire triangular area represents 100% of all the scores on a set of exams. About what percentage of these exam scores are below 400? If a grand total of 200 people took this exam, how many of them scored less than 400? This triangle is not really a histogram, because it is not made of rectangular bars. It cannot be made from a real set of data, but it can serve as an idealized smooth model for a data set.

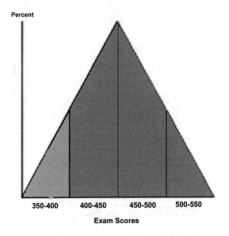

A set of data whose histogram looks pretty much like this is said to have a **triangular distribution**.

e. The entire symmetric bell-shaped area represents 100% of all the scores on a set of exams. The shaded percentage is given in the graph. Determine the approximate percentage of scores that are:

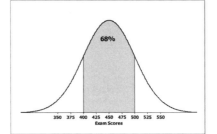

  i. less than 400;
  ii. less than 450;
  iii. less than 500;
  iv. between 450 and 500.

f. The entire symmetric bell-shaped area represents 100% of all the scores on a set of exams. The shaded percentage is given in the graph. Determine the approximate percentage of scores that are:

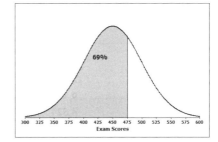

  i. less than 425;
  ii. less than 450;
  iii. between 425 and 475.

7. The figures shown are special back-to-back histograms called **population pyramids**. The bars represent age groups, the lowest bar representing children aged 0 to 4.

a. Compare and contrast these population pyramids. What's going on in these countries?

b. Use the data tables to determine the percentage of the population in each country that is less than 15 years old.

c. Which country has the greatest percentage of women 90 years old and older?

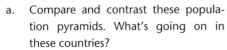

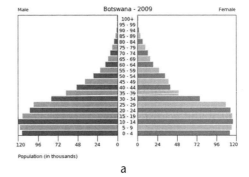

a

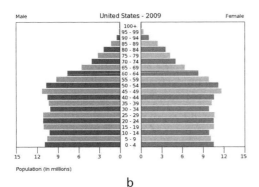

b

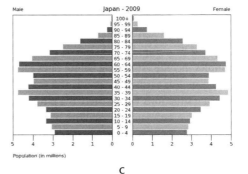

c

2. (Small group activity.) Invent two dice experiments, one of which you expect to produce a symmetric probability distribution, and one to produce a distribution that is not symmetric. Conduct each experiment a sufficient number of times to generate frequency tables and graphs to support your hypotheses. Prepare a clear description of your experiments to share with the class.

3. Based on the data in Figure 1.9, what is the probability that the next earthquake will have magnitude 5 or greater?

A Variety of Other Graphs

When you use a graph to help tell the story of some investigation, you are allowed to be creative. A look at graphs in the media will quickly show that people invent all kinds of graphs and charts to make a point clearly. The field of graphical representation is evolving rapidly, especially now that graphics can be made interactive on the Internet. (For some examples, check the *New York Times* or the website FlowingData.com.) You should know the basic styles and name them properly so that you can teach about them in a consistent way in your classes, but there should be no ruling out a graph because it doesn't fit a standard type.

Two fine books on using graphs to portray data are Edward Tufte's *The Visual Display of Quantitative Information* and Howard Wainer's *Graphic Discovery: A Trout in the Milk and Other Visual Adventures*. Wainer's book also serves as a brief history of statistical graphs.

Exercises on a Variety of Other Graphs

1. Here is a style of graph, called a **floating bar graph**, that teachers have found useful in action research.

    a. These two graphs represent the same data. Compare the two graphs and comment on their differences. Can you extract a story here about the success of the intervention? Which of the two graphs would you prefer to use in a report? Why?

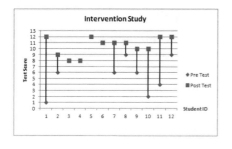 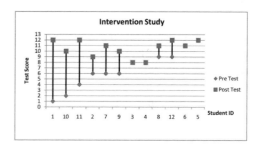

    b. This **timeline graph** for the life spans of four founding fathers is also a floating bar graph where the horizontal axis represents continuous time. Timeline graphs are convenient for investigating overlaps of several phenomena. What system was used to choose the order in which the bars were printed?

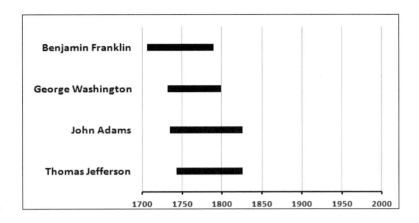

Per capita electricity sales in kilowatt hours per person

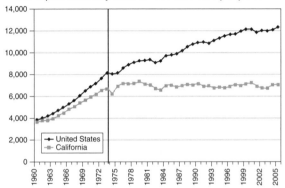

2. This graph shows time passing on the horizontal axis in equal increments. Such graphs are called **time-series graphs**. They are excellent for illustrating how a variable changes over time. In this graph the pattern for California is different from the national pattern.

    a. Summarize the difference in a sentence or two, but note how much easier it is to compare the trends visually.

    b. *Extra, for discussion:* List some possible reasons that might explain why the two patterns

Source: California Energy Commission 2007, 2007 Integrated Energy Policy Report Summary, CEC-100-2007-008-CMF-ES. Reprinted with permission.

are different. According to the source for the graph, California uses less electricity per person than any other state in the nation.

2

PERCENTAGES

Introductory Activity

The Luvly School

A six-week educational intervention at the Luvly School raised the number of students who were fluent with fractions by 50 percent. Is this wonderful news? Make up several examples showing 50 percent increases in the number of fluent children to support your opinion.

Percentages and Percentage Change

In this text the noun **statistic** refers to any number calculated or copied from a set of data. Some examples are: the mean of a set of data, the maximum value in a set of data, the sum of the numbers in a set of data, the percentage of numbers in a data set that are greater than 72. The two most common statistics used to summarize data are percentages and averages.

Percentages are the most common statistic for representing quantities proportionally. When we say that 3 out of 6 is 50 percent, we are saying that the ratio of 3 to 6 is the same as the ratio of 50 to 100.

We are quite used to reading percentages in statistical reports to tell us what portion of a group has some characteristic. But be aware that percentages and changes in percentages based on a small set of data may be misleading. Percent literally means "per hundred," and we grasp percentages most intuitively for sets that have at least 100 elements.

Many statistical results are given as **percentage change**. Percentage change measures change by the ratio of the amount of change to the original amount. For instance, if a price changes from $60 to $90, the amount of the increase is $30. As $30 is half the original price, the percentage change in price is 50. The price has increased by 50% of its original value.

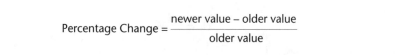

$$\text{Percentage Change} = \frac{\text{newer value} - \text{older value}}{\text{older value}}$$

If the newer value is smaller than the older value, the formula will yield a negative result, representing a percentage *decrease*.

Exercises on Percentage and Percentage Change

1. a. A test consists of two questions of equal value. What are the only possible test scores when given in percentages that are correct?

Number correct out of 2	Percentage correct out of 100%
0	
1	
2	

   b. What if the test has five questions? What are the only possible test scores in terms of percentages?

   c. A test consists of five questions of equal value. A student takes a retest and gets one more question correct than he did on the original test. By how much does his score go up in percentage points?

   d. How many questions must there be on a test so that getting one more question correct raises a grade by 2 percentage points?

2. A 3rd grade class in a small rural school consists of eight students. In 2008, six of them meet the standards in mathematics. The next year when they are in 4th grade five of them meet the standards.

   a. Express the change as a simple difference of percentages.

   b. Express the change as a percentage change.

   c. The answers in both parts a and b may seem misleading. What might be a better way to report the children's performance over these two years to the school board?

3. a. Class enrollment jumps from 10 children to 15 children. Express this change as a percentage increase.

   b. Class enrollment drops from 15 children to 10 children. Express this change as a percentage decrease.

   c. School enrollment jumps from 100 to 105. Express this change as a percentage change.

   d. School enrollment drops from 105 to 100. Express this change as a percentage change.

   e. Why are the two values in parts c. and d. so close to one another, but the two values in parts a. and b. so different?

4. Express each of the following changes as either a percentage increase or a percentage decrease.

   a. The male enrollment in a nursing program climbs from 1 to 2.

   b. The number of physicians in a rural community drops from 2 to 0.

   c. The female enrollment in a hockey program climbs from 0 to 1.

5. Every week for ten weeks, you take a test with only one question. The only possible scores each time are 0% and 100%. At the end of that period your final grade is the average of your ten scores. Is that the same grade you would get if you just took the percentage of the ten questions that you got right?

6. This box is similar to those found at the Buy.com website. This is their way of telling you that certain items have suddenly become very popular because of a price cut. How did they get that 14,400% figure? Is this really a percentage increase? Applying percentage change to ranks really doesn't make mathematical sense. (See Exercise 3 in "Math connections and extensions" below for more about this.)

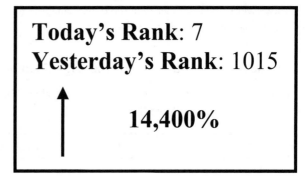

Today's Rank: 7
Yesterday's Rank: 1015

14,400%

7. *Per capita statistics:* Many statistical reports give results "per capita," which means per number of heads or per person. For example, crime statistics are often given per capita, but the ratio may be expressed not per one person but per 1,000 people or some other number of people. Table A below shows the countries with the highest murder rates. Table B below shows the countries with the highest number of murders. (*Source:* http://www.nationmaster.com, January 2008, based on UN data from 1998–2000.)

   a. Why aren't the tables identical?
   b. Interpret the value 0.617847 in the first row of Table A below. How was this value calculated?
   c. Express the murder rate in the United States per 100,000 people and also per million people.
   d. Why can't you use just the information in Table A to determine if there were more murders in Jamaica or Venezuela?

TABLE A Murder rate

Rank	Country	Murders per 1,000 people per year
1	Colombia	0.617847
2	South Africa	0.496008
3	Jamaica	0.324196
4	Venezuela	0.316138
5	Russia	0.201534
6	Mexico	0.130213
7	Estonia	0.107277
8	Latvia	0.103930
9	Lithuania	0.102863
10	Belarus	0.0983495
24	United States	0.042802

TABLE B Number of murders

Rank	Country	Murders per year
1	India	37,170
2	Russia	28,904
3	Colombia	26,539
4	South Africa	21,995
5	Mexico	13,829
6	United States	12,658
7	Venezuela	8,022
8	Thailand	5,140
9	Ukraine	4,418
10	Indonesia	2,204
17	Jamaica	887

Source: http://www.nationmaster.com (Jan. 2008) based on UN data from 1998–2000.

8. The general risk of dying from disease A is one in a million. However, if you have a certain bad habit the risk increases to three in a million. What is the percentage increase in the risk of dying for people with this bad habit? Is it worth giving up the habit?
9. The point of this exercise is that for certain contexts the *rate* is what matters most, but in other contexts the actual *number of cases* may be more important.

In Sick City the hospitalization rate for a certain disease is 100 people in a million during the month of July. In Fine City the rate is 10 people in a million. The population of Sick City is 500,000, and the population of Fine City is 5 million.

    a.   How many times more likely is a citizen of Sick City to be hospitalized for the disease in July than a citizen of Fine City?

    b.   How many hospital beds are required to cope with the affected citizens in each city?

    c.   If you are a citizen, in which city are you less likely to need hospitalization for the disease in July? That is, which city seems safer? If you are a city health official who needs to make sure there are sufficient hospital beds, which city is more needy?

    d.   Make up an example in an educational setting that shows two contexts, one in which the rate is more important and one in which the number of cases is more important.

10. Say what? Websites, newspapers, and TV often are sloppy about quantitative reporting, especially about percentages, percentage change, and per capita statistics. The *New Scientist* magazine collects such examples from its readers. Here are a couple of examples.

    a.   Reader Mike Rodgers sent this one in. It appeared on December 15, 2007. What is Rodgers getting at?

"By 2010, the production and sale of each bottle of water will actually result in a 120 per cent net reduction of carbon in the atmosphere," Thomas Mooney of Fiji Water told *The Guardian* newspaper in London. "Can nothing be done to stop these people," Mike Rodgers asks, "before it's too late?"

    b.   What's this reader making fun of?

Reader Peter Bell is puzzled by this claim on a website advertising a transport conference at bit.ly/billiondevices: "A recent report by *Analysys Mason* predicts that by 2020 there will be a rise from 6 billion (present day) to between 16 and 44 billion digitally identifiable, potentially linked, electronic devices per head of population on this planet."

    Peter is particularly intrigued by the assertion that we are already carrying around 6 billion devices each. "Given that I don't carry any more than two or three such devices at any one time, and I don't know anyone else who does, some people must be carrying a hell of a lot of devices for the average to be 6 billion. How do they do it?"

Math Connections and Extensions

1.   This exercise points up the non-symmetry of percentage change.

    a.   What is the percentage change if a price increases from $1 to $2? What is the percentage change if a price decreases from $2 to $1? Why are the two answers not the same? What is the ratio of the price decrease to the price increase?

    b.   Redo a. above, but assume the two prices are $8 and $10.

    c.   A price increases by a certain amount, and then decreases by that same amount. Which is smaller, the percentage increase or the percentage decrease? What is the ratio of the price decrease to the price increase?

2.   a.   A price is increased by 100%. What decrease will bring it back to its original price?

    b.   A price is increased by 25%. What decrease will bring it back to its original price?

    c.   A price is increased by r%. What decrease will bring it back to its original price?

3. The idea of percentage is based on the assumption of a well-defined "whole." This in turn implies that there is well-defined "nothing." From this you can say, for example, that 50% of a quantity represents twice as much as 25% does. In some measurement systems, though, zero does not mean "nothing." For example, an IQ of 100 is average on most intelligence scales. But an IQ of 0 has no meaning at all. And, therefore, an IQ of 140 does not represent twice the intelligence of an IQ of 70.

   a. You can convert temperatures in Fahrenheit to Celsius using $C = \frac{5}{9}(F - 32)$. Clearly, 80°F is twice the temperature of 40°F. But is it twice as hot? What happens when you convert these two temperatures to Celsius? Is the higher Celsius temperature twice the lower one? The difficulty stems from the fact that in both systems zero degrees does not mean "no heat." Ratios make sense only when zero really means "nothing."

   b. Name some other scale besides IQ and temperature (C or F) where zero does not mean "nothing." You should be able to see that ratios don't make good sense.

4. Suppose a new model car gets $30 \frac{\text{miles}}{\text{gallon}}$ when the old model got $20 \frac{\text{miles}}{\text{gallon}}$.

   a. What is the percentage change in fuel efficiency for this increase from $20 \frac{\text{miles}}{\text{gallon}}$ to $30 \frac{\text{miles}}{\text{gallon}}$?

   b. You commute 60 miles a day. With gas at $4.00 per gallon, what is the percentage change in cost if you switch from the old model car to the new model car? Is this the same answer you got in a. above?

   c. Suppose it takes 1/30 of a gallon of gas for a new model car to go one mile, when the old model took 1/20 of a gallon to go that far. What is the percentage change for this change

      from $\frac{1}{20} \frac{\text{gallon}}{\text{mile}}$ to $\frac{1}{30} \frac{\text{gallon}}{\text{mile}}$? Is this the same answer you got in b. above?

5. In computing percentage change we always assume that both values are positive. Weird things happen if we try to extend the concept of percentage change to include starting from a negative or zero value. Consider your answers to these three questions and see if they make sense.

   a. Your net worth changes from −$50 to +$50. What is the percentage change in your net worth?

   b. Your net worth changes from −$25 to −$50. What is the percentage change in your net worth?

   c. Your net worth changes from $0 to +$50. What is the percentage change in your net worth?

3

AVERAGES

Introductory Activity

The Cruise

Suppose that you won the grand prize in a local radio contest, an all-expenses-paid five-day cruise for two people. Because of your hectic schedule, there are only two possible weeks when you can take the cruise. Knowing that cruise companies occasionally have themed cruises, you call to find out if there is any difference between the two cruises. The only information that the cruise company will provide is that the average age of cruise-goers on the first cruise is 20 years, while the average age on the second cruise is 40 years.

1. Which cruise would you choose? Why?

2. a. For the cruise you have selected (with mean age of 20 or 40), create a data set of ten ages that would support your decision and would be a cruise you would happily take.
   b. Create another data set of ten ages, with the same mean age, that would horrify you when you boarded the boat.

3. Does knowing the mean age of cruise-goers help you to make an informed decision? Why or why not?

(This activity was adapted from a worksheet prepared by the Vermont Mathematics Partnership.)

Averages (Measures of Center or Location)

When working with large sets of numbers, a single statistic is often calculated to represent a "typical" or average value. The concept of an average is often useful, but, as was shown in the introductory "Cruise" activity, sometimes it makes no sense or is very uninformative by itself. As we mentioned in Chapter 1, it is risky to do any summarizing without first knowing the shape of a distribution.

In statistics, "average" is a concept that must be specified clearly – there are many kinds of averages. Other general terms for average in statistical terminology are "measure of center" and "measure of location." The three most common measures of location are mean, median, and mode. All three can be used when numerical variables are being described. Additionally, the mode (but not the mean and median) can be used for qualitative variables. Recall that a qualitative or categorical variable is one where the subject gives you a *name* or a *word* rather than a number as a response. You might ask "What is your job title?" The response would be a title such as "Teacher" or "Principal." The main summarizing you do with qualitative variables is to put them in categories and count them; the job category with the highest count is the mode.

Big idea: You should not decide which measure or measures of center to use until you know the reason you are doing it. Pick the one that helps you tell the story of your data. If you have a very small set of data, you may prefer not to do any of them, but just to show all the data.

Official Definitions

$$\text{Mean} = \frac{\text{sum of all the values in a distribution of numbers}}{\text{number of values in the set}}$$

In symbols, mean $= \frac{\Sigma x}{n}$, where Σ is the Greek uppercase sigma, which means "the sum of"
x represents a number in a distribution
Σx represents the sum of all the numbers in the distribution
n represents the number of values in the distribution

Median = the middle number after all the numbers in a set have been placed in numerical order.
If the set contains an even amount of numbers, the median will be the mean of the two middle ones.

Mode = the number or category that appears most often.

Note that the mode for a numerical variable may have nothing at all to do with the numerical "center" of a set of numbers. For instance, the lowest number could be the mode.

The main purpose of the mode is to notice if there is an outstanding value or category. For that reason, if many categories have the same maximum frequency, it is more common to say there is *no* mode, rather than that there are many modes.

"Unimodal" and "bimodal" are frequently used to describe the general shape of a distribution. These labels just mean that the graph has one or two "bumps." The bumps do not need to have the same height. Figure 3.1 is the graph of a bimodal distribution. A bimodal graph may mean there are two distinct subgroups contributing data.

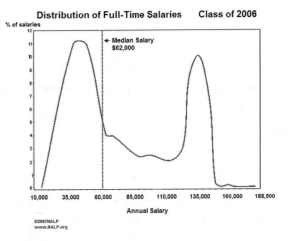

FIGURE 3.1 Bimodal distribution: starting salaries, graduates from law school in 2006

Source: www.nalp.org/apictureworth1000words. Graph reproduced with permission by NALP.

Note: $n = 22,665$ salaries.

Exercises about Measures of Center

Notation for data sets: We use two styles of notation to present data sets; one is more formal mathematically than the other:

Formal style: $X = \{4,7,2\}$

The name of the set is a capital letter. Following an equals sign, the elements of the set are enclosed in parentheses and separated by commas. In more advanced courses this style generalizes to $X = \{x_1, x_2, x_3\}$.

Informal style: X: 4,7,2

Following a colon, the elements are listed separated by commas.

Mathematical Properties of Means and Medians

1. Without doing any calculating, explain why these two distributions have the same median but not the same mean.
    X: 0,0,5,81   Y: 0,0,5,8100

2. a. What is the *position* of the median in a distribution that consists of 9 values? 19 values? 999? Write a rule to say how you locate the position in these cases.
    b. What is the position of the median in a distribution that consists of 10 values? 20 values? 1,000?
    c. What is the position of the median in a distribution that consists of *n* values?

3. True or false? The mean and the median for a list of numbers must be one of the numbers in the list. Support your choice by an illustration.

4. *Some mathematical puzzles about the mean:*

    a. A set of five numbers has a mean equal to 13. What is the sum of those numbers? If you replace each of the original numbers by 13, then what is the sum?
    b. True or false? If you replace each number in a list by the mean, then the sum is unchanged.
    c. What would the fifth number, *x*, have to be so that the mean of 20, 30, 40, 50, and *x* equals 40? 50? 20? How would your answers change if "mean" were replaced by "median"?
    d. The mean of five numbers is 10, and the mean of three of them is 9. What is the mean of the remaining two values? Can you determine the individual values of those two numbers?
    e. The mean of five numbers is 10. One number was removed from the set, and the mean increased to 11. What number was removed?

5. a. Show by a couple of examples that doubling each number in a list will double the mean.
    b. Show, using algebra, that the mean of the four values *kx*, *ky*, *kw*, *kz* is *k* times the mean of the four values *x*, *y*, *w*, *z*. State a principle in words that is illustrated by this exercise.
    c. Suppose $k = 1/2$ in b. above. What does this tell you about dividing every number in a list by the same number?

6. a. Show by a couple of examples that adding 5 to each number in a list will add 5 to the mean.

   b.   Show, using algebra, that the mean of the four values $x + k, y + k, w + k, z + k$ is k plus the mean of the four values x, y, w, z. State a principle in words that is illustrated by this exercise.

   c.   Suppose $k = -5$ in b. above. What does this tell you about subtracting a constant from every number in a list?

7.   Check that the mean of the six numbers 1, 4, 8, 9, 10, 16 is 8.

   a.   Subtract this mean from each number to get a new list of six numbers. Your new list should have some positive and some negative numbers and even a zero. What are the sum and mean of the six new numbers? What is going on here? Can you state a general principle? Demonstrate the principle with an example that you make up.

   b.   Can you prove the principle from a. above using algebra if the list contains just two numbers, a and b? How about three numbers, a, b, and c?

Applications of Means and Medians

8.   In July 1998, the following data were published for four categories of blue-collar workers in private industry in Huntsville, Alabama.

Blue-collar workers in private industry

Occupation	Number of workers	Mean hourly earnings
Precision production craft and repair occupations	7,235	$13.61
Machine operators, assemblers, and inspectors	13,122	$14.08
Transportation and material moving occupations	1,391	$10.87
Handlers equipment, cleaners, helpers, and laborers	2,910	$9.05

   a.   Based on these data find the mean hourly earnings, rounded to the nearest cent, of a blue-collar worker who worked in private industry in Huntsville, Alabama, in 1998.

   b.   In which of these four occupation categories would you find the median hourly earnings for a blue-collar worker who worked in private industry in Huntsville, Alabama, in 1998?

(This problem is adapted from a sample test for quantitative reasoning needed to graduate from a VT state college.)

9.   A joker said, "The average American has fewer than two legs." What's the person getting at? What are some accurate ways to describe this phenomenon?

10. For each of these graphs, *estimate* the mean and median exam scores, and justify your estimate. Why is the verb in the previous sentence "estimate" rather than "compute"?

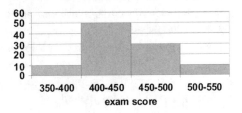

Percent of exam scores

11. One semester a teacher gives three quizzes, a midterm exam, and a final exam. The final exam counts for 50% of the grade. The midterm counts for 25%, and the quizzes count for the rest. What is this student's final grade?
    $Q_1 = 80$, $Q_2 = 80$, $Q_3 = 92$, $M = 76$, $F = 70$.

12. a. The mean salary for the 15 female teachers at a school is $35,000. The mean for the 5 male teachers is $25,000. What is the mean salary for the 20 teachers in the school?
    b. Three-quarters of the teachers at a school are female. Their mean salary is $35,000. The mean salary for the male teachers is $25,000. What is the mean salary for all the teachers in the school?

13. This table is taken from a teacher-leader workshop presented by Dr. Ray Garcia in June 2007. The data are from research by John Hollingsworth and Silvia Ybarra in California. The cell entries represent the percentage of tasks at various grade levels that were actually assigned in specific grades. For example, the 23 in the math table indicates that 23% of the tasks assigned in the 2nd grade were at the 1st grade level.

Grade	Mathematics GLS %						Av. Gr. Level	Language Arts GLS %						Av. Gr. Level
	K	1	2	3	4	5		K	1	2	3	4	5	
K	100							100						K
1st		100					1.0	100						1.0
2nd		23	77				1.8		20	80				1.8
3rd			45	55			2.6		2	14	84			2.8
4th			40	40	20		2.8		2	30	35	33		3
5th			2	35	59	2	2	2.7		28	60	10	2	2.9

Hollingsworth & Ybarra, 2000

   a. Describe the story told by this table. Dr. Garcia calls this the slippage phenomenon.
   b. What are the values in the columns labeled "Av. Gr. Level"? How did the table authors compute the numbers in this column?

14. *Trimmed mean:* We have seen that the median is less sensitive to outliers than the mean. Other such "robust" measures of center are also used. An example is the trimmed mean. To calculate a 10% trimmed mean you discard the highest and the lowest 10% of the data and then compute the mean. Similarly, to calculate a 5% trimmed mean you discard the highest and the lowest 5% of the data and then compute the mean.

    In 1882 Simon Newcomb (US Naval Academy) carried out experiments to measure the speed of light. His data, shown here, have since been used to investigate statistical procedures for estimation. (My source for the data was: Stephen M. Stigler, Do Robust Estimators Work With *Real* Data?, *Annals of Statistics*, 1977.)

    The 66 numbers shown here represent the variable part of Newcomb's measurements of the time it took light to travel a total of 7,442 meters (from Fort Myer on the west bank of the Potomac to a fixed mirror at the base of the Washington monument and back again). His measurements were not always exactly the same because he was pushing the limitations of his equipment.

    This table shows how each of the 66 measurements deviated from .000024800 seconds. Basically, Newcomb always got a value a little bit off from .000024800 seconds. So, for instance, the 16 represents .000024800 + .000000016 = .000024816 seconds.

TABLE T13 Variable part of Newcomb's measurements of the speed of light

-44	-2	16	16	19	20	21	21	22	22	23
23	23	24	24	24	24	24	25	25	25	25
25	26	26	26	26	26	27	27	27	27	27
27	28	28	28	28	28	28	28	29	29	29
29	29	30	30	30	31	31	32	32	32	32
32	33	33	34	36	36	36	36	37	39	40

a. To see why the median and the trimmed means are considered more robust than the mean, compare the mean, median, and 5% and 10% trimmed means for Newcomb's measurements. For example, to get the 10% trimmed mean you would throw out the top and the bottom 7 numbers, because 10% of 66 is 6.6.

b. Sometimes a researcher just omits obvious outliers if they are obvious errors of measurement. What would the mean of these measurements be if you just omitted the −44 and the −2?

c. All of Newcomb's measurements are approximately .0000248 seconds. What estimate of the speed of light follows from this time?

Math Connections for Means

1. The mean can be thought of as a mathematical function, but one for which you input several numbers at once. You could play "function machine," where you put in two numbers and get out their mean.

   This process is not invertible. If you have the output you can't tell what the input was. Check the question marks in the table to see this point.

TABLE T14 Mean function machine

Input	Output
3, 7	5
−1, 0, 1	0
2, 4, 6	?
?	5

2. We teach children to add fractions using a common denominator: $\dfrac{1}{2}+\dfrac{5}{2}=\dfrac{1+5}{2}$. Wouldn't it be nice to remind them that this is an equality and that therefore you can decompose a fraction into the sum of other fractions with the same denominator? Example: $\dfrac{1+5}{2}=\dfrac{1}{2}+\dfrac{5}{2}$. More generally, $\dfrac{a+b}{c}=\dfrac{a}{c}+\dfrac{b}{c}=\dfrac{1}{c}a+\dfrac{1}{c}b.\cdot$

   a. The mean of 3 and 5 is $\dfrac{3+5}{2}=4$. Notice that $\dfrac{3+5}{2}=\dfrac{1}{2}(3)+\dfrac{1}{2}(5)=1.5+2.5=4$. In expressions like this the ½ is called a *weight*. The mean of two numbers can be thought of as a sum where each number gets a weight of ½. How would you express the mean of 3, 5, and 10 as such a sum? What weight would each number get?

   b. Show that the mean of 5, 5, and 8 can be expressed as $\dfrac{2}{3}(5)+\dfrac{1}{3}(8)$. In this case, the 5 and the 8 are not weighted equally. The 5 carries greater weight. In general, when you find a mean where the weights are not equal, you say that you have computed a **weighted mean**. The ordinary mean is the special case when all the weights are equal.

   c. A set of numbers consists of 200 4s and 100 7s. Find the mean and the sum. How would you express the mean of these numbers as a weighted sum of 4s and 7s?

d. A large set of numbers consists solely of 4s and 7s. One-third of the numbers are 7s. What is the mean of all the numbers? Can you find the sum of all the numbers?

3. A collection of numbers consists of twenty 1s and thirty 0s. What is the mean of this set of numbers? The mean of a set of numbers that consists entirely of 1s and 0s tells you something about a percentage. What does it tell you?

4. a. Consider the set of consecutive numbers 1, 2, 3, . . . , 7, 8, 9. We are looking for a shortcut to find their sum. If you know the mean of nine numbers, how would you find their sum? Confirm that the mean of these nine values is the same as the mean of just the first number and last number. Why then must the sum of these nine numbers be 9 × 5 = 45?

    b. Following the reasoning of a. above, explain why $1 + 2 + 3 + \cdots + n$ must be $n\left(\dfrac{n+1}{2}\right)$. You may have seen this formula before. It is often associated with the mathematician Carl F. Gauss.

    c. Find a formula for this sum: $a + (a + 1) + (a + 2) + (a + 3) + \ldots + (a + m)$.

5. True or false? The mean of two different numbers is exactly halfway between them. Prove or disprove this statement.

Means and Geometry

6. If you have a fixed amount of material arranged into a shape like the front arrangement in the figure, then, if you even out all the bars (keeping the original total amount of material) as shown in the back arrangement, the height of the "evened out" version is the mean of the original heights.

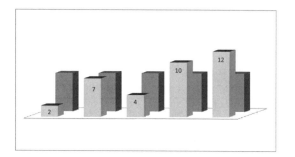

    a. Explain why this is so using some specific example.
        (Note how this evening out corresponds to replacing each value in a list by the mean of the list. We have seen earlier that this preserves the sum.)

    b. This second figure shows the same story but in two dimensions, as if you were looking at the first figure straight on. If you even out the heights of the bars, then you get one large rectangle whose area is equal to the total area of the original bars. From this it follows that, if you know the total area of the bars and you know the base of the large rectangle, then, by division, you can calculate the mean height of the bars.

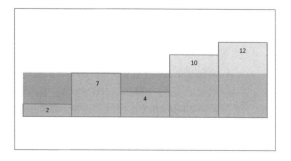

$$\text{mean height of bars} = \frac{\text{total area of original bars}}{\text{base of large rectangle}}$$

Assume the base of each bar is 1 unit wide, and find the total area of the bars and the mean height of the bars in the second figure. What happens if you assume the base of each bar is 3 units wide?

Calculus connection: The approach described in b. above may be used to find the mean height of curves which continuously change height. An example would be the measurement of temperature during a day, where a graph of temperature in the morning might look like this figure. By the calculus function called an integral we can measure the shaded area. Dividing it by 4, the base, will then yield the mean temperature between 8 a.m. and noon.

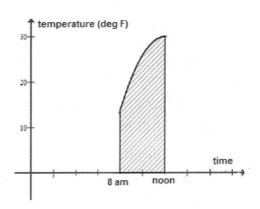

Less Familiar Means

There are many different means, each with its own special characteristics. They all share one property: the mean of a set of numbers falls between the lowest and highest values. The three most widely used means are the arithmetic mean, the geometric mean, and the harmonic mean. As a group they were known in ancient Greece and together are called the Pythagorean means.

The next few exercises concern the geometric and harmonic means, which find application in many field of mathematics, so they are included here just for fun. They will not play a role in this statistics course, though they do in more advanced statistics. For example, the harmonic mean is used in some cases as the best value to use for the "average" sample size when you combine information from different samples. The geometric mean is used in water quality sampling at public beaches to represent the average contamination over a given time period.

Exercises on Less Familiar Means

1. The usual mean we compute is more specifically called the **arithmetic mean** (put the stress on the syllable "met"). The adjective "arithmetic" is associated with the operation of addition. To find an arithmetic mean we add **n** numbers and then divide by **n**. The adjective "geometric" is associated with the operation of multiplication. To find a **geometric mean** we multiply **n** numbers and then take the **n**th root.

    a. A rectangle has dimensions 4 inches by 9 inches. If you "averaged out" the sides so that the rectangle became square, what should the side of the square be, so that the square has the same area as the original rectangle? That number is called the geometric mean of 4 and 9. Which is larger, the arithmetic mean of 4 and 9 or their geometric mean?

    b. What is the geometric mean of 1 and 25?

    c. Find two numbers whose geometric mean is 10. Now find two more.

    d. A rectangular solid has dimensions 2 × 6 × 18. If you "averaged out" the sides so that the solid became a cube, what should the dimensions of the cube be, so that both figures have the same volume? That number is called the geometric mean of 2 and 6 and 18.

    e. Find the geometric mean of 1, 5, and 10.

    f.   Why is the geometric mean defined only for positive numbers? What happens if you try to find the geometric mean of −5 and +5?

    g.   Take any two numbers, a^2 and b^2, that are perfect squares (such as 9 and 16). What is their geometric mean?

2.   a.   Find a formula for the geometric mean of **a** and **b**.

    b.   Find a formula for the geometric mean of **a**, **b**, and **c**.

3.   a.   You drive 60 miles to work at 20 mph and you drive back home at 30 mph. What is your average speed for the round trip? Prove it by dividing your total distance by your total time. That average speed is called the harmonic mean of 20 and 30. The harmonic mean gives you a fixed speed that would accomplish the whole round trip in the same total time.

    b.   You drive to work at 20 mph and you drive back home the same distance at 30 mph. What is your average speed for the round trip? Why do you not need to know the distance? Why is the average speed closer to 20 mph than to 30 mph?

    c.   You drive to work at 30 mph. How fast do you need to drive back so that your average speed for the round trip is 60 mph? Watch out. People have come to blows over this one. If you think you have the answer, check it by recalculating the total distance divided by the total time to get the average speed.

    d.   Let there be a relay race between two teams each consisting of two athletes. In one of the teams, the speed of the first athlete is 10 mph, and that of the second is 15 mph. In the second team, two identical twins always run at the same speed. The question is, "What must be the speed of the runners in the second team so that the two teams finish at exactly the same time?"

4.   A formula for the harmonic mean (**H**) of **a** and **b** is $H = \dfrac{2}{\dfrac{1}{a} + \dfrac{1}{b}}$.

    a.   Show that this is the reciprocal of the arithmetic mean of the reciprocals of **a** and **b**.

    b.   Show that the formula can also be expressed as $\dfrac{2ab}{a+b}$.

    c.   In general, the **harmonic mean of n numbers** is the reciprocal of the arithmetic mean of their reciprocals. The formula for three numbers looks like $\dfrac{3}{\dfrac{1}{a} + \dfrac{1}{b} + \dfrac{1}{c}}$. Simplify this expression into a form like that in b. above.

5.   a.   An investor purchases $1,200 worth of stock every month for three months and the prices paid per share each month were $10, $20, and $30. Find the average price per share. Which mean is this?

    b.   An investor purchased 1,000 *shares* per month for three months, and the prices paid per share each month were $10, $20, and $30. Find the average price per share. Which mean is this?

6.   This semicircle shows the relationships among the arithmetic (A), geometric (G), and harmonic (H) means for two numbers, **a** and **b**.

    a.   Confirm these relationships for a = 8 and b = 2.

    b.   (Hard) Confirm these relationships strictly by algebra.

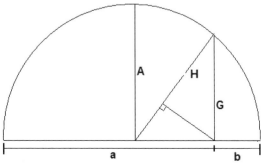

Means of Probability Distributions

We have been discussing how to find and interpret the mean of a given set of observations. We can extend the idea of the mean to random variables known by probability distribution rather than by a set of observations. The mean of such a random variable is also called its **expected value**, often symbolized as $E(X)$ It represents a "typical value" in the sense that it is the average of all the *potential* outcomes of a random experiment.

For example, in an experiment where you roll one die and record its value, the expected value is 3.5 because the six outcomes, 1, 2, 3, 4, 5, 6, are all equally likely and should each occur one-sixth of the times you roll the die. In other words, 3.5 is the long-run average of all the outcomes if you keep this game going forever.

In symbols: $X = \{1,2,3,4,5,6\}$. (These are the possible outcomes for the die.) Each outcome has a probability equal to 1/6.

$$E(X) = \frac{1}{6}(1) + \frac{1}{6}(2) + \frac{1}{6}(3) + \frac{1}{6}(4) + \frac{1}{6}(5) + \frac{1}{6}(6) = \frac{1+2+3+4+5+6}{6} = \frac{21}{6} = 3.5$$

In general,

Expected value of $X = E(X) = \Sigma p(x) \cdot x$,

where the *x*s are the possible outcomes and the *p(x)*s are the corresponding probabilities. In other words, the expected value of X is a weighted mean of all the potential values of X where the weights are the probabilities.

Exercises Involving Expected Value

1. You have a special die where the six faces are labeled 0, 0, 0, 1, 1, 1. You roll this die and record the value that comes up. This list of values represents a random variable X. Find the expected value of X. Is the expected value a number that can actually come up on the die?
2. Find the expected value for X where X represents the outcomes of a die labeled with two 5s and four 10s.
3. Let X represent the *sum* you get when you roll two regular dice. Find the probability distribution of X. Use this information to find the expected value of X and explain what that number tells you.
4. Let X represent the absolute value of the *difference* when you roll two regular dice. Find the expected value of X.
5. Let X represent the *product* you get when you roll two regular dice. Find the expected value of X.
6. a. A random variable X has only two possible values, 0 and 1, each with probability ½. Find the expected value of X.
   b. Suppose the probability of 0 is .4 and the probability of 1 is .6. What is the expected value of X?

7. *Mean of random walk:* A certain kind of bug lives and dies on the number line. These bugs are born at 0. On its birthday a bug hops randomly exactly 1 unit either to the left or to the right. Little does the bug know that at −2 and +2 there are death traps. As soon as the bug arrives at either of these numbers its life is over.

   a. What are the shortest and longest possible lifetimes for this kind of bug?
   b. Can the lifetime of a bug be 3 years? What are the only possible lifetimes?
   c. (Hard) What is the mean lifetime for this kind of bug?

Comparing the Mean, Median, and Mode According to the Concept of Minimum Distance

Each of these three measures of center finds a single number that is "typical" of all the numbers in a data set. Each, in its own way, is that value which comes closest overall to all the numbers in the original list. The three statistics differ by the mathematical way we decide what "closest" is. The median uses the absolute value of the difference of two numbers to say how close they are. The mean uses the square of the difference of two numbers to say how close they are. The mode simply says the only degrees of closeness are 0 and 1. Two numbers either are equal or are not. The following three exercises let you explore these ideas.

Exercises on Comparing Measures of Center According to the Concept of Minimum Distance

1. *How the median minimizes distance:* Use this set of numbers: 1, 2, 6.

    a. Show that the sum of the *absolute* deviations (or differences) from the median is smaller than the sum of the absolute deviation from the mean. That is not an accident. The sum of the absolute deviations from the *median* is always less than or equal to the sum of the absolute deviations from any other fixed number.

    b. Use a graphing calculator to sketch $y = (1 - x)^2 + (2 - x)^2 + (6 - x)^2$ and see that the smallest value of y occurs when $x = 2$, which is the median of 1, 2, and 6.

2. *How the mean minimizes distance:* Use this set of numbers: 1, 2, 6.

    a. Show that the sum of the *squared* deviations from the mean is smaller than the sum of the squared deviations from the median. That, also, is not an accident. The sum of the squared deviations from the *mean* is always less than or equal to the sum of the squared deviations from any other fixed number.

    b. Use a graphing calculator to sketch $y = (1 - x)^2 + (2 - x)^2 + (6 - x)^2$ and see that the smallest value of y occurs when $x = 3$, which is the mean of 1, 2, and 6.

    c. If you algebraically simplify the expression in b. above, the resulting expression will be a familiar quadratic, whose graph is a parabola with vertex at the mean of 1, 2, and 6. What is the connection between the value of the y-intercept and those three numbers? What is the connection between the y-value of the vertex and those three numbers?

3. *How the mode minimizes distance:* Use this set of numbers: 1, 2, 6, 6.

    a. For each number in the set complete this table. The "distance" between two numbers is 0 if the numbers are equal, but 1 if they are not equal.

x	"Distance" from each number in the set {1,2,6,6}				y = sum of distances
	1	2	6	6	
1	0	1	1	1	3
2					
6					

    b. The mode of the list is that value of x which yields the smallest value of y, the total distance. Which value of x satisfies this requirement?

4

SPLITTING A DISTRIBUTION OF NUMBERS INTO EQUAL PARTS

Introductory Activity

Money

There are two points to this activity: first, to figure out what is meant by the word "quintile," and, second, to point out that it is very difficult to construct consistent and meaningful measures of wealth and income.

1. Table 4.1 is adapted from one given by the US Census Bureau. What is the root meaning of the prefix "quint"? How many words can you come up with that start with "quint"? What is the meaning of the value 20,453 in the table? Be as specific as possible and make use of the number 117,538 in your answer.

    TABLE 4.1 US household income distribution 2009

No. of households (thousands)	Upper limit of each quintile (dollars)				
	Lowest	Second	Third	Fourth	Lower limit of top 5%
117,538	20,453	38,550	61,801	100,000	180,001

    Note: Income in 2009 adjusted dollars.

2. Read this explanation of household income taken from Wikipedia, and give an example of a circumstance where household income might not be an accurate representation of wealth.

    Household income is a measure commonly used by the United States government and private institutions, that counts the income of all residents over the age of 18 in each household, including not only all wages and salaries, but such items as unemployment insurance, disability payments, child support payments, regular rental receipts, as well as any personal business, investment, or other kinds of income received routinely. The residents of the household do not have to be related to the head of the household for their earnings to be considered part of the household's income. As households tend to share a similar economic context, the use of household income remains among the most widely accepted measures of income. That the size of a household is not commonly taken into account in such measures may distort any analysis of fluctuations within or among the household income categories, and may render direct comparisons between quintiles difficult or even impossible.

(Wikipedia, http://en.wikipedia.org/wiki/U.S._Household_Income)

Splitting a Distribution of Numbers into a Given Number of Equal Parts: Quartiles, Deciles, Quintiles, Percentiles

The median essentially splits a set of ordered numbers into 2 equal parts. This splitting idea may be generalized to any given number of equal parts. The idea of splitting becomes more useful when you deal with large sets of numbers, in which case you would use computer software to do the work.

Quartiles: 4 equal parts (25% of the values are in each part).
Quintiles: 5 equal parts (20% of the values are in each part).
Deciles: 10 equal parts (10% of the values are in each part).
Percentiles: 100 equal parts (1% of the values are in each part).

General case: quantiles or *n*-tiles: *n* equal parts ($\frac{100}{n}$% of the values are in each part).

It is common to see quartiles used in many areas of educational research, while quintiles are more often seen in financial and economic studies.

Exercises for Quintiles and Deciles

1. This table is typical of those found in US Census Bureau summaries of income. Based on this table:

    a   What is the total number of households accounted for in the table? (Check the units carefully.)
    b. Why does the number 22,629 appear five times in the table?
    c. What percentage of US households have income greater than $88,030? About how many households is this?
    d. What percentage of US households have income less than $34,738?
    e. Examine the table and write down two (or more) stories you can imagine it tells. For example, what's going on with home ownership if you look at the highest and lowest quintiles?

Data	All households	Lowest fifth	Second fifth	Middle fifth	Fourth fifth	Highest fifth	Top 5%
Households (in 1,000s)	113,146	22,629	22,629	22,629	22,629	22,629	5,695
Lower limit	$0	$0	$18,500	$34,738	$55,331	$88,030	$157,176
Median number of income earners	1	0	1	1	2	2	2
Tenure							
Owner occupied	62.4%	49.0%	58.8%	68.9%	80.5%	90.0%	92.8%
Renter occupied	29.2%	48.3%	39.7%	29.9%	18.7%	9.6%	6.9%

Continued overleaf

			Type of household			
Family households	68.06%	41.06%	59.97%	70.04%	80.87%	88.35%	90.61%
Married-couple families	51.35%	19.03%	38.89%	51.00%	67.05%	80.08%	85.59%
Single-male family	4.32%	3.08%	4.64%	5.69%	4.89%	3.30%	2.47%
Single-female family	12.38%	18.94%	16.43%	13.35%	8.93%	4.24%	2.54%
Non-family households	31.93%	58.92%	40.02%	29.96%	19.12%	11.64%	9.36%

Source of table: Household Income in the United States (June 20, 2007), in *Wikipedia, The Free Encyclopedia,* http://en.wikipedia.org/w/index.php?title=Household_income_in_the_United_States&oldid=139348832; accessed June 23, 2007.

Source of data: US Census Bureau, 2000.

2. a. Explain the meaning of the numbers 2,566 and 2.26% in the first row of this table of US household income for 2009.

    b. From this table, estimate the quintiles of this income distribution for US households. Interpret what each quintile tells you.

Income range	Households (thousands)	Percentage	Income range	Households (thousands)	Percentage
Under $2,500	2,566	2.26%	$55,000 to $57,499	2,420	2.13%
$2,500 to $4,999	1,389	1.22%	$57,500 to $59,999	1,786	1.57%
$5,000 to $7,499	2,490	2.20%	$60,000 to $62,499	2,566	2.26%
$7,500 to $9,999	3,360	2.96%	$62,500 to $64,999	1,774	1.56%
$10,000 to $12,499	4,013	3.54%	$65,000 to $67,499	2,101	1.85%
$12,500 to $14,999	3,543	3.13%	$67,500 to $69,999	1,637	1.44%
$15,000 to $17,499	3,760	3.32%	$70,000 to $72,499	1,978	1.74%
$17,500 to $19,999	3,438	3.03%	$72,500 to $74,999	1,413	1.24%
$20,000 to $22,499	4,061	3.58%	$75,000 to $77,499	1,802	1.59%
$22,500 to $24,999	3,375	2.98%	$77,500 to $79,999	1,264	1.11%
$25,000 to $27,499	3,938	3.48%	$80,000 to $82,499	1,673	1.47%
$27,500 to $29,999	2,889	2.55%	$82,500 to $84,999	1,219	1.07%
$30,000 to $32,499	3,921	3.46%	$85,000 to $87,499	1,418	1.25%
$32,500 to $34,999	2,727	2.41%	$87,500 to $89,999	984	0.86%
$35,000 to $37,499	3,360	2.96%	$90,000 to $92,499	1,282	1.13%
$37,500 to $39,999	2,633	2.32%	$92,500 to $94,999	917	0.81%
$40,000 to $42,499	3,378	2.98%	$95,000 to $97,499	1,023	0.90%
$42,500 to $44,999	2,294	2.02%	$97,500 to $99,999	846	0.74%
$45,000 to $47,499	2,700	2.38%	$100,000 to $149,999	11,194	9.89%
$47,500 to $49,999	2,371	2.09%	$150,000 to $199,999	3,595	3.17%
$50,000 to $52,499	3,071	2.71%	$200,000 to $249,999	1,325	1.17%
$52,500 to $54,999	2,006	1.77%	$250,000 and above	1,699	1.50%

3. Just for fun. Make up a set of numbers that satisfies:

    a. First quintile = 10, second quintile = 50, third quintile = 60, fourth quintile = 85.

    b. First quintile = 10, second quintile = 10, third quintile = 10, fourth quintile = 10.

Quartiles and Box Plots

We devote some extra attention to the computation of quartiles now because of its connection to a useful graph called a box plot.

Quartiles

A 2nd grade class has 11 students. They are assessed on math and reading. Table 4.2 shows the results.

a.   Interpret what you see in the data.
b.   Find the median of each set of scores.
c.   Find the quartiles of each set of scores. (You weren't shown how to do this – just do something reasonable and say why you did it. Probably not everyone will do the same thing.)

TABLE 4.2   Scores of 11 students on two assessments

Student ID	1	2	3	4	5	6	7	8	9	10	11
Math	98	100	101	99	100	101	99	100	100	101	102
Reading	80	110	90	120	100	105	85	118	100	82	100

One conventional way to find quartiles:

The quartiles are officially called Q_1, Q_2, and Q_3 going from smallest to largest. Here's how it goes for the reading scores.

Original scores: 80 110 90 120 100 105 85 118 100 82 100

	Bottom half	Median	Top half
Put them in order:	80 82 **85** 90 100	**100**	100 105 **110** 118 120
	Q_1	Q_2	Q_3

To calculate Q_1 we use just the bottom half of the data, and we do not include the median itself in the bottom half or in the top half. Q_1 is the median of the bottom half, and Q_3 is the median of the top half.

Note: Some people (and some software and calculators) *do* include the median in both the top half and the bottom half. Their results for Q_1 and Q_3 may be different from yours, but the difference will be slight, and is not usually important, especially for large sets of numbers.

Terminology: The word "quartile" has two meanings (as do "decile" and "percentile"); you will have to judge the meaning from the context. For example, Q_3 means the particular value that cuts off the top quarter of a set. We would say "Q_3 equals 110." But we also say that "Joe is *in* the top quartile," which means his score is one of those in the top quarter of all the scores.

Exercises for Quartiles

1.   Find the quartiles for the math scores in Table 4.2 using the procedure given above.

2. This is a distribution of ages of people arrested for speeding in one month in a large community.

Age	Frequency	Percentage or relative frequency	Cumulative percentage
11–20	42		
21–30	103		
31–40	75		
41–50	37		
51–60	14		
61–70	8		
71–80	1		
81–90	1		
Total	281		

    a. Convert the frequencies to percentages and calculate the cumulative percentage column. Round the percentages to the nearest tenth of a percent.

    b. In which age group will you find Q_1, Q_2, and Q_3? Do you prefer to answer this question by referring to the third or fourth column in the table?

Box Plot (Also Called Box and Whiskers Plot)

A histogram allows us to represent frequency distributions for individual numerical variables. The next type of statistical graph we consider, the **box plot**, does this too, but also allows us more easily to picture and compare several distributions at once – a task which is clumsy using histograms. Histograms and box plots are good complementary ways to graph the distribution of a numerical variable.

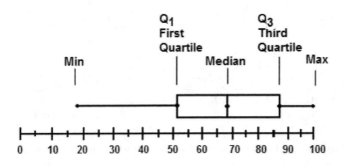

Box plot for data where the minimum value was 18, the median was 68, and the maximum was 100. Q_1 was 51, and Q_3 was 87.

FIGURE 4.1 Box plot

    The box plot for a data set depends directly on a **five-number summary** of the data, consisting of the three quartiles and the minimum and maximum values. See Figure 4.1.

Box plots are excellent for comparing two or more groups of people, or one group before and after some intervention. They give a nice summary of a group as a whole but little information about individuals within the group.

    There are two common versions of the box plot, one which specifically points out any outliers and one which does not. K-12 textbooks vary on this topic. Some graphing calculators let you choose which kind you want. Most statistical software will automatically draw the one that shows outliers if there are any. Figure 4.2 illustrates these two versions. In either case, you can choose to orient the graph horizontally or vertically.

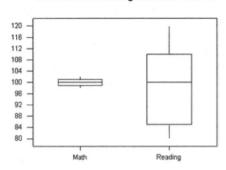

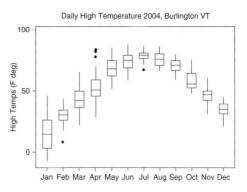

FIGURE 4.2 Box plot: no outliers (left) and with outliers (right)

Rules for constructing a box plot

Version 1 (simple box plot – does not show outliers):

The box extends from Q_1 to Q_3.

A line is drawn inside the box at the median.

The "whiskers" extend from the ends of the box to the minimum and maximum values in the data set.

Version 2 (shows outliers if there are any):

The box extends from Q_1 to Q_3.

A line is drawn inside the box at the median.

The "whiskers" extend from the ends of the box to the smallest and largest values that are *not* outliers.

The outliers are indicated by dots.

What is an **outlier** for a box plot? By convention, a number that is more than 1.5 box lengths beyond the box is an outlier. The length of the box is $Q_3 - Q_1$. The box plot was invented by John Tukey in the 1970s, and several variants exist for determining outliers. The one we have given is widely used now.

Box Plot Exercises

1. How many temperature readings were used to make the January box plot in the Burlington temperature data shown in Figure 4.2? What did each of those readings represent?

2. Give the five-number summary and draw a box plot for the following data. The data represent weights in milligrams (mg) of the active ingredient in a diet supplement pill labeled 3.5 mg. How many weights are in this set of data?

Weight (mg)	Frequency
3.8	3
3.7	4
3.6	6
3.5	8
3.4	7
3.3	1
3.0	1

3.   This box plot illustrates annual salaries in thousands of dollars for 60 members of a social club who responded to a salary survey. Give the range, the five-number summary, and the inter-quartile range (IQR).

   a.   About how many respondents earned less than $40,000? More than $90,000?
   b.   What percentage of these people earn more than $45,000? More than $90,000?

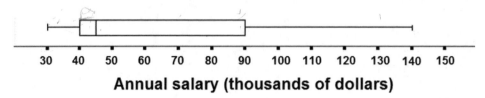

Annual salary (thousands of dollars)

4.   Box plots are good for comparing the overall performance of a class before and after an intervention. Here is an illustration from a teacher's action research paper about such an intervention.
   The "e" and "c" in the variable labels refer to the "experimental" and "control" groups. The vertical axis refers to scores on a test.
   What story do the box plots tell?

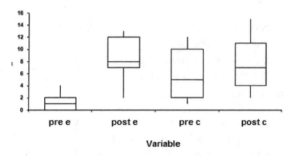

5.   Here are ten values: 20, 21, 22, 23, 24, 25, 26, 27, 28, 29. Insert an 11th number that is an outlier; then draw the box plot showing that outlier as a separate dot. Confirm that your new value is an outlier by showing it is more than 1.5 box lengths outside the box.

5

MEASURING VARIABILITY

Introductory Question

Who Did Best?

Here are the test results for the students of three teachers in the same grade at the same school. Which class did best? Why?

Class 1: 50 55 55 60 60 60 65 65 65 65 70 70 70 70 70 75 75 75 75 80 80 80 85 85 90 70

Class 2: 50 50 50 50 55 55 55 60 60 65 90 75 80 80 80 85 85 85 85 90 90 90 90 50 55 60

Class 3: 70 70 70 70 70 70 70 70 70 70 70 70 70 70 70 70 70 70 70 70 70 70 70 70 70 70

Measuring Variability

Why Do We Care about the Variability in a Set of Data?

When you collect data in the real world, you see variability. This can be a critical issue when you try to assess learning. After you have taught your class a topic you give an assessment. Not all the students get the same score. The scores vary from one student to the next. Why does this happen?

There are at least two plausible reasons:

1. The students do not all have the same mastery of the topic. A large amount of variability means that mastery is all over the place in this class. A small amount of variability means the class is pretty much together on this topic. Statistics provides ways to quantify the amount of variability in a data set.
2. The assessment tool was not very good. Maybe the students got right or wrong answers partly or mainly by luck. The resulting variability is more an indication of the quality of the test than the ability of the students. You can see that if school performance is measured unreliably you will have a mess trying to compare schools. Statistics provides some tools to deal with the fact that no assessment tool is perfectly reliable.

Note: Variability of human ability or talent or any quality is a fact of life. It is perhaps the most basic fact of life. Anything we make up about the "average" person, or the average ability in a classroom, is just that – *made up*. Averages are a mathematical invention to help us understand large amounts of data, but, if you are not careful, averages can lead to dangerous *mis*understanding. You can see, for example, that the average height of the people in a family consisting of two parents and two toddlers is not a useful number. And it is certainly confusing to phrase the result as the height of "the average person" in the family. There is no average person.

A simple example of getting in trouble with averages is one sociologists call the **ecological fallacy**. This is the fallacy of assuming that a randomly chosen person from a group must be like the "average person" in that group. For example, suppose it is true in a school that the average score for boys on a standardized test is higher than for girls. It is still quite possible that, if you randomly picked a particular boy and girl, the girl would score higher and, in fact, many of the girls may have higher scores than a large number of the boys.

Introductory Investigation

How Can You Measure and Summarize Variability?

Just as people have invented multiple ways to describe the "center" of a set of numbers by a summary statistic, you can invent multiple ways to measure the variability (or **spread** or **dispersion**) in a set of numbers by a summary statistic.

Here are three key features for any statistic designed to measure variability:

- If the numbers in a set are all the same, the statistic must equal 0. There is no variability in the data set.
- If the numbers are not all the same, the statistic is positive. There is some variability in the data set.
- If list A is more variable than list B, then the statistic for A is larger than the statistic for B.

Activity

With a partner or two, invent some statistic that measures variability and use it to compare the variability of the reading and the math scores shown here. The basic idea is to use the information in each set of scores to come up with a single number for that set that summarizes the amount of variability in it. Then you can use those two statistics to compare the variability in the two lists. If you have time, make up a different statistic that will also work.

Scores of 12 students on two assessments

Student ID	1	2	3	4	5	6	7	8	9	10	11	12
Math	98	100	101	99	100	101	99	100	100	101	102	99
Reading	80	110	90	120	100	105	85	118	100	82	100	110

Some Statistics That Are Used to Measure Variability

Here are several statistics for measuring variability that you may see in published research. You will probably notice a similarity to ones invented in the previous activity.

The **range** and the **interquartile range (IQR)** both summarize variability as a *distance from a representative low value to a representative high value.*

Range = Maximum value − Minimum value

This is not the ordinary way we use the word "range" in conversation. For the set of numbers 4, 5, 7, 12, the range statistic is 8. But in conversation we say the numbers range from 4 to 12. In strict statistical lingo, "the" range is a numerical statistic, a single value. Note that the range statistic for the set 104, 105, 107, 112 is also 8.

$$IQR = Q_3 - Q_1.$$

It is the difference between the first and third quartiles, rather than the difference between the very smallest and the very largest value. Geometrically, the IQR is the length of the box in the box plot. The IQR is not influenced by outliers as much as the range statistics is.

Another approach to measuring variability is to describe how the numbers tend to spread out from the center. This type of statistic measures the amount of **dispersion** or **scatter** in the data.

- **The mean absolute deviation**: The amount by which any number in a set differs from the mean is called its **mean deviation**. The mean absolute deviation is the mean of the absolute values of all the individual mean deviations.

  Example: X: 4, 5, 7, 12
  Mean = 7
  Mean deviations: −3, −2, 0, 5
  Absolute values of the deviations: 3, 2, 0, 5 or, by putting them in order, 0, 2, 3, 5
  Mean absolute deviation: $\dfrac{0 + 2 + 3 + 5}{4} = 2.5$

- **The standard deviation** (*SD*): The *SD* also summarizes how the individual numbers in a set differ from the mean of the set, but it is based on the squares of the deviations rather than their absolute values.
  SD = square root of the mean of the squared deviations.

  Example: X: 4, 5, 7, 12
  Mean = 7
  Mean deviations: −3, −2, 0, 5
  Squares of the deviations: 9, 4, 0, 25
  Mean of the squares: $\dfrac{9 + 4 + 0 + 25}{4} = \dfrac{38}{4} = 9.5$
  SD = square root: $\sqrt{9.5} = 3.08$

  This sequence of steps is summarized by the formula:

  $$SD = \sqrt{\frac{\sum (x - mean)^2}{n}} \text{ or } SD = \sqrt{\frac{\sum (x - \bar{x})^2}{n}}, \text{ where } \bar{x} \text{ represents the mean of a set of } xs.$$

- **The variance**: The square of the standard deviation is called the variance. It is also used as a measure of dispersion, mainly in more advanced work. It does not have a direct interpretation that is intuitive, because its units are the squares of the original units – "square pounds," for example, if the original data are weights in pounds. In short, the variance is the mean of the squares of the deviations. In the previous example, the variance of the data set is 9.5.

Some comments about the standard deviation:

- The standard deviation and the variance are the two most frequently used measures of variability in statistical research. That is mainly because their mathematical properties are well understood, particularly their connection to many probability distributions. These properties come into play, for instance, when you assign a margin of error to a survey.
- The units for the standard deviation are the same as the units for the data in the original data set. For instance, if your numbers represent ages in years, the standard deviation is also in years.
- What does the standard deviation tell you? Roughly speaking, it gives a typical amount by which the individual numbers are dispersed from the mean. In many research data sets it is unusual to see numbers more than about 2 standard deviations away from the mean. For example, if $SD = 3$, then you should expect to see a sizeable fraction of the numbers about three units away from the mean and very few of the numbers would be more than about six units away from the mean.

Calculation note: There are two slightly different formulas for standard deviation. One involves dividing by n, as we have shown, and one involves dividing by $n-1$. The SD that you usually see in published research is the one that divides by $n-1$. It is usually symbolized as s. There are reasons to prefer it in inferential statistics, where you consider your subjects to be representative of some larger group of people. For now, we will use the formula that uses n and symbolize it by SD because it makes more sense intuitively and is more likely to appear in texts at the K-8 level. The two versions give practically the same numerical answer except for very small data sets.

Which Measurement of Variability Should I Use?

The mean absolute deviation is gaining in popularity as the best way to introduce measuring variability in grades K-12, saving standard deviation for more advanced work.

In research, the mean absolute deviation is often chosen as the measure of variability when the median is used as the measure of center, while the standard deviation is used when the mean is the measure of center.

Exercises about Standard Deviations

Most of these exercises involve short lists of numbers so that you can do them easily by hand, but you should learn how to get the standard deviation on a calculator like a TI-83 or by computer using a program like Excel. They will produce the answer automatically and reduce errors, especially when the list of numbers is long.

Mathematical Properties of the Standard Deviation

In these exercises the standard deviation should be calculated using n as the divisor.

1. a. Measure the variability in this data set by calculating the standard deviation. Assuming these numbers are given in centimeters, confirm that the correct answer is 2 centimeters.

   X: 3, 4, 5, 6, 7, 8, 9

   b. Ignoring signs, what are the smallest and largest deviations that entered into your calculation of the standard deviation? This may help you see why 2 is a reasonable value for SD.

   c. Which numbers in the list are more than 1 standard deviation away from the mean?

d. If the original numbers in the data set had all been in inches, what would the units be for the standard deviation?

2. Confirm that *SD* for this list is 2.

X: −3, −2, −1, 0, 1, 2, 3

Compare this to the data and results in the previous exercise. Why do both lists have the same *SD*?

3. a. What happens to the standard deviation and the range if you add 4 to each of the numbers in a set? Demonstrate by adding 4 to each number in Exercise 1 above and computing the new range and *SD*. Write a sentence to explain why your answer makes sense.
    b. What happens to the standard deviation and the range if you subtract 6 from each of the numbers in a set? Demonstrate by subtracting 6 from each number in Exercise 1 above and computing the new range and *SD*.
    c. What happens to the standard deviation and the range if you add *k* to each of the numbers in a set? Demonstrate by adding *k* to each number in Exercise 1 above and computing the new range and *SD*.
    d. Using the results of a., b., and c. above, explain why – without doing any calculation – the two data sets, *X* and *Y*, have equal *SD*s. X = {1.2, 4.7, 9.0, 11.5} and Y = {4.3, 7.8, 12.1, 14.6}.

4. a. What happens to the standard deviation if you multiply each of the numbers in a set by 10? Demonstrate by multiplying each number in Exercise 1 above by 10 and computing the new *SD*.
    b. What happens to the standard deviation if you divide each of the numbers in a set by 10? Demonstrate by dividing each number in Exercise 1 above by 10 and computing the new *SD*.
    c. What happens to the standard deviation if you multiply each of the numbers in a set by *k*? Demonstrate by multiplying each number in Exercise 1 above by *k* and computing the new *SD*.
    d. What happens to the standard deviation if you divide each of the numbers in a set by the standard deviation of that set? Demonstrate by dividing each number in Exercise 1 above by the *SD* and computing the new *SD*.

5. a. Given X: 3, 4, 5, 6, 7, 8, 9, find the mean and standard deviation of *X*.
    b. Create *Y* by subtracting the mean of *X* from each number. Find the mean and standard deviation of *Y*.
    c. Create *Z* by dividing each number in *Y* by the standard deviation of *X*. Find the mean and standard deviation of *Z*.
    d. Summarize the work of a., b., and c. above in this table.

Variable	Values	Mean	SD
X	3, 4, 5, 6, 7, 8, 9		
Y			
Z			

e. Repeat a., b., c., and d. above for X: 1, 3, 5, 7.

Variable	Values	Mean	SD
X	1, 3, 5, 7		
Y			
Z			

f. Explain how you might have known the results for variable Z without doing any calculations. State a general principle about what happens to the mean and standard deviation of
a distribution when you subtract the mean from every value and then divide each by the
standard deviation to rescale it.

6. a. Can two sets of numbers have the same mean but different standard deviations? Explain
or give an example.

   b. Can two sets of numbers have different means but the same standard deviation? Explain
or give an example.

   c. What happens if you try to calculate the standard deviation of a set with only one number
in it? Does this make sense? Why or why not?

7. a. Which of these two variables would you guess has more variability when measured by the
standard deviation? When measured by the range? Do the calculations to check your
intuition.

   X: 40, 40, 40, 40, 50, 60, 60, 60, 60
   Y: 40, 49, 49, 49, 50, 51, 51, 51, 60

   b. In each list find all the numbers that are more than 1 standard deviation away from the
mean.

8. a. True or false? If two sets of numbers have the same
mean and the same standard deviation, then their
distributions must have the same shape.
     To investigate this question we have calculated
several statistics for these two sets of data, X and
Y, as shown on the right side of the table. Note
that X and Y have the same means and standard
deviations.
     Graph the data in some reasonable way, and
decide if the two distributions have the same shape.

   b. Here is another simple example. Confirm that
these two sets have the same mean and the same
SD but different shapes.

   X: 5, 9
   Y: 4, 5, 6, 7, 8, 9, 10

X	Y		X	Y
31.0	52.5	Mean	75.0	75.0
47.4	55.6	SD	19.4	19.4
61.3	57.6	Minimum	31.0	52.5
72.6	65.8	Q_1	61.3	57.6
81.0	68.9	Median	81.4	70.4
81.4	70.4	Q_3	91.3	84.7
87.4	77.1	Maximum	92.6	125.0
87.7	79.1			
91.3	84.7			
91.4	88.4			
92.6	125.0			

Standard Deviation in Research

1. Suppose you wanted to assess your students' skill in addition but you gave a test that was
way too easy for their grade level. What might you expect to see for the mean and standard

deviation of the test scores? Suppose, in contrast, that the test was way too hard. Then what would you expect for the mean and standard deviation?

2.   The table below shows summary statistics from an action research paper.

   a.   What do you think the topic of this teacher's research might have been? What might the units in this study be?
   b.   What do the two standard deviations tell you about what happened?

	Before training	*After training*
Mean	3.43	2.59
Standard deviation	1.61	0.73
Number of observations	16	16

   c.   Here are the raw data. Draw two parallel box plots to see how they help portray the change that was suggested by the standard deviations.

Time to complete problem set (minutes)

Student ID	1	2	3	4	5	6	7	8	9	10	11	12	13	14	15	16
Before training	1.15	1.62	2.00	2.35	2.37	2.55	2.55	2.90	3.08	3.23	3.48	4.02	4.95	5.95	6.12	6.67
After training	1.12	1.13	1.28	1.43	1.77	1.88	2.23	2.25	2.25	2.27	2.68	2.92	2.97	2.98	3.13	3.46

3.   Every Friday for 20 weeks a teacher gives her class of 16 children a math quiz. Each Friday she calculates the standard deviation for the scores that day. What does this standard deviation tell her? At the end of 20 weeks she writes down the 20 means and computes their standard deviation. What does this standard deviation tell her? Which standard deviation do you expect to be smaller? Explain why.

4.   Write a few sentences to explain the concept and purpose of the standard deviation to a school board member.

5.   In many medical studies groups given different treatments are compared to one another. The data from such an experiment are easiest to interpret when the groups are as alike as possible at the beginning of the study. The characteristics of the patients at the start of the study are called **baseline** characteristics. Here are a few lines adapted from a very long table of patient characteristics from a study that compared four different types of diets. Where does the standard deviation appear in this table, and why is it important? (*Source:* Frank M. Sacks, M.D., et al., Comparison of Weight-Loss Diets with Different Compositions of Fat, Protein, and Carbohydrates, *New England Journal of Medicine*, February 26, 2009.)

Baseline Characteristics of the Study Participants*

Characteristic	Low-Fat, Average Protein Group (N=204)	Low-Fat, High-Protein Group (N=202)	High-Fat, Average Protein Group (N=204)	High-Fat, High-Protein Group (N=201)	All Participants (N=811)	Participants Who Completed the Study (N=645)
Age-yr	51±9	50±10	52±9	51±9	51±9	52±9
Sex-no. (%)						
Female	126 (62)	135 (67)	125 (61)	129 (64)	515 (64)	397 (62)
Male	78 (38)	67 (33)	79 (39)	72 (36)	296 (36)	248 (38)
Weight-kg	94±16	92±13	92±17	94±16	93±16	93±16

* Plus–minus values are means +/– *SD*

6. This graph is based on one in an action research paper by a 4th grade teacher. The height of a bar gives the mean for a group of students. The error bar extends one standard deviation above and below the top of the bar. What can you say about these two groups of students based on their mean scores and the standard deviations?

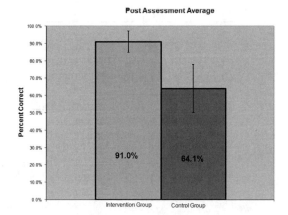

7. The following discussion appeared on a diabetes management website:

> There seems to be a lot of buzz about the fact that it's not just about A1C's anymore; rather, it's about using the Standard Deviation to evaluate the success of your diabetes management. If you think about it, it's common sense really: a simple average of your blood glucose over the past three months doesn't tell you how far you've strayed from the ideal range. You may get an excellent "average" number that is nothing but a middle point between the highs and lows you've been experiencing.
>
> . . .
>
> The theory is that the greater the deviation in your blood sugars, the more likely you are to experience microvascular damage in eyes, kidneys, etc. Dr. Hirsch suggests that diabetics should aim for an *SD* of one-third of their mean blood sugar. So, if your mean blood sugar were 120 mg/dl, you would want your standard deviation to be no more than 40 mg/dl, or one-third of the mean.
>
> (*Source:* http://www.diabetesmine.com/2005/07/standard_deviat.html)

Does it make intuitive sense to you that the severity of the condition is related to the standard deviation? Why might this be so?

Math Explorations Involving Standard Deviations

1. a. Find a set of two numbers that has $SD = 3$.
   b. Find a larger set of numbers that has $SD = 3$.

2. (Wicked hard) The *SD* for the arithmetic sequence 1, 2, 3, 4, 5, 6, 7 is 2. For what other arithmetic sequences 1, 2, 3, . . ., *n* is *SD* an integer?

3. An alternative formula for the variance is $var = \frac{\sum x^2}{n} - \left(\frac{\sum x}{n}\right)^2$. This formula is algebraically equivalent to the usual formula and produces the same result.

   a. Use this formula to show that the SD for X: 1, 2, 3, 4, 5, 6, 7 is 2.
   b. A set of ten numbers has mean 50 and SD = 5. If the number 60 is removed from that set, what are the resulting mean and SD?

4. A theorem by the Russian mathematician Pafnuty Chebyshev implies that the difference between the mean and the median for a set of data can never be more than 1 standard deviation. Play around with sets of numbers and see how close you can get to this limit.

The Standard Deviation of a Probability Distribution

In the same way that we were able to define the mean of a random variable known by its probability distribution, we can define the standard deviation. The mean of a probability distribution is intended to describe the mean we would get in an infinite number of outcomes of some experiment. Similarly, the theoretical standard deviation describes the amount of variability we would get if we recorded all the outcomes "forever."

Here's how that calculation works where X represents the outcomes of rolling a single regular die. As with raw data, the standard deviation is the square root of the mean of the squared deviations.

The probability distribution for X consists of all the possible values and their probabilities.

Probability distribution: rolls of a regular die						
Outcome, x	1	2	3	4	5	6
Probability, p	$\frac{1}{6}$	$\frac{1}{6}$	$\frac{1}{6}$	$\frac{1}{6}$	$\frac{1}{6}$	$\frac{1}{6}$

First we confirm that the mean = $E(X) = 3.5$.

$$\text{Mean} = E(X) = \tfrac{1}{6}(1) + \tfrac{1}{6}(2) + \tfrac{1}{6}(3) + \tfrac{1}{6}(4) + \tfrac{1}{6}(5) + \tfrac{1}{6}(6) = \frac{1+2+3+4+5+6}{6} = \frac{21}{6} = 3.5$$

Next we find the deviations:

Probability distribution: rolls of a regular die						
Outcome, x	1	2	3	4	5	6
Probability, p	$\frac{1}{6}$	$\frac{1}{6}$	$\frac{1}{6}$	$\frac{1}{6}$	$\frac{1}{6}$	$\frac{1}{6}$
Deviation from E(X)	1−3.5	2−3.5	3−3.5	4−3.5	5−3.5	6−3.5

Variance = Expected value of the squared deviations

$$= \tfrac{1}{6}(1-3.5)^2 + \tfrac{1}{6}(2-3.5)^2 + \tfrac{1}{6}(3-3.5)^2 + \tfrac{1}{6}(4-3.5)^2 + \tfrac{1}{6}(5-3.5)^2 + \tfrac{1}{6}(6-3.5)^2$$

$$= \frac{6.25 + 2.25 + 0.25 + 2.25 + 6.25}{6} = \frac{17.5}{6} = 2.917$$

Standard deviation = $\sqrt{\text{Variance}} = \sqrt{2.917} = 1.708$

This method of finding the standard deviation is parallel to the approach we used for an ordinary data set.

Exercises for Standard Deviations of Probability Distributions

1. For the example of the die above, how many of the six possible outcomes are more than 1 standard deviation from the mean?

2. You have a special die where the six faces are labeled 0, 0, 0, 1, 1, 1. Let X represent the outcome when the die is rolled. Find the expected value and the standard deviation of X.

3. Find the expected value and the standard deviation for X where X represents the outcomes of a die labeled with two 5s and four 10s.

4. Let X represent the *sum* you get when you roll two regular dice. Find every possible value of X and the probability for each such outcome. Use this information to find the expected value and standard deviation of X. How many of the possible outcomes are more than 1 standard deviation away from the mean?

5. Let X represent the absolute value of the *difference* when you roll two regular dice. Find the expected value and standard deviation of X.

6

PLACEMENT OF INDIVIDUALS IN A GROUP

Introductory Activity

Talking to Mom

The results of a really important test have just come back, and you need to tell your mother how you did. On this test a perfect score is 100.

What would you tell Mom if you were Alix? Frankie? Jeslie? Write down the exact words you would use.

Here are the class results:

Alix	Barry	Cassandra	Derrick	Ethan	Frankie	Guy	Halle	Indira	Jeslie
100	50	45	45	45	45	45	45	45	44

Placement of One Value in a Whole Set of Values

In many assessment situations you may need to describe how a particular individual compares to others in a group. Examples include giving the standing of a child in a classroom, or a school within a district. In doing so you are giving a **relative placement**. Not surprisingly, several statistics have been invented to do this.

Perhaps the two most popular relative placement statistics are the **percentile** and the **z-score**, both of which make the most sense for large data sets. For small data sets these statistics may be overkill, or even misleading, and it may be best just to say something like "Hannah ranked 3rd out of 12" and present a table showing all the student scores.

Percentiles

Percentiles are commonly used in reporting results of national standardized tests such as NAEP or SAT. A child's score on a standardized test may be *at* the 87th percentile or *in* the 87th percentile. In either case the intention is to indicate that, roughly speaking, the child scored *higher than* 87% of the people who took the exam. In short, this student scored high *compared to others*. We may also say that the **percentile rank** for that child is 87. Percentiles make most sense for large data sets where one individual makes up only a tiny percentage of the entire group; they can be essentially meaningless if the group is too small. By definition, the percentiles split a distribution into 100 equal parts.

A formula for calculating the percentile rank (*PR*) of a data value, *x*, is:

$$PR = \frac{\text{(number of values less than } x) + \text{(half the number of values equal to } x)}{\text{total number of values in the data set}} \times 100$$

Percentile ranks are often rounded to the nearest whole number.

You can see from this formula that the definition of a percentile is intended to take into account scores that are tied with the one you are referring to. In many applications the fraction of scores exactly equal to the one you care about is small enough to ignore.

The median of a set of data, because it splits the data into equal upper and lower parts, is by definition the same as the 50th percentile. Similarly, the first and third quartiles are the 25th and 75th percentiles.

Exercises about Percentiles

1. This table was taken from the NAEP website (http://nces.ed.gov/nationsreportcard/nde).

    a. What is the subject matter of this NAEP test? What group of students does this table describe?
    b. Interpret the number 213 in the first line of the table. What percentage of the males scored lower than 213?
    c. What was the median score for the male students? For the female students?
    d. About what percentage of the male students scored higher than 280?
    e. About what percentage of the female students scored between 230 and 263 points?

    NAEP results: Percentiles for mathematics, Grade 4, gender, by jurisdiction, 2007

Gender	Jurisdictions	Year	10th percentile	25th percentile	50th percentile	75th percentile	90th percentile
Male	Vermont	2007	213	231	250	266	280
Female	Vermont	2007	211	230	247	263	276

2. In a set of 1,000 test scores your own test score is 400. It turns out that 610 of the test takers scored lower than you, and that 49 other people also got a 400. What is your percentile rank?

3. (Not quite a trick question)

    a. You scored at the 90th percentile on an algebra test. How good are you at algebra?
    b. Jasmine scored at the 89th percentile. How much better are you than Jasmine?
    c. What does a percentile tell you? What does it *not* tell you?

4. A class consists of ten students. Here are their grades on a test:

Name	Noah	Emma	Jacob	Elizabeth	Benjamin	Ava	Logan	Olivia	Mason	Emily
Grade	40	41	74	75	76	90	91	92	92	93

Find the percentile rank for Emily and Logan. What do you think about using percentile ranks here to describe relative placement?

5. You score at the 90th percentile on an algebra test and at the 50th percentile on a reading test. Therefore your average percentile is 70. Explain what each of these three scores means. Explain why the 70 is almost certainly meaningless. Be very careful about interpreting averages of percentile ranks: such measurements may be bogus, yet they appear in school reports.

6. Refer to the accompanying growth chart.

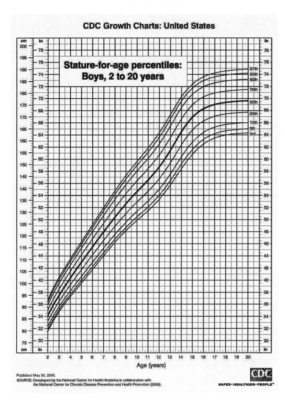

a. A 15-year-old boy is 5 feet 5 inches tall. About what percentage of 15-year-old boys are taller than him?

b. About what height will put a 10-year-old boy at the 95th percentile for height?

c. At about what age is a boy half his final height?

Standardized Scores (Z-Scores)

A second statistic used to describe relative placement is the **z-score**, which depends on the mean and the standard deviation of the data set. The z-score is designed to tell you how far away from average a given score is. The larger the magnitude of the z-score, the farther from the mean it is.

The z-score is an example of a **standardized score** (or standard score). When you standardize a score you re-express it in terms of some specified unit. The z-score as it is used in statistics converts everything to "standard deviation units." This allows us to compare relative placement in data sets which have different units to begin with. For example, we could compare the relative standing of a student's reading score and mathematics score even though the two tests were based on different scales.

The z-score for a given value, x, tells you the number of standard deviations above or below the mean that x is. For example, if your z-score on an assessment is -2, then you came in 2 standard deviations below the mean score. In some school districts, eligibility for certain services is determined by standardized scores on particular assessments. See Box 6.1 for one example.

BOX 6.1

Eligibility for special education services for children with autism (Vermont)

For all adverse effect measures, a student must have documented performance levels determined to be among the lowest 15% compared to average performing grade level peers *or*
have a standard score that is at least 1 standard deviation below the mean on a norm-referenced test.

(*Source:* http://education.vermont.gov/new/pdfdoc/pgm_sped/
data_reports_pubs/autism/asd_sped_eligibility.pdf)

In short, z-scores give placement using the *SD* as the unit of measurement. So, $z = 1.5$ means 1.5 standard deviations. If a set of ages has mean = 50 months and *SD* = 7 months, then the age of a subject with $z = 1$ is 57 months. The age of a subject with $z = -1$ is 43 months. In this illustration, $z = 1$ means 7 months above average, not 1 month. You measure placement by groups of 7 because the *SD* of the set of ages is 7 months.

This transformation can be visualized by a sketch like the one in Figure 6.1.

In contrast to the standardized scores, the original data (the ages in this case) are called the **raw scores**.

The formal definition for a z-score is given in Box 6.2.

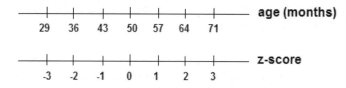

FIGURE 6.1 Raw scores and corresponding z-scores

BOX 6.2

Definition of z-score

$$z = \frac{\text{individual deviation}}{\text{standard deviation}} = \frac{\text{value} - \text{mean}}{\text{standard deviation}} = \frac{x - \bar{x}}{SD}$$

Because positive z-scores represent values which are above the mean, and negative z-scores represent values below the mean, the order of the terms in the numerator of the formula is important.

In many data distributions the majority of the values are no more than 1 standard deviation from the mean, and it is very rare to find individuals more than 3 standard deviations away from the mean. In many circumstances standardized scores with absolute value more than 2 raise some kind of flag for researchers.

Notation convention: When we get to the sections of this book that deal with inferential statistics, we will need to distinguish between situations where we know or pretend we know a true value for a mean or standard deviation of a distribution and situations where we are estimating those values from a limited available data set. At that point we shall sometimes see the formula for the z-score written as $z = \dfrac{x - \mu}{\sigma}$. The Greek letters μ (mu) and σ (sigma) are used specifically to indicate that the mean and standard deviation are assumed to be true.

Exercises for Z-Scores

1. In 2009 the mean score on a job skills test taken by about a thousand people was 130 points with standard deviation 16 points. On this exam Mila scored 162 points. The next year she took the 2010 version of the test and scored 159 points, but that year the mean score was 135 points with a standard deviation of 12 points.

   a. In which year did she do better? What does "better" mean?
   b. Find her placement each year in terms of standard deviation units – that is, *how many standard deviations* above the mean was she placed each year? What were the z-scores for each of her raw test scores?

2. Many babies are evaluated for length and weight. Draw sketches of the five babies named in the table.

	z-score for weight		
	−3	0	3
z-score for height −3	Anna		Brad
0		Edmund	
3	Corinne		Dempsey

3. a. Standardize this set of quiz scores by re-expressing each original score as its z-score. What are the largest and smallest z-scores?

   X: 66, 68, 70, 72, 74, 76, 78

   b. The teacher decides to give everyone 10 extra points. Let Y stand for the new set of grades. Standardize the Y grades and compare this set of z-scores to the ones in a. above. Why does your answer make sense?

4. Convert these seven quiz scores to z-scores: 1, 2, 3, 4, 5, 6, 7. How would you explain to a parent the distinction between a quiz score of 1 and a quiz score that had a standardized score of 1?

5. Take some set of data from your own classroom and standardize it. What are the largest and smallest z-scores? Did any of the z-scores have magnitude more than 2? Make a histogram and a box plot for your data.

6. These graphs show a peaked and a flat distribution of test scores.

   a. For each of these find the percentage of scores that have $z > 2$. You can use the information that both means are 6.5 and that the standard deviations are 3.45 and 1.88 for the flat and peaked distributions respectively. Why is the z-score for the 12 not the same in both distributions?

   b. Confirm the values given for the means and standard deviations.

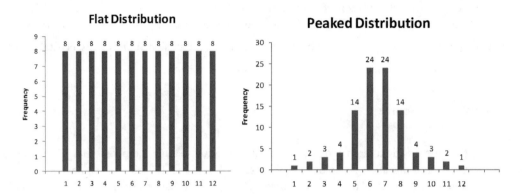

Exercises 7-10: The formula $z = \dfrac{x - \text{mean}}{SD}$ describes a relationship among four algebraic variables. Given any three of them you can solve for the fourth.

7. Do the necessary algebra to find the missing value in each row of this table. As noted above, the equation may be written as $z = \dfrac{x - \mu}{\sigma}$ where we use the Greek lower-case mu (μ) for mean, and sigma (σ) for standard deviation.

Data value	Mean	Standard deviation	Z-score
x	μ	σ	z
12	18	2	
88		6	1.5
	5	3	2.5
77	70		1.75

8. A car has a fuel economy rating of 34 mpg, which places it 2 standard deviations above the national average. If the standard deviation of fuel economy ratings is 6, what is the mean fuel economy rating?

9. The finishing time of runners in a marathon has a mean of 169 minutes, with variance also equal to 169. If someone finished with a time that was 2 standard deviations above the mean, how long did it take her to finish the race?

10. Carl and Carla took the same test, and Carl's score of 52 equated to a z-score of -3, while Carla's score of 79 was 1.5 standard deviations above the mean. If Beverly scored 91, what is her z-score?

Math Explorations Involving Z-Scores

1. (Z-scores and linear functions) For the set of data X: 66, 68, 70, 72, 74, 76, 78, the mean is 72 and the standard deviation is 4. We know therefore that $z = \frac{x - 72}{4}$ is a linear function that transforms x into z.

   a. Plot the line determined by this function and find its slope and the intercept.

   b. Determine the relationship that converts z into x.

2. a. Make up any set of data where at least one value has a z-score greater than 3.

   b. (A tough one) What is the smallest set of numbers for which this is possible?

3. Show that the sum of the squares of the z-scores for the data set X: 2, 3, 4, 5, 6, 7, 8 is 7, which happens to be n. Make up any other set of numbers and find the sum of the squares of their z-scores. Do you always get n?

7

THE NORMAL CURVE

Introductory Activity

A Predictable Pattern?

Some phenomena that are essentially random nevertheless generate predictable patterns in the long run. This activity – with any luck – will provide a taste of that experience.

Part 1: A Thought Experiment

Imagine that you toss a fair coin 16 times. It is impossible to predict the number of heads that any group of 16 tosses will show. It could be any number from 0 to 16. But perhaps if we collect the results of many sets of 16 tosses a familiar pattern may emerge.

Draw a sketch of what you anticipate a frequency graph of the results might look like. Use the axes shown for your sketch. Assume you will have the results from about 100 groups of 16 tosses, so that the total of the frequencies is about 100. Explain how you decided what shape graph to make.

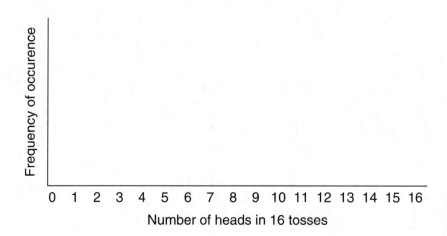

Part 2: Data-Based Experiment

Here are two options for collecting data. You can go ahead and actually toss a coin 16 times, record the number of heads, and then repeat this until the class has collected about 100 frequencies, or you can choose random rows from Table A.4 (in the Appendix), which were generated by computer randomization. Draw the frequency graph for these data. Discuss how well or how poorly this data-based graph matches the hypothetical one you made in Part 1.

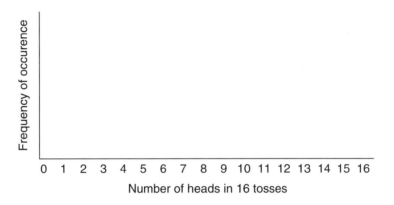

Normal Curve

The normal curve represents the most important theoretical distribution in statistics. At this point in the statistics course it serves to bring together the basic concepts of shape, measure of center, and measure of variability. It is useful in descriptive statistics because many naturally occurring distributions may be represented by normal curves, and it plays a crucial role in statistical inference because it is used to determine margins of error for many estimates.

1. *The histograms for many real sets of data are close to normal curves in shape.*
   Distributions of many human, animal, and plant characteristics have normal distributions. For example, if a sample of your blood was passed through a machine that counts red blood cells, the machine would show the distribution of red blood cells of different sizes in that sample. It would print out a curve like this one. That tail on the right side results from multiple cells going through the machine together and getting recorded as one large cell. The units for cell size (by volume) on the horizontal axis are femtoliters (fL). A femtoliter is one-quadrillionth of a liter (.000 000 000 000 001 liter). "REL#" is the abbreviation for "relative number."

Red Blood Cell Histogram

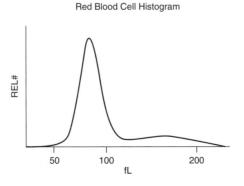

Because the normal curve is so well studied, working with data becomes simpler when the histogram of the data is close to the shape of a normal curve. The simple phrase "These data are normally distributed" conveys a quick intuitive image of the data.

In some technical areas, especially engineering, normal curves are called "Gaussian," because the mathematician Gauss made major contributions in the use of this family of functions, particularly with regard to describing errors in astronomical measurement.

2. *Normal curves are crucial in statistical inference.*

When you make an inference from sample data to a larger population it is crucial to have some idea of the likely magnitude of any error you may be making. The calculations used to determine the margin of error in a survey are based on the normal curve, as indicated by Figure 7.1. The figure shows the margin of error when a survey has a reported percentage of 50%. The details for this will be discussed later.

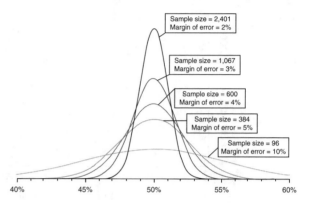

FIGURE 7.1 Normal curve used to determine margin of error in a survey

(*Source of image:* Margin of Error, in *Wikipedia, The Free Encyclopedia*, retrieved June 29, 2007, from http://en.wikipedia.org/w/index. php?title=Margin_of_error&oldid=140566111.)

Properties of the Normal Curve

When we say data are normally distributed, we are referring to the appearance of a histogram of the data. Clearly, histograms can have many shapes, but one type comes up very often: it is symmetric, peaks in the middle, and drops fairly rapidly on both sides as you get further from the middle. The figure shown in Table 7.1 below is typical. A smooth curve passing through the tops of the bars may remind you of a bell. There are specific bell shapes that are called **normal curves**, and when the histogram of a data set comes close to this shape we say that the data are approximately normally distributed. Because a normal curve is smooth and a histogram is not, no histogram can have precisely the shape of a normal curve, but many are very close to it.

One of the first scholars to recognize that many human characteristics had approximately normal distributions was the Belgian scientist and sociologist Adolphe Quetelet, who published the following data in 1817. They are chest circumference measurements for 5,732 Scottish soldiers. Table 7.1 shows a frequency table for his data, and a histogram is also shown. A normal curve fits the histogram very well, so we say that the data are *approximately* normally distributed. In more casual speech we may say that the chest circumferences *are* normally distributed.

Strictly speaking, a normal curve is the graph of a specific mathematical function. It is a fairly unusual-looking equation, but, like a linear function, it contains exactly two constants that determine its shape. One constant determines where the peak is, and the other determines how wide

TABLE 7.1 Approximately normal frequency distribution of chest-circumference measurements for 5,732 Scottish soldiers

Chest circumference (inches)	Frequency	Percentage
33	3	0.1
34	19	0.3
35	81	1.4
36	189	3.3
37	409	7.1
38	753	13.1
39	1,062	18.5
40	1,082	18.9
41	935	16.3
42	646	11.3
43	313	5.5
44	168	2.9
45	50	0.9
46	18	0.3
47	3	0.1
48	1	0
Total	5,732	100

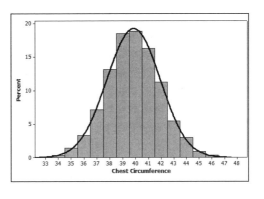

Source: Quetelet data, 1817.

the curve is. By changing the values of these constants you can produce a whole variety of normal curves. Only curves determined by this function are correctly called "normal."

Here is the equation: $y = f(x) = \dfrac{1}{\sqrt{2\pi b}} e^{\frac{-(x-a)^2}{2b^2}}$

The value of *a* determines the center of the curve, and the value of *b* determines how wide the curve is. We call *a* the mean of the curve and *b* the standard deviation. For our purposes you never need to work with this formula. We show it here as a reminder that "normal curve" and "normal distribution" are actually strictly defined mathematical concepts.

Here are various normal curves superimposed on histograms. The horizontal scale is the same on all three graphs. Curves A and B have the same mean but different standard deviations. Curves A and C have different means but the same standard deviation. The total number of observations is the same in all three histograms.

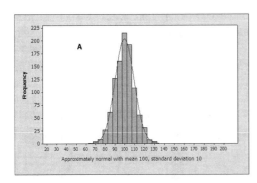

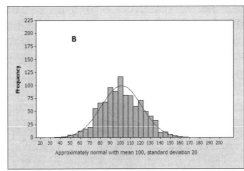

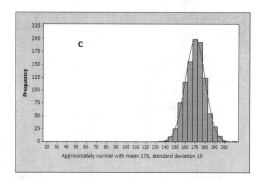

The next figure shows a generic normal curve on which the two **inflection points** have been marked. Mathematicians say the curve changes concavity at the inflection point. The middle part of the curve is called concave down; the outside parts are concave up.

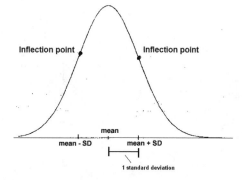

The distance along the horizontal axis from the mean to the point directly under the inflection point is the standard deviation of the normal curve.

When we approximate a specific histogram by a normal curve, the mean and standard deviation of the normal curve are taken to be the same as the mean and standard deviation of the data in the histogram. For the table of the chest circumferences the 5,732 measurements have mean 39.8 inches and standard deviation 2.1 inches, and their histogram is very close to a normal curve. The normal curve superimposed on it has the same mean and standard deviation as the data set. We have redrawn the normal curve by itself without the underlying histogram.

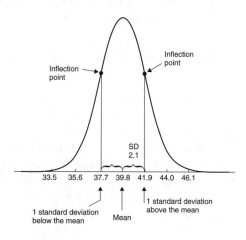

The peak is directly above 39.8 on the horizontal axis, and the inflection points are 2.1 units to the left and to the right of the mean. By the time you reach 3 standard deviations from the mean (33.5 and 46.1 on the axis) the graph is quite close to the axis, indicating that chest circumferences smaller than 33.5 inches or larger than 46.1 inches are rarely, if ever, observed in this population.

Big idea: Because of its mathematical formula, every normal curve has the same percentage of area within a given number of standard deviations from the mean.

For practical purposes, every (approximately) normal distribution of data has (approximately) the same percentage of data values within a given number of standard deviations from the mean.

Some of these percentages are given in the so-called 68–95–99.7 rule.

Box 7.1

Normal curve rule (68–95–99.7 rule)

When the histogram of a data set is well approximated by a normal curve:
about 68% of the values are within 1 standard deviation of the mean,

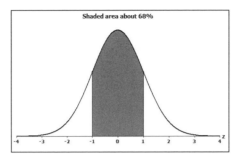

about 95% of the values are within 2 standard deviations,

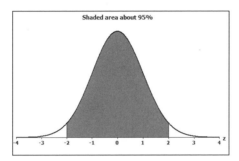

and practically all (99.7%) of the values are within 3 standard deviations.

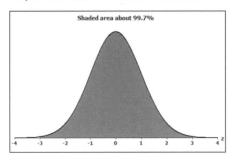

The closer the curve approximates the histogram, the more accurately these percentages hold.

Conversely, if a histogram is *not* well approximated by a normal curve, then these percentages may not be correct.

Application of the 68–95–99.7 Rule

This rule allows us to estimate fractions of data sets that fall into specified groups *without having to do any counting.*

Illustration Based on the Chest Circumference Data

The chest circumference data are approximately normal, with mean = 39.8 and standard deviation = 2.1 inches.

a. Estimate the percentage of soldiers who have a chest circumference between 37.7 and 41.9 inches.

b. About what percentage have a chest circumference between 39.8 and 41.9 inches?

c. About what percentage have a chest circumference smaller than 37.7 inches?

Solution:

It will be helpful to show a sketch with two labeled axes for each question.

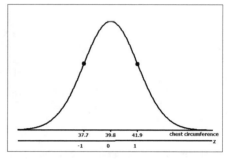

FIGURE 7.2 Chest measurements and corresponding z–scores

a. In Figure 7.2 the two axes are labeled "chest circumference" and "*z*." The curve is centered over 39.8 on the top axis and 0 on the bottom axis. The chest circumferences corresponding to the mean ± 1 standard deviation are 39.8 ± 2.1, or 37.7 and 41.9 inches.

   The percentage of soldiers whose chest circumference is between 37.7 and 41.9 inches is represented by the percentage of the total area under the normal curve that is contained within 1 standard deviation of the mean. By the 68–95–99.7 rule that is 68%. In Figure 7.3 we emphasize that this represents an *area* under the curve by shading it.

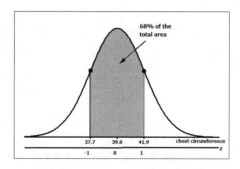

FIGURE 7.3 Percentage of soldiers with chest circumference between 37.7 and 41.9 inches

b. Figure 7.4 shows a normal curve with the area corresponding to the interval 39.8 to 41.9 shaded. By symmetry, this area is one half of 68%, or 34%. Thus about 34% of the soldiers have chest circumference between 39.8 and 41.9 inches.

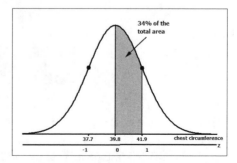

FIGURE 7.4 Percentage of soldiers with chest circumference between 39.8 and 41.9 inches

c. The shaded area in Figure 7.5 represents those soldiers whose chest circumferences were smaller than 37.7 inches.

The entire left side of the graph represents 50% of the total area, and from b. above we know that the unshaded part of the left half represents 34% of the total area. Therefore the shaded area is equal to 50% − 34% = 16% of the total area. So about 16% of the soldiers have chest circumferences smaller than 37.7 inches.

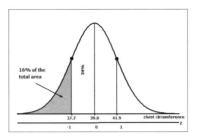

FIGURE 7.5 Percentage of soldiers with chest circumference smaller than 37.7 inches

Exercises Using the 68–95–99.7 Rule

1. A large set of exam scores is approximately normal. The mean score is 500, and the standard deviation is 100.

    a. Estimate the percentage of the scores that are higher than 500, higher than 600, and higher than 700.
    b. Estimate the percentile ranks for exam scores of 500, 400, and 300.
    c. About what percentage of the scores are between 500 and 600? Between 400 and 600? Between 300 and 600? Between 300 and 700?
    d. Suppose this set of exam scores was *not* normally distributed. Say its shape was *flat*. How would this affect your answer to a. above?

2. a. A large school district establishes a policy that any student whose z-score is less than −2 on a certain test qualifies for special assistance. It turns out that 200 students meet this criterion. A parent demands that the cut-off score be changed to $z = -1$. If you assume that the set of scores for all students in the district has a normal distribution, then how many additional students would qualify for assistance? If the cost of this service is $1,000 per student, how much would changing the cut-off increase the budget? Express this increase both in dollars and as a percentage increase.
    b. If the district had another $200,000 to spend on this assistance, approximately what z-score should it set as the cut-off for a student to qualify? (Use Table 7.2 below to get a more precise answer.)

More Precise Percentages for a Normal Curve

For certain calculations you may want a more precise set of z-scores and areas for a normal curve. Such values are built into many graphing calculators and into much spreadsheet software. There are also many versions of printed normal curve tables. Table 7.2 is called a *cumulative* distribution table because the areas given in the table accumulate all the way from the extreme left until the tabled z-value. The shaded picture indicates how the table works.

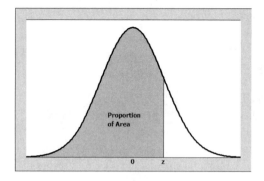

TABLE 7.2 Cumulative normal distribution table

z	Area	z	Area
0	0.500	1.5	0.933
0.1	0.540	1.6	0.945
0.2	0.579	1.645	0.950
0.3	0.618	1.7	0.955
0.4	0.655	1.8	0.964
0.5	0.691	1.9	0.971
0.524	0.700	1.96	0.975
0.6	0.726	2.0	0.977
0.674	0.750	2.1	0.982
0.7	0.758	2.2	0.986
0.8	0.788	2.3	0.989
0.842	0.800	2.33	0.990
0.9	0.816	2.4	0.992
1.0	0.841	2.5	0.994
1.036	0.850	2.6	0.995
1.1	0.864	2.7	0.997
1.2	0.885	2.8	0.997
1.28	0.900	2.9	0.998
1.3	0.903	3.0	0.999
1.4	0.919		

Exercises (Use the More Precise Normal Curve Table)

1. Why is the area on the $z = 0$ line equal to 0.500? If you shade all the area under the curve that is to the left of $z = 0$, what percentage of the total area will be shaded?
2. According to Table 7.2, what percentage of the area under the curve is between $z = -1$ and 1? Between –2 and 2? Between –3 and 3? Check that your answers are very close to the approximations given by the 68–95–99.7 rule.
3. In a normal distribution of weights of 3rd grade boys, find the percentage of weights whose z-scores are:

   a. Less than $z = 2.33$.
   b. More than $z = 1.65$.
   c. Between the mean and $z = 2.5$.
   d. Between $z = 0$ and $z = -1.6$.
   e. Less than $z = -1.6$.
   f. More than $z = -1.6$.
   g. Between $z = 2$ and $z = 2.5$. Between $z = -2$ and $z = -2.5$.
   h. More than 1 standard deviation from the mean.
   i. If these were the weights of 4th grade girls, would the answers be different? Explain.

4. Decide if each statement is true or false, and justify your decision.
   For a normal curve:

   a. The area between $z = 0$ and $z = 1$ equals the area between $z = 0$ and $z = -1$.
   b. The area between $z = 0$ and $z = 1$ equals the area between $z = 1$ and $z = 2$.
   c. The percentile rank of $z = 1$ equals the percentile rank of $z = -1$.

5. a. In any normal distribution approximately what z-score cuts off the top 10%? The bottom 20%?

   b. What two z-scores cut off the middle 30%? The middle 50%?

6. Label the raw scores corresponding to the z-scores given on the axis of this graph.

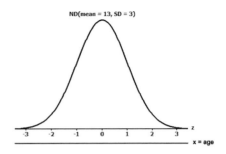

ND(mean = 13, SD = 3)

7. Label the z-scores corresponding to the raw scores given on this graph.

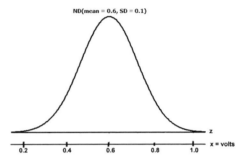

ND(mean = 0.6, SD = 0.1)

8. A large set of exam scores is approximately normal. The mean score is 500, and the standard deviation is 100.

   a. What percentage of the scores are between 450 and 550? Between 550 and 650? Why do you get two different answers when the gap in both cases is 100 points?

   b. What percentage of the scores are higher than 550? Higher than 650?

   c. What is the percentile rank for an exam score of 710? Round to the nearest whole percentage.

9. A large set of exam scores is approximately normal. The mean score is 500, and the standard deviation is 100.

   a. Jill's exam was ranked at the 80th percentile. Estimate her exam score.

   b. Jack's exam score was at the 30th percentile. Estimate his exam score.

10. A large school district establishes a policy that any student whose z-score is less than –2 on a certain test qualifies for special assistance. It turns out that 200 students meet this criterion. If the cost of this service is $1,000 per student, how much would the budget drop if the cut-off were changed to z = –2.5? Assume that the set of scores for all students in the district has a normal distribution.

11. Boris Gudenov entered a Russian literature contest. Last year's competition results are symbolized by ND(mean = 230, SD = 11) or more simply ND(230, 11). If the results are similar this year and Boris wants to score in the top 10%, what score will be good enough for Gudenov?

12. The distribution of scores on a test that assesses XXXX is normal, with mean equal to 50 points and standard deviation = 10 points.

   a. On this assessment approximately what test score cuts off: the top 5%? The bottom 5%? The bottom 2.5%? The top 2.5%?

b.   Why does it not matter for this exercise what the purpose of the assessment is? Make up a purpose if you like.

13. A quality control engineer for an electronics manufacturer evaluates each item produced in a particular run, each time recording a voltage reading. The engineer finds that the collection of readings is approximately normally distributed, with mean about 7.4 volts and SD about 0.6 volts.

   a.   What fraction of the readings were between 7.0 and 8.0 volts?
   b.   What is the probability that a reading taken at random will be over 8.6 volts?
   c.   What is the probability that a random reading will be outside the range of 6.9 to 7.9?

14. The results on a certain blood test performed on healthy people are known to be normally distributed, with mean = 60 and SD = 18. Approximately what are the chances that a healthy person will have a result more than 89? If that happens he or she will be called back for further testing. Such tests, done on a general population to locate people at risk, are called **screening tests**. Possibly familiar examples include mammograms and colonoscopies.

15. The lifetimes of a certain brand of floodlights are normally distributed, with mean = 210 hours and SD = 56 hours. Let X be the lifetime of a light picked at random. The company guarantees that its light will last at least 120 hours. What percentage of the bulbs does it expect to have to replace under this guarantee?

16. a.   In a distribution of grades, mean = 80 and SD = 10. Yet it is not true that 34% of the distribution is between 80 and 90. In fact, we cannot find what percentage of the grades lie between 80 and 90 from the above information. Why?

   b.   The distribution of professors' salaries at a large college has mean = $67,000 and SD = $4,000. What percentage of the professors earn between $67,000 and $71,000? Be careful.

Math Connections for Normal Curves

1.   The two parallel axes under the earlier normal curve sketches of the soldiers' chest measurements show that the transformation from an original set of scores, x, to standardized scores, z, is a linear function. A change of 2.1 units on the x-scale consistently corresponds to a change of 1 unit on the z-scale.

   The function is given by $z = f(x) = \dfrac{x - \bar{x}}{s}$ where $\bar{x}$ is the mean, and s is the standard deviation.

   For the chest measurement data we have $z = \dfrac{x - 39.8}{2.1}$ or $z = \dfrac{1}{2.1}x - \dfrac{39.8}{2.1}$ or $z = .476x - 18.952$.

   a.   Use any one of these formulas to graph z as a linear function, $f(x)$.
   b.   Find $f(40)$ and explain what it means.
   c.   What is a reasonable domain for the function in this context?

2.   (Graphs based on the normal curve formula) The general formula for a normal curve is $y = f(x) = \dfrac{1}{\sqrt{2\pi b}}e^{\frac{-(x-a)^2}{2b^2}}$, where a is the mean and b is the standard deviation.

   a.   The simplest version, the so-called *standard* normal (the graph of z-scores), has mean = 0 and standard deviation = 1. Therefore its formula is $y = \dfrac{1}{\sqrt{2\pi}}e^{\frac{-x^2}{2}}$. Use a graphing calculator to show this normal curve.

   b.   Use a graphing calculator to plot the normal curve that describes the chest measurements. The mean is 39.8 inches, and the standard deviation is 2.1 inches.

8

CORRELATION

Introductory Investigation

Do You See It?

What does this graph mean? Read all the labels carefully. Why would a researcher print these two scatter plots side by side?

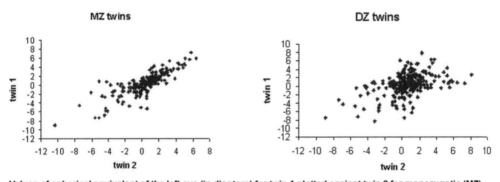

Values of spherical equivalent of the left eye (in diopters) for twin 1 plotted against twin 2 for monozygotic (MZ) and dizygotic (DZ) twin pairs. Minus values represent myopic subjects; plus values represent hyperopic ones.

Correlation

Many studies are designed to see how two variables are related. Here are a few familiar examples:

Study	Are these variables related?	
1	Free lunch status	Reading ability
2	Teacher salary	School performance
3	Class size	Dropout rate
4	Smoking	Lung cancer
5	Echinacea dose	Cold symptoms
6	Father's eyesight	Child's eyesight

To conduct such a study, you need a set of subjects, and you need to record their scores on *two* variables. In the specific language of statistics such investigations are called **correlational studies**. Correlational studies attempt to describe how two variables are *associated*. The primary graph for such studies is the **scatter plot**, and the primary statistic is the **correlation coefficient**.

When statisticians say "correlation" they are usually referring to one particular kind of relationship between two *numerical variables*, namely, a *linear* relationship. By this they mean the same thing that mathematicians mean when they talk about linear functions. They are attempting to connect the two variables by a linear equation with a formula of the type $y = mx + b$. We say that $y = mx + b$ is a **linear model** of the relationship. We expect to see a picture of a line in such studies, and we expect to be able to make sense of the slope of that line.

It is important to remember that a mathematical model of some relationship such as the relationship between class size and dropout rate is a tremendously simplified version of reality. The model should help us think more clearly about what is going on in the real world, but the real world will always be more complex than what the model can account for.

Scatter Plots

A scatter plot consists of a bunch of dots. Each individual dot combines the two pieces of numerical information for one subject by using one piece as the *x*-coordinate and the other as the *y*-coordinate. When you focus on one dot in a scatter plot, you should be able to name the subject, and see two numerical scores for that subject. A data table used to construct a scatter plot therefore has *three* columns. One column identifies the subject and two columns contain the appropriate numerical data.

Exercises for Scatter Plots (1)

The scatter plot in this figure is based on one of the first data sets ever analyzed by correlation. It was collected in England by Karl Pearson 100 years ago. There are slightly over 1,000 dots in this scatter plot.

A couple of rows in Pearson's data table might look like this:

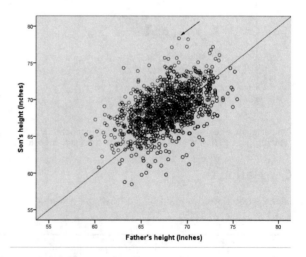

Father–son pair ID	Father's height (inches)	Son's height (inches)
1	70	71
2	74	72

1. Look at the highest dot in the plot and report what information it contains.
2. By looking at the overall pattern of the dots, interpret the story this scatter plot tells. How precise a story is this?
3. We have superimposed a 45-degree line onto this plot. What distinguishes the points above the line from the points below the line? What points would be right on the line?

Positive and Negative Correlation

When the pattern of dots in a scatter plot tends to slant up to the right we say they exhibit **positive correlation** in accord with the concept of the positive slope of a line. Similarly, a pattern that tends to slant down to the right is called **negative correlation**. When neither tendency is present we say there is **no correlation**.

Positive correlation   Negative correlation   No correlation

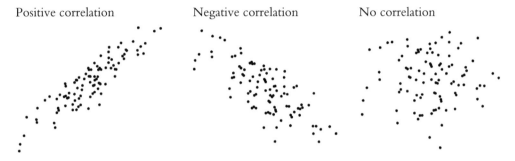

It follows from these definitions that in positive correlation individuals with high values on one variable tend to have high values on the other. In negative correlation individuals with high values on one variable tend to have low values on the other. In the case of no correlation individuals with high values on one variable are scattered among those that have both high and low values on the second variable.

Correlation and Causation

The popular saying most associated with the concept of correlation is "Correlation is not causation." You may already know this, but it can't hurt to mention it explicitly here. You will have a chance to think about correlation and causation in some of the next exercises and even more so in Chapter 16 on statistical regression. The basic point is that a scatter plot that shows a clear relationship between two variables does not, by itself, tell you *why* the relationship exists. The "why" may be very tough to identify. For example, data may show a strong correlation between family income and educational achievement. But why does this happen? And because sincere policy makers disagree about the why, they disagree about how to fix inequalities in education. The presence of the correlation helps define the problem, but it is not a substitute for wisdom.

Exercises for Scatter Plots (2)

1. In a data set for the ages of married couples, each wife is exactly four years younger than her husband. Will the scatter plot of husband's age (vertical axis) versus wife's age (horizontal axis) indicate positive, negative, or no correlation? Give a specific data set for five such couples and draw the scatter plot.

   a. As the ages of the wives increase the ages of the husbands _____ (increase or decrease?).
   b. If you use the horizontal axis for the husband's age and the vertical axis for the wife's age, will the nature (positive versus negative) of the correlation change?

2. The dots in this scatter plot represent individual students in three classes. Each class took a test before and after an educational intervention.

    a. Describe how the intervention affected the test scores in each class.

    b. In which class was the intervention most successful? Explain your choice.

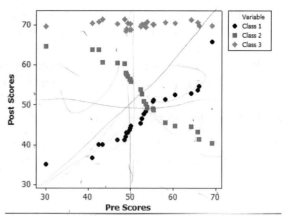

3. This scatter plot that shows math achievement scores for tests taken in 2005 and 2007 allows you to see four different subgroups. (Thanks to Michael Hock, Vermont Department of Education, for sharing this graph.)

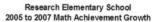

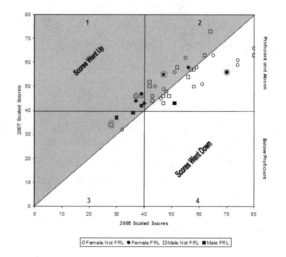

    a. The points for four students have been circled. Describe each student and state how the math achievement score changed for each of them from 2005 to 2007.

    b. In the graph legend FRL stands for "free or reduced lunch," indicating lower family income. Does there seem to be a math achievement problem in this school in the progress of students on these lunch programs?

    c. Do you agree with this quote from Dr. Hock?

    > I think we've been paying too much attention to the students in quadrant 2 (started proficient and stayed there). But the real success stories are the students in quadrant 1 (started in the basement and moved up) and the students above the diagonal in quadrant 3 (still in the basement but makin' it up the stairs). Schools should be focusing on those students and asking themselves how they contributed to that movement.

4. Medical correlational studies investigate the relationship between disease and some factor of interest. The graph shown here was one of the first to suggest a relationship between cigarette smoking and heart disease. Each point represents one state in the US. CHD is an abbreviation for coronary heart disease.

    a. Does there seem to be positive, negative, or no correlation?

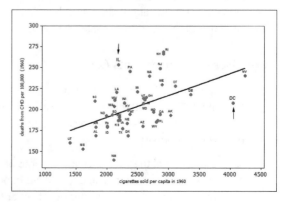

b. The trend line indicates *on average* what the relationship is. Describe and contrast the information about DC and IL, two points which are relatively far off the trend line. Such outliers often lead to further study.

(*Source:* Adapted from G. D. Friedman, Cigarette Smoking and Geographic Variation in Coronary Heart Disease Mortality in the United States, *Journal of Chronic Diseases*, October 1967.)

5. Data were collected to compute the mean salary for head football coach in a given college football conference as well as the mean salary for a full professor at that conference.

(*Source:* http://www.aaup.org/AAUP/comm/rep/Z/ ecstatreport2007–08)

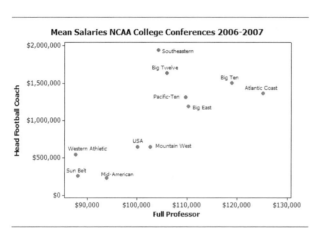

Mean Salaries NCAA College Conferences 2006-2007

Conference	Mean salary ($)	
	Head football coaches	Full professors
Atlantic Coast	1,363,450	125,044
Big East	1,184,851	110,263
Big Ten	1,504,176	118,851
Big Twelve	1,631,022	105,961
USA	649,552	100,074
Mid-American	226,475	93,783
Pacific-Ten	1,311,968	109,654
Southeastern	1,941,612	104,229
Sun Belt	255,069	87,983
Western Athletic	546,508	87,596
Mountain West	645,632	102,627

a. What is the nature of the correlation? Positive or negative? If that makes sense to you explain why.

b. In which conference is the ratio of coach to professor salary greatest? Lowest? If that makes sense to you explain why.

6. The number of coffee shops in a certain metropolitan area and the number of tickets given out there for speeding have both been increasing over the past ten years.

a. A scatter plot of these two variables shows a positive correlation, but is it likely that coffee consumption is causing the increase in speeding offenses? What third (unmentioned) variable might be considered? A variable that influences the outcome of a study but that is not accounted for in the analysis is called a **confounding variable**.

b. Draw a fictional scatter plot that would illustrate this story. What would each dot represent? How many dots would there be?

7. The accompanying table and scatter plot show the percentage of children who received a DPT vaccine, for protection against diphtheria, whooping cough, and tetanus, and the mortality rate for children under 5 in 20 selected countries for the years 1995–98.

Source: United Nations Children's Fund, *State of the World's Children*, 2000.

a. Which country is represented by the highest dot in the scatter plot? By the leftmost dot?

Nation	Percentage immunized against DPT by age 1	Under 5 mortality rate per 1,000 live births
Bolivia	42	85
Brazil	94	42
Canada	97	6
China	98	47
Egypt	96	69
Ethiopia	58	173
Finland	86	5
France	96	5
Greece	85	7
India	73	105
Italy	95	6
Japan	100	4
Mexico	94	34
Poland	95	11
Russia	97	25
Senegal	65	121
Turkey	79	42
United Kingdom	95	6
United States	94	8
Yugoslavia	94	21

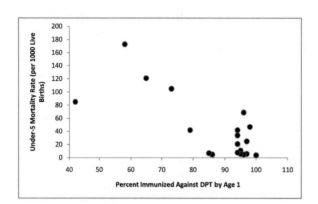

b.   Describe any trend you see. Explain why you cannot conclude from this graph alone that increasing the immunization rate *causes* a drop in the mortality rate. What might be another reason that explains this trend? Why do you think the trend breaks up when the percentage immunized is near 100%?

8.   In this exercise you will use your imagination to make up three tables and the three scatter plots that go with them. Each new table changes one column in the previous table. You will make up the numbers: there are no calculations involved. You will just be thinking about trends and relationships.

Table and scatter plot 1: The table will have three columns: month, mean of the daily high temperatures for that month in your city, and number of ice cream cones sold in an ice cream shop in your city that month. The table will have 12 rows of data, one for each month from January to December. Label both axes, and also label each of the 12 points with the name of the month it represents.

Table and scatter plot 2: Same idea, but replace the column about ice cream by a column for the number of flu cases there that month.

Table and scatter plot 3: Same idea, but the three columns are now month, number of flu cases, and number of ice cream cones sold. (Use the numbers you have already made up.)

Questions:

a. Does scatter plot 3 show that the number of cones sold is correlated with the number of flu cases? Does it show that the number of cones sold influences the number of flu cases? Explain the distinction.

b. We have a tendency to think that the variable on the horizontal axis is the one "causing" the results on the vertical axis. What two stories would you get if you switch the roles of the two axes in scatter plot 3?

9. The data below (*source:* http://nces.ed.gov/programs/digest/d07/tables/dt07_137.asp) show the mean SAT math scores for seniors in the 2006–07 academic year versus the percentage of high school graduates taking the test for each of the states.

   a. Construct a scatter plot for these data.

   b. Describe the relationship between the two variables.

State	Mean math SAT	Percentage taking SAT	State	Mean math SAT	Percentage taking SAT
Alabama	556	9	Montana	543	28
Alaska	517	48	Nebraska	585	6
Arizona	525	32	Nevada	506	41
Arkansas	566	5	New Hampshire	521	83
California	516	49	New Jersey	510	82
Colorado	565	24	New Mexico	546	12
Connecticut	512	84	New York	505	89
Delaware	496	72	North Carolina	509	71
District of Columbia	462	78	North Dakota	596	4
Florida	496	65	Ohio	542	27
Georgia	495	69	Oklahoma	571	6
Hawaii	506	61	Oregon	526	54
Idaho	539	19	Pennsylvania	499	75
Illinois	611	8	Rhode Island	498	68
Indiana	507	62	South Carolina	496	62
Iowa	613	4	South Dakota	602	3
Kansas	590	8	Tennessee	569	13
Kentucky	565	10	Texas	507	52
Louisiana	567	7	Utah	556	6
Maine	465	100	Vermont	518	67
Maryland	502	70	Virginia	511	73
Massachusetts	522	85	Washington	531	53
Michigan	579	9	West Virginia	507	20
Minnesota	603	9	Wisconsin	598	6
Mississippi	549	4	Wyoming	571	8
Missouri	594	6			

Source: NCES, National Center for Education Statistics Census, Revenues and Expenditures for Public Elementary and Secondary Education: School Year 2000–2001 (NCES 2003–362).

The Correlation Coefficient

In the same way that mathematicians have invented statistics to describe the center and the variability of a data set, they have invented statistics to summarize the degree of correlation revealed in a scatter plot. The basic concept is the same: use the information in the data to produce a single summary value.

The magnitude or strength of a correlation is most commonly measured by a statistic called the **correlation coefficient**, r, that is defined mathematically so that it always is between -1 and $+1$. The calculation of r involves a lot of arithmetic, so we usually compute it using a calculator or computer. The formula is explained below. For now we just indicate how to interpret r.

If the dots in a scatter plot are exactly in a straight line, then r is 1 or -1, depending on whether the correlation is positive or negative. If r is close to 1 or -1 we say there is strong correlation. If there is no tendency for the dots to form a line, then r is near 0, and we say there is no correlation or weak correlation. Figure 8.1 gives some examples.

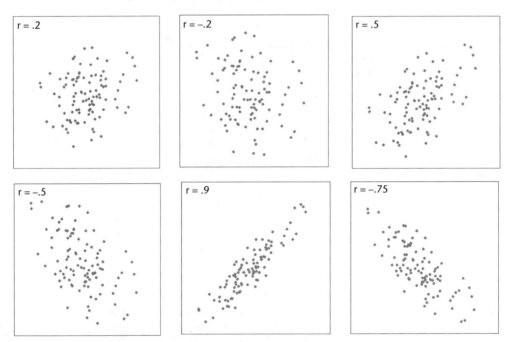

FIGURE 8.1 Scatter plots with different values of r, the correlation coefficient

How the Correlation Coefficient, r, Is Calculated

The correlation coefficient is defined as the mean of a set of products of z-scores. Each dot in the scatter plot contributes the product of the two z-scores for that dot. The correlation coefficient is the mean of these products. We illustrate this procedure next.

Figure 8.2 is a scatter plot for the two variables X and Y based on the data in Table 8.1.

We split the scatter plot into four quadrants by drawing a set of perpendicular axes centered at the two means as shown. This gives four quadrants.

TABLE 8.1 Data for scatter plot

	X	Y
	1	5
	3	9
	4	7
	5	1
	7	13
Mean	4	7
SD	2	4

Figure 8.3 is the scatter plot for the corresponding z-scores. In the z-score scatter plot, because the mean always gets a z-score of zero, the splitting occurs at the origin (0,0).

Notice that the two scatter plots show the same overall pattern. Converting to z-scores does not change the relationship between X and Y. Only the numbers on the axes change.

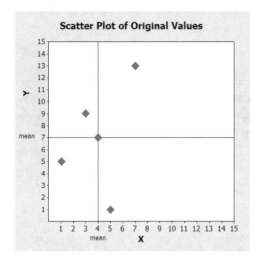

FIGURE 8.2 Scatter plot (original data) **FIGURE 8.3** Scatter plot (z-scores)

In the z plot, points in the first and third quadrants contribute positive products. Points in the second and fourth quadrants contribute negative products. Points on the axes contribute zeros to the list of products. If the points with the positive products predominate, then r is positive. If the points with the negative products predominate, then r is negative.

Table 8.2 shows the data and the z-scores for the scatter plots. You calculate r by finding the mean of the five products on the z plot.

TABLE 8.2 Calculation of correlation coefficient

Calculation of correlation coefficient

Raw data		z-scores		Products	
X	Y	z_x	z_y	$z_x z_y$	
1	5	−1.5	−0.5	0.75	
3	9	−0.5	0.5	−0.25	
4	7	0	0	0	
5	1	0.5	−1.5	−0.75	
7	13	1.5	1.5	2.25	
Sum	20	35	0	0	2
n	5	5	5	5	5
Mean	4	7	0	0	0.40	← r, correlation
SD	2	4	1	1		coefficient

Why Can't the Absolute Value of r Be Bigger Than 1?

A mathematical proof that $|r|$ can't be more than 1 is beyond the level of this text, but here are two ways to support its truth:

- No variable is more highly correlated with x than x itself. So the value of r for a data set with two identical variables should yield the maximum possible value of r.
  Make up any small data set, and call it x. Copy that set, but call it y. Show that $r = 1$.

- In the context of vector mathematics, the correlation coefficient, r, can be interpreted as the cosine of an angle. Cosines of angles are always between −1 and +1. Geometrically it is always possible to measure the angle between two lines as an angle between 0 degrees and 90 degrees. The closer that angle is to 0 degrees, the more "alike" the lines are. The cosine of 0 degrees is 1. By analogy, the more "alike" two data sets are (meaning that there is a linear relationship between them), the closer their correlation is to 1.

Correlation Calculation Exercises

1. The correlation coefficient is a number without units. We have shown previously that the correlation coefficient, r, is 0.40 for the pairs of numbers in the table here, but this time we assume that X represents lengths of some objects in feet, and Y represents their weights in pounds. We still say that the correlation coefficient is 0.4: just plain 0.4, with no units.

	X: Length	Y: Weight
Object 1	1 foot	5 pounds
Object 2	3 feet	9 pounds
Object 3	4 feet	7 pounds
Object 4	5 feet	1 pound
Object 5	7 feet	13 pounds

 a. Convert the lengths to inches and the weights to ounces and recalculate the correlation coefficient. Explain why your answer makes sense. A scatter plot might help.
 b. Convert the lengths and weights to their squares. For example, 3 feet becomes 9 square feet. Recalculate the correlation coefficient. Explain why your answer makes sense.

2. We have seen earlier that r for these data is 0.40.

 a. What happens to r if each value of X is multiplied by 5? Do the calculation.

X	Y
1	5
3	9
4	7
5	1
7	13

 b. What happens to r if you add 5 to each value of X?
 c. Summarize the effect on r if you rescale the variables by adding a constant or multiplying by a constant. You can get some insight if you start with a set of points that are in a straight line on a scatter plot and see what happens when you change the X- or Y-values of the points by adding or multiplying by a constant. Remember the job of the correlation coefficient is to measure linearity.

3. Draw a scatter plot with four points arranged in a square. Compute r. Why does your answer make sense?

4. Draw a scatter plot with four points arranged precisely

 a. in a slanted line;

b. in a horizontal line;

c. in a vertical line.

For each case calculate *r* and explain why the result is sensible.

Person	x	y
A	3	20
B	8	25
C	2	15
D	9	30
E	0	0
F	−4	1

5. *Just for routine practice:*

a. Use a computer or calculator to show that the correlation coefficient for this set of data is *r* = 0.93 (rounded to 2 decimal places).

b. Do the same calculation "by hand."

6. *Challenge problem with little educational value:* The prize goes to the person who finds a set of five dots on a scatter plot with *r* closest to 0.8.

7. F. J. Anscombe invented these four data sets to demonstrate the importance of graphing the data before interpreting the correlation coefficient. Confirm that each of the four pairs of variables has the same correlation coefficient and that the corresponding means and standard deviations are equal. Show how important Anscombe's advice is by constructing the four scatter plots. (*Source:* F. J. Anscombe, Graphs in Statistical Analysis, *American Statistician*, 1973, 27, 17–21.)

	x1	y1		x2	y2		x3	y3		x4	y4
	10	8.04		10	9.14		10	7.46		8	6.58
	8	6.95		8	8.14		8	6.77		8	5.76
	13	7.58		13	8.74		13	12.74		8	7.71
	9	8.81		9	8.77		9	7.11		8	8.84
	11	8.33		11	9.26		11	7.81		8	8.47
	14	9.96		14	8.1		14	8.84		8	7.04
	6	7.24		6	6.13		6	6.08		8	5.25
	4	4.26		4	3.10		4	5.39		19	12.5
	12	10.84		12	9.13		12	8.15		8	5.56
	7	4.82		7	7.26		7	6.42		8	7.91
	5	5.68		5	4.74		5	5.73		8	6.89
Mean	9.0	7.7		9.0	7.5		9.0	7.5		9.0	7.5
SD	3.32	2.03		3.32	2.03		3.32	2.03		3.32	2.03
r		.82			.82			.82			.82

8. (Correlation activity) In groups of four, make up a fake set of data with a scatter plot that shows a correlation between two variables. Prepare a poster to display for the class. Your group should be prepared to give a three-minute "lecture" on your findings. Be sure to indicate whether you have found positive or negative correlation. Check that the axes on the scatter plot are correctly labeled. Be sure you are clear about what any single point represents. Put a label on at least one point. Feel free to make up ridiculous or silly examples.

Math Extension for Correlation

1. If the points in a scatter plot are in a straight line, then two facts follow: first, the correlation coefficient *r* is equal to 1; second, at each point the z-scores for *x* and *y* are equal, so each point contributes z^2 to the total. Use these two facts to show that the sum of all the z-squares must equal *n* for any data set.

9

PROBABILITY

Introductory Investigation

Birthdays

Usually there is no way for a college teacher to know if two students in a new class have the same birthday. If we assume that we are talking about a regular non-leap year, there are 365 possible birthdays. If we further suppose that all 365 birthdays are equally likely for any individual student, then depending on the size of the class it may seem unusual for two of the students to have the same birthday. How do we know if something that happens is something unusual or something we should have expected? This activity may demonstrate (with any luck) that something that seems surprising to most of us is not really that unusual.

Using the rules of probability it can be shown that the chances for at least two people in a group to share a birthday passes 50% as soon as the group size reaches 23. Here is a graph that shows the probabilities for various size groups:

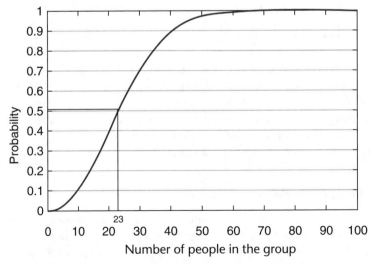

Probability that at least two people in a group have the same birthday

1. Realizing that the results are not guaranteed, determine whether there are any shared birthdays in your class.
2. According to the graph what are the chances for a shared birthday if there are 50 students in a class?
3. One reason people are surprised at the result is that they instinctively misinterpret the problem. The question is not whether someone has the same birthday as *you*. That is not very likely. We are asking: what are the chances that there is a match between *some* pair of people in the group?
4. Here is one way for you to do an experiment that might make the result more believable. Let the birthdays be identified by day of the year from 001 to 365. Use a random number generator to select 23 three-digit numbers in that range. Record whether there is a match. Repeat this experiment as many times as you can. According to probability theory you should see a match about half the time. If you don't have access to a random number generator you can use Table 9.1, which was constructed using such a generator. You will need to devise some way to take 23 random numbers repeatedly from the table.

TABLE 9.1 Random numbers from 1 to 365 (generated by RANDBETWEEN function in Excel)

	1	2	3	4	5	6	7	8	9	10	11	12	13	14	15
1	317	208	39	205	347	230	297	131	141	56	307	270	198	152	188
2	282	318	276	248	329	123	86	96	135	260	23	53	261	125	292
3	308	239	137	243	232	89	78	194	174	59	276	14	268	27	260
4	185	212	69	60	62	79	114	228	92	106	91	3	324	297	222
5	275	189	85	179	206	185	170	97	30	206	30	344	277	145	11
6	101	37	279	254	195	310	58	94	332	207	220	137	158	69	304
7	229	126	270	8	97	189	138	17	312	56	94	182	63	284	221
8	340	209	328	203	88	63	50	93	85	57	314	218	285	161	158
9	7	166	291	42	78	49	132	5	154	29	144	123	78	18	103
10	237	247	84	67	309	182	221	93	92	356	175	286	246	74	180
11	186	334	244	120	244	296	88	226	179	334	292	326	131	166	125
12	94	71	206	171	140	264	145	24	333	22	189	257	71	282	254
13	98	256	24	42	82	106	265	46	232	175	176	365	317	9	189
14	339	160	271	253	53	26	218	122	270	59	34	314	99	362	92
15	8	149	239	279	302	3	201	212	46	189	264	47	26	182	22
16	336	24	32	88	172	276	86	52	249	262	232	13	270	174	270
17	102	76	318	109	250	214	345	105	245	18	11	96	164	161	55
18	294	347	271	352	164	137	182	243	200	252	359	260	205	12	90
19	47	8	301	342	263	201	340	234	70	292	359	264	108	363	70
20	329	362	151	124	44	319	356	150	209	197	85	48	213	298	90
21	131	342	176	283	241	156	72	345	255	126	197	36	62	46	7
22	239	83	41	111	78	47	165	297	49	330	44	152	21	143	116
23	207	304	306	284	263	335	220	220	126	216	164	345	338	98	277
24	118	218	343	98	346	232	342	223	73	176	66	156	228	174	67
25	141	164	221	340	244	83	359	70	194	268	226	11	87	275	220
26	27	221	52	208	48	118	116	106	129	131	50	315	333	91	352
27	240	111	306	354	155	254	268	21	96	141	187	236	116	263	308
28	240	215	61	228	209	335	118	337	96	219	176	23	82	296	2
29	50	63	314	5	184	198	193	189	194	135	145	137	152	64	205
30	340	154	205	298	137	45	219	231	243	317	116	178	95	278	77
31	16	33	107	319	255	230	17	361	345	81	156	181	297	84	202
32	134	149	181	106	258	9	81	76	179	284	102	253	220	75	278
33	329	229	73	221	348	362	273	300	209	41	307	2	255	253	74
34	313	51	111	104	185	303	308	269	98	5	86	52	220	264	209
35	163	164	347	211	358	285	344	276	314	2	278	339	78	295	198
36	343	251	326	309	138	189	363	272	129	51	249	190	353	124	272
37	260	137	318	37	110	92	364	97	213	295	17	173	338	159	335
38	83	162	184	69	140	49	307	118	35	144	240	113	244	250	252
39	355	150	121	43	148	328	28	106	20	362	363	135	19	291	108
40	287	143	230	274	188	73	351	275	300	334	352	51	9	103	153

Probability and Statistics

Why are the two labels "probability" and "statistics" often linked in the math curriculum? One basic reason is that *probability theory provides models against which we test data*. We can use such models to help make decisions when we have incomplete information. The phrase **statistical inference** refers to the procedures by which we make such decisions. In educational assessment, for instance, the tools of statistical inference allow us to say when some school is performing unusually well or unusually poorly. We can do that only if we have in mind a model that tells us how schools *usually* perform. This model will tell us how much deviation from average is to be considered unusual. If we don't have such a model, then we have more trouble identifying extraordinary cases.

We'll begin by looking at some simple situations to see how we can interpret data in the light of a probability model. One very simple model is based on spinning a perfectly balanced spinner or tossing a coin, so we'll start there, but it should become evident that many other applications are similar.

First, we use probability theory to describe how a given spinner or coin *should* behave. Then when we test it (that is, when we collect data) we can compare the data to what the theory predicted. For instance, if we toss a coin 100 times and get 45 heads, is that consistent with the usual behavior of a fair coin? What about 20 heads in 100 tosses?

Similarly, we can take the results of an actual political poll and compare it to a theoretical model. For instance, if we poll 100 voters in a big city and find that 45 of them approve of the president's performance, is that consistent with a city population in which 50% approve? What about a poll where 20 out of 100 people approve of the president's performance? Is that consistent with a population in which 50% approve?

The questions about the coin and about the presidential poll are mathematically equivalent, and they both can be analyzed by finding areas under a normal curve. The two questions would lead to Figures 9.1 and 9.2 below.

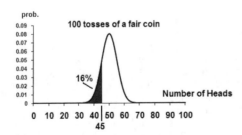

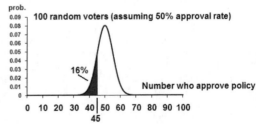

FIGURE 9.1 Probabilities of all possible numbers of heads in 100 tosses of a fair coin

FIGURE 9.2 Probabilities of all possible "approves" in a poll of 100 voters if the true approval rate is 50%

We have marked the edge of the shaded tail area at 45 heads in Figure 9.1 and at 45 voters in Figure 9.2. That edge corresponds to the information in the data. The overall curve is the probability model. The answer to our original questions about how well the data agree with the model depends on how much area has been shaded. By current practice, if such a shaded tail area is less than 5% of the total area, the result is considered unusual given the theoretical model. That 5% area implies that there is less than a 5% chance the observed data came from the assumed population. In Figure 9.1 the shaded area is 16% of the total, so 45 heads in 100 tosses is not considered "suspicious" behavior for a fair coin. The coin may be all right. We hesitate to say it's not. In contrast, you can see that 20 heads is far enough in the tail of the curve to raise doubts about the coin.

Analogously, 45 out of 100 votes in favor of a policy is not "off" enough from 50% to decide that the real approval rating is lower than 50%. But it's a different story if only 20 out of 100 voters approve.

In Figures 9.1 and 9.2, the values on the vertical scale, which determine the height of the curve, are determined so that the total area under the curve is one square unit. It is a property of probability models that the sum of the probabilities of all possible outcomes is 1 and that therefore the total area bounded by a probability model graph is 1. In practice we rarely show the vertical scale for a normal curve. We just assume that the total area represents 100% of the possible outcomes.

The values on the horizontal axis are another matter. To get these right you need to know the mean and the standard deviation for the curve. In Figure 9.1 the mean of the curve is 50 heads and the standard deviation is 5 heads. These numbers were calculated from the next two formulas, where n stands for the total number of tosses and p represents the probability of heads on any *one* toss. We will see soon why these formulas work.

Mean number of heads $= np$

So, mean $= np = 100(.5) = 50$

Standard deviation for the number of heads $= \sqrt{np(1-p)}$

So, standard deviation $= \sqrt{100(.5)(.5)} = \sqrt{25} = 5$

Because this mean and standard deviation are characteristics of a theoretical model and not computed from data, they are called **parameters** (more about this later) rather than statistics, and the usual symbols are μ (Greek mu) for mean, and σ (Greek sigma) for standard deviation.

We can summarize the results by saying that the **mean and standard deviation of the probability model for a coin toss** are as follows:

Mean $= \mu = np$

Standard deviation $= \sigma = \sqrt{np(1-p)}$

We will make use of these formulas as we learn more about statistical inference.

The rest of this section is intended to let you see one way that mathematicians realized that the normal curve was the right model for modeling the coin toss and the political poll. The first mathematician to show that the normal curve was the correct model was Abraham de Moivre in about 1730.

We start with some straightforward probability models and calculations and hope that the path to the normal curve is well lit. Along the way you will be able to see where the mean and standard deviation formulas come from.

Exercises Based on a Simple Probability Model: A Two-Color Spinner

Exercises 1 to 5 should all be done completely so that you can see an important pattern developing and so that you can learn some new symbols. Be patient.

1. Imagine a perfect spinner where one-quarter of the face is red and the rest is green. There are two possible color outcomes for any one spin *but they are not equally likely*. It is customary to identify one of the two possible outcomes in an experiment like this as "success." By default, the other gets called "failure." In this exercise we will (arbitrarily) call red "success." It is also customary to let p stand for the probability of success on any *one* try. So for this spinner we have $p = \frac{1}{4}$. Then the probability of failure is $1 - p = \frac{3}{4}$. Note that the sum of these two probabilities must be 1.

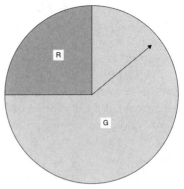

Red/green spinner

Complete the pattern of Rs and Gs in Table A to list all 16 possible sequences of red and green in four spins of the spinner. Then fill in the rest of the table. We use S for the *total* number of successes in four spins.

The basic probability rule is that if A and B are independent events then the probability of both A and B happening is the *product* of the two individual probabilities. Thus the probability of spinning the sequence "red, green" is $\frac{1}{4} \times \frac{3}{4} = \frac{3}{16}$.

TABLE A All 16 possible outcomes in $n = 4$ spins

Outcome ID	1st spin	2nd spin	3rd spin	4th spin	S = total number of reds	Probability of this outcome
1	R	R	R	R	4	$p*p*p*p* = p^4 = \left(\dfrac{1}{4}\right)^4 = \dfrac{1}{256}$
2	R	R	R	G	3	$ppp(1-p) = p^3(1-p) = \left(\dfrac{1}{4}\right)^3\left(\dfrac{3}{4}\right) = \dfrac{3}{256}$
3	R	R	G	R	3	$pp(1-p)p = p^3(1-p) = \left(\dfrac{1}{4}\right)^3\left(\dfrac{3}{4}\right) = \dfrac{3}{256}$
4	R	R	G	G		
5	R	G	R	R		
6	R	G	R	G		
7	R	G				
8	R	G				
9	G					
10	G					
11	G					
12	G					
13	G					
14	G					
15	G					
16	G					

You can also see the 16 possible outcomes by looking at a tree diagram as shown in Figure 9.3.

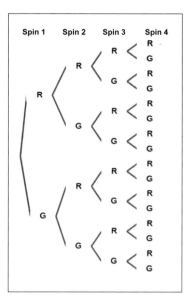

FIGURE 9.3 Tree diagram for four spins of a red/green spinner

Use the information in Table A to complete the probability distribution, P(S), in Table B. Then graph it with S on the horizontal axis and P*(S)* on the vertical axis. Hint: To find P(1), for example, you add the probabilities for each line of Table A that represents S = 1.

TABLE B Probability distribution for the number of reds in n = 4 spins

S = Total number of reds in 4 spins	0	1	2	3	4	Total
P(S) = Probability of S reds in 4 spins	81/256					1
nCs = Number of different outcomes that yield S	1					16

Use the information in Table A or Table B to find the mean and standard deviation for S. (You should get 1 and $\sqrt{\frac{3}{4}} \approx .866$.) Note that you would get the same answers from the formulas on page 81: mean of S = np and SD of S = $\sqrt{np\,(1-p)}$

2. Repeat Exercise 1 but replace 4 by 3, so that you are analyzing three spins of the spinner. You will need to make a whole new table (with fewer rows) to start.
3. Repeat Exercise 1 but replace 4 by 2, so that you are analyzing two spins of the spinner.
4. Repeat Exercise 1 but replace 4 by 1, so that you are analyzing one spin of the spinner.
5. Look back at Exercises 1 through 4 and copy the nCs rows into Table C. Can you guess what the next row would look like? Can you arrange the entries into a pleasing triangle?

TABLE C List of nCs sequences for various numbers of spins

Number of spins (n)	nCs sequence	Number of terms in the sequence
1		
2		
3		
4	1, 4,	5
5		

6. a. What is the probability of spinning more than two reds in four spins of a spinner? (In symbols this can be written $P(S > 2)$ for "Probability of more than two successes.")
    b. Suppose 25% of the voters in a town are registered plundercrats. What is the probability that, if you pick four at random, more than two of them will be plundercrats?

7. a. What is the probability of spinning more than three reds in five spins of a spinner?
    b. Suppose 25% of the voters in a town are registered plundercrats. What is the probability that, if you pick five at random, at least four of them will be plundercrats?

8. Suppose 25% of the employees in a large organization are incompetent.

    a. What is the probability that if you pick four employees at random none will be incompetent?
    b. What is the probability that if you pick four employees at random no more than one will be incompetent?

9. These three problems are all equivalent. Solve one and you solve them all.

    a. What is the probability of tossing more than two heads in four tosses of a fair coin? (A fair coin behaves just like a spinner with two *equal* color areas, so both p and $1-p$ equal $\frac{1}{2}$.)
    b. Suppose that for a given family the probability that a woman gives birth to a male child is $\frac{1}{2}$. If the woman bears four children what is the probability that more than two of them will be male?
    c. Four people each have a 50–50 chance of getting the flu tomorrow. What is the probability that more than two of them will do so?

Pascal's Triangle

You probably noticed this pattern for the nCs sequences.

This triangle may be familiar to you. Here are two familiar versions:

row 0	1
row 1	1 1
row 2	1 2 1
row 3	1 3 3 1
row 4	1 4 6 4 1
row 5	1 5 10 10 5 1
etc	

row 0	1
row 1	1 1
row 2	1 2 1
row 3	1 3 3 1
row 4	1 4 6 4 1
row 5	1 5 10 10 5 1
etc	

The pattern is called Pascal's triangle in honor of the seventeenth-century French mathematician Blaise Pascal. He was not the first to study it, but he published many findings about it in 1653 in a book called *Traité du triangle arithmétique*.

Exercises with Pascal's Triangle

1. The entries in the triangle are called **binomial coefficients** because of their connection to certain algebraic expansions. An expression of the form $p + q$ is called a binomial expression. Investigate this connection by expanding these binomial expressions:

    $(p + q)^2$, $(p + q)^3$, $(p + q)^4$.

2. We use the symbols nCs to refer to individual elements in the triangle. For example, $_4C_0 = 1$ and $_4C_1 = 4$. Find the value of $_4C_2$. (The letter C is used because nCs gives the number of distinct *combinations* you can make if you pick s items from a group of n items.)

3. (Shortcuts to the binomial coefficients) Follow the pattern and complete these tables. With this algorithm you can find the entries in any row of Pascal's triangle without knowing the entries above it.

$_5C_0$	$_5C_1$	$_5C_2$	$_5C_3$	$_5C_4$	$_5C_5$
1	$\dfrac{5}{1} = 5$	$\dfrac{5\times4}{1\times2} = 10$	$\dfrac{5\times4\times3}{1\times2\times3} = 10$		

$_6C_0$	$_6C_1$	$_6C_2$	$_6C_3$	$_6C_4$	$_6C_5$	$_6C_6$
1	$\dfrac{6}{1} = 6$	$\dfrac{6\times5}{1\times2} = 15$				

4. Find each of these: $_7C_3, \, _7C_7, \, _{10}C_0, \, _{40}C_2$.

5. One line of Pascal's triangle shows 1, 4, 6, 4, 1. What do the 4s signify?

6. (This is just about notation. You already know how to calculate it.) A *formula* for nCs is $\dfrac{n!}{s!(n-s)!}$.

   For example, $_7C_3 = \dfrac{7!}{3!4!} = \dfrac{7 \times 6 \times 5 \times 4 \times 3 \times 2 \times 1}{(3 \times 2 \times 1)(4 \times 3 \times 2 \times 1)} = \dfrac{7 \times 6 \times 5}{3 \times 2 \times 1} = 35.$

7. (Also about notation) Look back at Table B and check that in each cell

   $P(S) = {}_4C_s p^s (1 - p)^{4-s}.$

Binomial Random Variables

The random variable S in the spinner exercises above is called a **binomial random variable**. A binomial random variable tells the *total number of successes*, S, in n trials of an experiment such as spinning a spinner.

In general, a situation where you repeat some action that has exactly two possible outcomes (heads/tails, for example, or red/green) is called a **binomial experiment**. The individual repetitions are called **trials**. One of the outcomes of a trial is arbitrarily called "success" and the other "failure." With this general language we don't need to say specifically whether we are thinking about coins or spinners or voters.

Two properties characterize a binomial experiment:

1. What happens on one trial does not affect what happens on another.
2. The probability of success does not change from one trial to the next.

To identify a binomial random variable you state the number of trials n and the probability of success on each individual trial, p. For example, if you write that S is a binomial random variable with $n = 5$ and $p = 1/2$, you are describing an experiment equivalent to counting the total number of heads in five tosses of a fair coin.

Exercises for Binomial Experiments

1. A binomial experiment has four trials. On each trial the probability of success is .25. What is the probability you will have exactly two successes?

2. A binomial experiment has four trials. On each trial the probability of success is .25. What is the probability you will have fewer than two successes?

Large Numbers of Trials (Normal Approximation of the Binomial Distribution)

In principle you can now answer a question such as: "What is the probability of getting more than 20 heads in 30 tosses of a fair coin?" It would mean finding row 30 of Pascal's triangle, calculating all the separate probabilities from $S = 21$ to $S = 30$ and taking their sum.

Table 9.2 shows that row of Pascal's triangle, and all the associated probabilities. To answer the question we simply add the shaded cells to get 0.0214. There is about a 2% chance that you will get more than 20 heads in 30 tosses of a fair coin. It's not very likely. Conversely, if you do toss a coin 30 times and get more than 20 heads, you might decide the coin is unbalanced.

TABLE 9.2 Probabilities for 30 tosses of a fair coin

Row 30 of Pascal's triangle:

Index	Value	Index	Value	Index	Value
0	1	11	54,627,300	22	5,852,925
1	30	12	86,493,225	23	2,035,800
2	435	13	119,759,850	24	593,775
3	4,060	14	145,422,675	25	142,506
4	27,405	15	155,117,520	26	27,405
5	142,506	16	145,422,675	27	4,060
6	593,775	17	119,759,850	28	435
7	2,035,800	18	86,493,225	29	30
8	5,852,925	19	54,627,300	30	1
9	14,307,150	20	30,045,015		
10	30,045,015	21	14,307,150		

	S	P(S)	S	P(S)	S	P(S)	S	P(S)	S	P(S)
$S =$	0	0.0000	6	0.0006	12	0.0806	18	0.0806	24	0.0006
number	1	0.0000	7	0.0019	13	0.1115	19	0.0509	25	0.0001
of heads	2	0.0000	8	0.0055	14	0.1354	20	0.0280	26	0.0000
in 30	3	0.0000	9	0.0133	15	0.1445	21	0.0133	27	0.0000
tosses of	4	0.0000	10	0.0280	16	0.1354	22	0.0055	28	0.0000
a fair	5	0.0001	11	0.0509	17	0.1115	23	0.0019	29	0.0000
coin									30	0.0000

You can see, though, that this approach gets unwieldy quickly as n increases. For 100 tosses of a coin, we would have to compute all 101 entries of the 100th row of Pascal's triangle.

Fortunately, there is a convenient way out of all the computation. It may be evident if you look at Figure 9.4, the graph of $P(S)$ for 30 tosses of a fair coin. The heights of the bars are taken from the table above. The graph is clearly bell-shaped.

Using the formulas given earlier we can compute the mean and standard deviation for S.

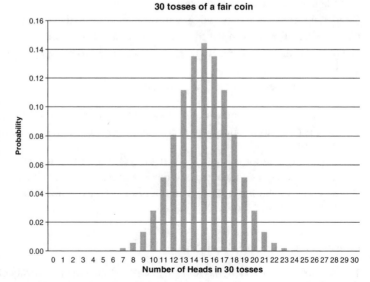

FIGURE 9.4 Binomial probability distribution for 30 tosses of a fair coin

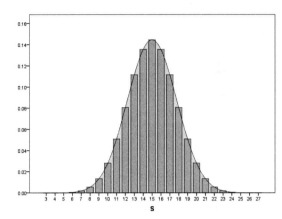

FIGURE 9.5 Normal curve approximation to binomial with $n = 30$ and $p = .5$, mean $= \mu = np = 15$, $SD = \sigma = \sqrt{np(1-p)} = 2.74$

We get mean $= \mu = np = 30(5) = 15,$

and

$$SD =$$
$$\sigma = \sqrt{np(1-p)} = \sqrt{30(.5)(.5)} = \sqrt{7.5} = 2.74.$$

Let's fit the normal curve with that mean and standard deviation on top of the binomial graph (Figure 9.5). The graphs are so close in shape that you can get accurate area *approximations* of the binomial distribution from the normal curve table.

To approximate the probability of getting *more than* 20 heads in 30 tosses of a fair coin, we can measure the area to the right of 20 under the normal curve. For better accuracy we should take the area to the right of 20.5 on the normal curve. This compensates for the slight mismatch between the continuous normal curve and the discrete binomial histogram.

First we get the z-score corresponding to 20.5 heads. Then we find the area to the right of that z-score.

$$z = \frac{20.5 - 15}{2.74} = 2.01$$

The area to the right of $z = 2.01$ is 2.2%. This is very close to the exact answer 2.1% that we got earlier using all the binomial data.

We got a good approximation with the fair coin example where $p = \frac{1}{2}$. If you reconsider the spinner problem with $n = 30$ and $p = .25$, you will find that the

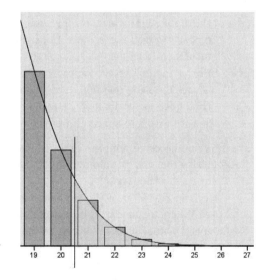

normal approximation still is good. See Table 9.3 and the accompanying figure. In this figure we take the mean of S to be $\mu = np = 30(.25) = 7.5$ and the standard deviation to be

$$\sigma = \sqrt{np(1-p)} = \sqrt{30(.25)(.75)} = \sqrt{5.625} = 2.37.$$

The approximation of the binomial by the normal is very good once n is large enough even when p is not $\frac{1}{2}$.

TABLE 9.3 Binomial distribution
with $n = 30$ and $p = .25$

S	P(S)	S	P(S)	S	P(S)
0	0.000	11	0.055	21	0.000
1	0.002	12	0.029	22	0.000
2	0.009	13	0.013	23	0.000
3	0.027	14	0.005	24	0.000
4	0.060	15	0.002	25	0.000
5	0.105	16	0.001	26	0.000
6	0.145	17	0.000	27	0.000
7	0.166	18	0.000	28	0.000
8	0.159	19	0.000	29	0.000
9	0.130	20	0.000	30	0.000
10	0.091				

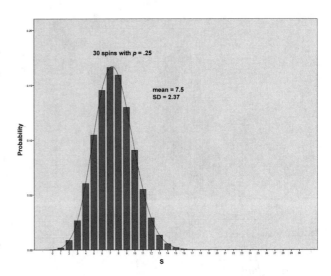

Exercises on Approximating a Binomial Distribution by a Normal Distribution

1. a. Use Table 9.3 above to find the exact probability that the spinner lands on red more than 10 times.
   b. Use a normal curve approximation to answer the same question. (See Table 9.4.) For a good approximation draw the cut-off line at $S = 10.5$ to indicate "more than 10."

2. Use a normal curve approximation to find the probability that you get more than 55 heads in 100 tosses of a fair coin.

3. In a certain city 50% of the students meet or exceed the math standards. In one class of 36 students, 10 students meet or exceed the standards. Is this different enough from the city rate to raise the possibility that something unusual is going on in this class? Use a normal curve approximation approach.

4. Some students invent a game of chance that gives the player an 80% chance of winning. They expect that on parents' night the game will be played about 600 times. They intend to give out a small prize for each win. They are going to stock 490 prizes. What is the probability that if the game is played 600 times they will not have enough prizes for the evening?

TABLE 9.4 Normal curve cumulative areas

z	Area	z	Area
0	0.500	1.5	0.933
0.1	0.540	1.6	0.945
0.2	0.579	1.645	0.950
0.3	0.618	1.7	0.955
0.4	0.655	1.8	0.964
0.5	0.691	1.9	0.971
0.524	0.700	1.96	0.975
0.6	0.726	2.0	0.977
0.674	0.750	2.1	0.982
0.7	0.758	2.2	0.986
0.8	0.788	2.3	0.989
0.842	0.800	2.33	0.990
0.9	0.816	2.4	0.992
1.0	0.841	2.5	0.994
1.02	0.846	2.6	0.995
1.036	0.850	2.7	0.997
1.1	0.864	2.8	0.997
1.2	0.885	2.9	0.998
1.28	0.900	3.0	0.999
1.3	0.903		
1.4	0.919		

10

INFERENCE AND MARGIN OF ERROR

Introductory Investigation

How Many Lefties?

1. Design a study to determine the percentage of teachers in your state who are left-handed. How would you go about it? What information would you record? How would you come up with your final figure? What difficulties, if any, might you anticipate?
2. Suppose, just for this exercise, that you can survey only the people in this class for this study. Go ahead and conduct the survey. Organize and summarize the data, and show a table or graph to describe your results. List the strengths and weaknesses of your study. How close do you think your final figure is to the truth about the state percentage? What do we mean by "the truth"?

Statistical Inference

Samples and Populations

Simply put, statistical inference means using data from part of a population to make decisions about the entire population. A part of a population is called a **sample**. As soon as you draw some conclusion about a population when you have information from only a sample of it, you lose certainty, and you need to attach probabilities to your conclusions. This kind of inference is what statisticians mean when they say they are making decisions based on incomplete information.

For a concrete example, you might use data about the percentage of left-handed people in one class to estimate the percentage of left-handed people in a school. The job of the statistican is to say how far off target the estimate is likely to be, and to clarify what is meant by "likely." We will see that the answer depends on how the sample was chosen and on how many people were in the sample.

Figure 10.1 illustrates the relationship between the sample and its population. Next to the figure we introduce some notation useful in inference.

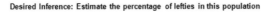

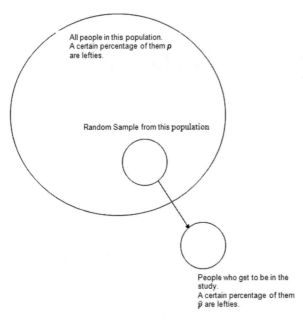

FIGURE 10.1 Logic of statistical inference

A survey usually includes only a small fraction of the people in a larger population. A survey that includes everyone in the population is called a **census**. We need symbols to distinguish whether we are talking about just the people in the survey or all of the people in the larger population. We use the symbol $\hat{p}$ (pronounced "p hat") to represent a percentage recorded in the survey, and we use p to represent the corresponding percentage in the entire population; $\hat{p}$ serves as an estimate of p.

More generally, a number computed from sample data is called a **statistic**, and the population value it estimates is called a **parameter**. So $\hat{p}$ is a statistic, and p is a parameter.

We have mentioned earlier that the mean and standard deviation of theoretical probability models are also parameters – and not based on sample data.

For a second illustration of inference, you might generalize from the results of an intervention done this year on students in one 3rd grade classroom to all 3rd graders in the district or to students you expect to be in 3rd grade in the future. Again, the statistical issue is to describe the likelihood that the inference is "off the mark" by any given amount. In this sense you imagine that the students who were actually in a study are a sample of a larger population of similar students.

A related idea in educational research is that all assessments are imperfect. Every measurement we make of a student's ability is "off" a bit from the student's "true" ability because it is affected by random interference such as the student's concentration at that moment, the wording of a question, or inconsistency on the part of the evaluator. That leaves us having to infer a student's true ability from imprecise data. Such inference is also likely to entail some amount of error. We can imagine that the score the student actually gets on a test is a sample of a population of all the scores the student would get with varying slight random disturbances. We say more about such measurement error later in the text.

The major thrust of our attention to statistical inference now is to learn how to make reasonable inferences from sample data while accounting for possible sources of imprecision.

Margin of Error in an Opinion Poll

In the next few sections, we are going to develop some formulas useful in interpreting data from samples. These formulas will be based on the concept of a **simple random sample (SRS)**. This is a sample in which the subjects have been picked randomly from a target population. In fact, professional polls taken over large populations are usually not chosen quite this way. For example, the polling company may deliberately pick a certain percentage of high or low income people, rural or urban dwellers, and so on, and then choose randomly *within* these groups, rather than just picking subjects directly from the population of the United States. These more complex sampling schemes have names such as **stratified sampling** or **cluster sampling**. The calculations appropriate to such sampling schemes are correspondingly more complex. For simplicity in this text, we will assume that all samples are simple random samples. We will also assume that the populations are much larger than the samples.

A National Opinion Poll

Perhaps the most familiar example of statstical inference is the national opinion poll. Typically, the poll is administered to about 1,000 adults selected from around the country. The number of people in a sample is called the **sample size**, and is often symbolized by n. Most such polls are conducted by telephone, but an increasing number are conducted by online techniques. Based on what the polled group says an inference is made about the entire US adult population (over 200 million people).

Here is an excerpt from the results of a *Time* poll on the state of public education in America (*source:* http://www.time.com/time/nation/article/0,8599,2016994,00.html). We show the figures for just one question in the poll.

Box 10.1

Time poll results: Americans' views on teacher tenure, merit pay and other education reforms (September 9, 2010)

What do you think would improve teacher effectiveness the most?

- Better training in universities: 30%.
- Mentoring by more experienced teachers: 30%.
- Merit pay: 20%.
- Higher salaries: 11%.
- No answer/don't know: 8%.

This *Time* magazine poll was conducted by telephone on August 17–19, 2010, among a representative national random sample of 1,000 Americans, ages 18 and older, throughout America. *The margin of error for the entire sample is approximately +/– 3 percentage points. The margin of error is higher for subgroups.* Surveys are subject to other error sources as well, including sampling coverage error, recording error, and respondent error.

What does the sentence in italics mean? Roughly speaking, it means that the figures in the poll are not likely to be off by more than 3 percentage points from what a poll of every single American adult would show. Strictly speaking, it means that the *procedure* used by the polling agency gets a result within 3 percentage points of the truth about 95 percent of the times it is used. This probability is usually expressed as: We have *95% confidence* that the results of this particular poll are within 3 points of the truth. This is a bit of an abstract concept, but the bottom line is that you can be reasonably sure (but not absolutely positive) that these results are not far off from "the truth."

Why 95%? Why not some other percentage? This value gives a level of confidence that has been found convenient and practical for summarizing survey results. There is nothing inherently special about it. If you are willing to change from 95% to some other level of confidence, and consequently change the chances that your poll results are off from the truth, you will therefore change the resulting margin of error. At present, 95% is just the level that is commonly used in a great variety of polls and research projects.

The published margin of error in most surveys refers specifically to the deviation of a statistic from "the truth" that occurs simply because the random collection of subjects who ended up in the sample may not perfectly represent the population. This kind of deviation from the truth is called **sampling error**. "Error" in this sense does not mean someone has done something wrong. The *Time* magazine report also indicates that other kinds of error in the survey can creep in from a variety of sources. The published margin of error does not usually take those into account. It is assumed that such errors do not distort the results significantly.

Box 10.2

Look for subgroups too

It is often important to consider how various subgroups respond to a survey. The breakdown shown in Figure 10.2 is revealing of the components that went into President Obama's overall approval rating of 40% in August 2011. You can see that this overall rate is based on three quite distinct rates for special subgroups.

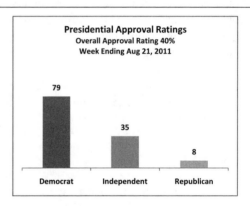

Presidential Approval Ratings
Overall Approval Rating 40%
Week Ending Aug 21, 2011

FIGURE 10.2 Obama approval rating

Every statistic is assumed to be imperfect and therefore to have an associated margin of error. This margin of error is computed from a formula that is particular to that statistic.

For example, a formula for the margin of error in a survey like a political poll is shown in Box 10.3. In this text we will be pretty casual about the meaning of the words "proportion" and "percentage." We may sometimes refer to a decimal like .25 as a proportion and sometimes refer to it as 25%. In formulas we will use the decimal representation.

We present the formula here without saying how it was derived, so that you can concentrate on how it is used, but we will say something about the derivation later.

Box 10.3

Approximate margin of error for a percentage statistic in a typical poll

$$\text{Margin of error} \approx 2\sqrt{\frac{\hat{p}(1-\hat{p})}{n}},$$

where $\hat{p}$ represents the percentage observed in the survey, and n represents the number of people in the survey. The "$\approx$" symbol means "is approximately."
    A rougher approximation for the margin of error is $\frac{1}{\sqrt{n}}$.

Climate Change Survey

A survey of 500 randomly picked adult Vermonters found that 400 of them believe climate change is a crucial issue. Announce the results of this survey as a percentage and calculate the margin of error for this estimate.

$n = 500$

$\hat{p} = 400/500 = .80 = 80\%$

$$\text{Margin of error} = 2\sqrt{\frac{\hat{p}(1-\hat{p})}{n}}$$

$$= 2\sqrt{\frac{.80(1-.80)}{500}} = 2\sqrt{\frac{.80(.20)}{500}} = 2\,(.01789) = .035 = 3.5\% \approx 4\%$$

The press release would simply say "The survey found that 80% of Vermonters think climate change is a crucial issue. The margin of error for the survey was 4%."

Let's just clarify a bit what this means. Based on this data one can say with 95% confidence that between 76% and 84% of Vermont adults hold this belief. In other words, it is quite likely that if we had been able to survey the entire population of Vermont adults we would have found the exact percentage who held this belief to be a value between 76% and 84%. In technical terminology we say that based on the statistic $\hat{p} = .80$ we estimate that the parameter p is between .76 and .84.

Comments on Estimating Percentages

It is remarkable that the margin of error when you estimate a percentage depends only on $\hat{p}$ and n. This explains why a national random sample of 1,000 people can accurately represent 200 million people. The $\hat{p}$ from the sample of 1,000 people is not likely to be more than 3% off from what you would find if you did include all 200 million. The size of the population, 200 million, does not appear in the formula at all. In that same vein, whether your population is 20 thousand or 20 million people, if you want to be confident that your survey is accurate within 3% you will need to sample about 1,000 people. Most critically, this conclusion assumes that you have really picked the sample *randomly* from the population, and not systematically included or excluded any groups or individuals.

In general, larger random samples will produce smaller margins of error. However, in the real world of research where a study takes time and costs money, at a certain point you just can't afford to increase the sample size. Your study will take too long or you may decide the increase in precision isn't worth the expense. For instance, if you increase the sample size from 1,000 to 4,000 the margin of error will drop from about 3% to about 2%, but you might quadruple the cost of your survey.

> *Big idea:* Every statistic used to estimate a parameter should have a margin of error assigned. If you don't know the margin of error you cannot properly interpret the statistic.

Determining Sample Size Needed for a Given Margin of Error

If you set $\hat{p} = .5$ the margin of error formula simplifies to $\frac{1}{\sqrt{n}}$. No other value of $\hat{p}$ will give a larger result. (You are asked to confirm this in Exercise 3 in the "Math extensions and connections" set of exercises below.)

For the climate change example above we get margin of error $= \frac{1}{\sqrt{n}} = \frac{1}{\sqrt{500}} = .045$ instead of .035. This simplified formula is called "conservative" because it yields a larger margin of error. You take less risk of being wrong when you say your survey is probably within 4.5% of the truth than if you say it is probably within 3.5%.

The conservative formula is useful when you need to determine how many people to include in your sample and you have no preconceived idea about p. For example, if you are willing to tolerate a 6% margin of error you can solve $\frac{1}{\sqrt{n}} = .06$ for n to find $n = 278$. You need to poll at least 278 people.

Recap of Terminology for Inferential Statistics

1. *Sample and population.* The **sample** for a study is the actual group of people from whom we get information. They may also be called "subjects" from whom we get "observations." In general, the subjects of a study do not have to be people – they can be animals or plants, or objects, or readings from laboratory instruments. The **population** for the study is the larger group from which the sample is taken. We hope that the sample is a good representation of the population. The number of subjects we select from the population is called the **sample size**, and is denoted by n. The simplest kind of random sample is the **simple random sample (SRS)**.

2. *Statistics and parameters.* A **statistic** is a number calculated from a sample of values taken from a larger population. It is used to estimate some value in the population that you can't get exactly (usually because the population is too big to deal with). The exact value you are trying to estimate with the statistic is called a **parameter** for the population. In short, *we use statistics to estimate parameters.* The tools and techniques of **statistical inference** help you evaluate the dependability of those estimates.

Exercises on Margin of Error for Estimating a Percentage

1. Liping Ma, in *Knowing and Teaching Elementary Mathematics*, describes a study in which only 9 out of 21 American elementary school teachers solved $1\frac{3}{4} \div \frac{1}{2}$ correctly. Assume the study was based on a random sample of American teachers.

   a. Estimate the percentage of all American elementary school teachers who could solve this problem correctly.

   b. Find the margin of error for your estimate. Does this study indicate conclusively that fewer than 50% of American elementary school teachers can do this problem correctly? Why, or why not?

   c. In this context distinguish between the statistic and the parameter.

2. In estimating a population percentage, if you increase the size of the sample will the margin of error become greater or smaller or remain the same? Why? Base your explanation on the formula for the margin of error.

3. You want to know the percentage of K-6 teachers in your state who have taken a statistics course in the last five years. You therefore interview a random sample of 120 K-6 teachers in the state. You find that 30 of them have taken a statistics course in the last five years.

   a. What percentage of your sample took such a course? Would the correct symbol for this be p or p-hat? Distinguish between the population and the sample in this survey. Distinguish between a statistic and a parameter in this investigation.

   b. What is the margin of error for this estimate?

   c. After you do your survey, you read in your favorite newspaper that "fewer than 10% of K-6 teachers in your state have recently taken a statistics course." Do your data tend to support or not support that statement? Why? What is it about your survey that makes you so sure of your response?

4. The following quotation was taken from the *Cincinnati Enquirer* (November 7, 2009). It was part of a report about a primary election campaign between Trey Grayson and Rand Paul for the Republican Senate nomination in Kentucky. Use $\hat{p} = .5$ to confirm their margin of error. What do they mean by saying the race is "effectively even?"

    > The poll was conducted Oct. 30 to Nov. 2 by Survey USA for WHAS-TV in Louisville. Of 448 likely voters polled, 35 percent said they would vote for Paul and 32 percent said they'd vote for Grayson if the primary were today. Paul's three-point lead falls well within the 4.7 percentage point margin of error, making the race effectively even.

5. a. A random sample of 400 teenagers will be asked if they have purchased any music online in the previous month. If this survey is used to estimate the percentage of all teenagers who have done so, what is the approximate margin of error we expect the survey to have? Because you have no preconceived idea what the survey percentage might be, use .5 for $\hat{p}$.

    b. If the sample is doubled to 800, will the margin of error be cut in half?

    c. By intuition, trial and error, or algebra find a sample size, n, that will yield a margin of error that is half of the one in a. above; then show by calculations that your value of n is correct.

6. Determine the approximate sample sizes necessary to achieve the following margins of error:

    a. 1%;
    b. 3%;
    c. 10%.

7. In May 2001, Senator James Jeffords of Vermont announced he was leaving the Republican Party to become an Independent. The media covered this controversial decision with great interest, and there was a vigorous exchange of opinions in the Vermont newspapers. The following quotation is taken from a letter to the editor that appeared in the Montpelier, VT *Times Argus* on May 28, 2001. How would you respond to the writer? Is he basically correct? Is he wrong? Is polling 400 people in Vermont (population about 600,000) equivalent to polling 2 people from the town of Brandon (population about 4,000)? Specifically, consider the role the sample size plays in the formula for the margin of error.

    > Enough already with your bogus surveys, most recent being the 400 plus Vermonters you surveyed about the Jeffords defection. I do not care what statistical formula you [use], that small of a sample compared to the total population is a pathetic misuse of common sense.
    >   Statistically it is no different than going to Brandon or Waterbury and asking one or two people. . . .
    >   To add insult to injury, you then use this bogus survey's results to produce your headlines and lead stories. You should be reporting the news, not producing it. Shame on you.

8. (Activity) With a colleague decide on some characteristic for which the percentage of people in this room who have that characteristic can be used to estimate the percentage in a larger population. Conduct the survey, summarize the data, and present your results to the class. Write up your results "professionally" as a news release.

Math Extensions and Connections

1. In an earlier example we computed a margin of error as $2\sqrt{\dfrac{.80(1-.80)}{500}} = .035$. We used .80 to represent 80% in decimal notation. What would have happened if we had just put 80 into the formula instead of .80? What would we need to substitute for the 1 to be consistent?

2. Compare these two expressions: $A = \sqrt{ab}$ and $B = \sqrt{(100a)(100b)}$. How many times bigger is B than A? What is the connection to the previous exercise?

3. We said earlier "If you set $\hat{p} = .5$ the margin of error formula simplifies to $\dfrac{1}{\sqrt{n}}$. No other value of $\hat{p}$ will give a larger result."

   a. Show that $\sqrt{x(1-x)}$ reaches its maximum value when $x = .5$. What is that maximum value? What is the graph of $\sqrt{x(1-x)}$?

   b. Do $\sqrt{x(1-x)}$ and $x(1-x)$ reach their maximum points for the same value of x?

   Compare the graphs of $y = \sqrt{x(1-x)}$ and $y = x(1-x)$. (*Hint:* Only one of these is a parabola.)

Where Does the Margin of Error Formula Come From?

This section deals with some fairly abstract notions. It is not simple to digest. Don't freak out. We will return to these concepts over and over again. Remember, you already know how to calculate a margin of error for a percentage. This section provides some background for these calculations.

Earlier we said that the formula for the margin of error for a percentage was:

$$\text{margin of error} \approx 2\sqrt{\dfrac{\hat{p}(1-\hat{p})}{n}}$$

How did anyone come up with this formula?

The formula for the margin of error for *any* statistic is based on the **sampling distribution** of that statistic. In general we refer to any collection of values in statistics as a *distribution* of values. The *sampling* distribution of a given statistic is a particular distribution of values related to that statistic. Different statistics may have differently shaped sampling distributions. For example, the sampling distribution of *r*, the correlation coefficient, is not the same as the sampling distribution for $\hat{p}$, and so these two statistics will have different formulas for their margin of error. One reason the normal curve is so important is that it is a good approximation to the sampling distribution of many statistics.

The sampling distributions of the most commonly used statistics have been established by professional statisticians. It takes fairly advanced statistical theory to derive the mathematical function for the sampling distribution of a given statistic. In this book we simply take the statisticians' findings as true, but we will indicate how such functions might be determined.

The Sampling Distribution of the Sample Percentage, $\hat{p}$

For an opinion poll like the previous one on climate change, the sampling distribution for the $\hat{p}$ statistic is the collection of percentages we would get if we could repeat the survey over and over endlessly, each time with a different randomly picked sample of 500 subjects from the target population. Because each survey picks up only *some* of the people in the population, we would expect to get a slightly different value each time for $\hat{p}$, the percentage who say "yes" to the question, "Is climate change a crucial issue?"

For this kind of survey, where we simply record the percentage of yeses in 500 subjects, it turns out that in repeated sampling we would end up with a list of percentages whose histogram would look like a normal curve. We summarize this by saying that the sampling distribution of the percentage statistic, $\hat{p}$, when n is 500, is a normal distribution. A bit later we will have an opportunity to see how this happens through a simulation experiment.

Recall that in order to work with a normal distribution we need to know its mean and its standard deviation. We get formulas for these from mathematicians.

The sampling distribution of the percentage statistic, $\hat{p}$, when n is "large," is approximately a normal distribution. In practice "large" is often taken to mean that the survey results included at least five "yes" responses and five "no" responses.

Shape, Mean, and Standard Deviation of the Sampling Distribution of $\hat{p}$

1. *Shape.*
    The sampling distribution of $\hat{p}$ is normal.
2. *Mean.*
    The mean of this normal distribution is p, the mean of the population.

    In other words, on average, these various surveys tend to be "on target" for the parameter they are intended to estimate. We say that $\hat{p}$ is an *unbiased* estimator of p. An unbiased estimator is a statistic whose mean value is on target. The statistic $\hat{p}$ is unbiased because with random samples it is just as likely that a survey would overestimate the true percentage (p) as underestimate it.

    It is also worth noting that the results of any one particular survey will only rarely be *way* off from the true population percentage. Survey percentages that are close to the true value would be more common than ones that are far away, leading to a bell-shaped distribution of survey percentages.

3. *Standard deviation.*
    The standard deviation for this normal sampling distribution is $\sqrt{\dfrac{p(1-p)}{n}}$.

    The expression $\sqrt{\dfrac{p(1-p)}{n}}$ also has another name, the **standard error (SE)** of $\hat{p}$.

    In general, the term "standard error" refers to standard deviations of sampling distributions. Every statistic has its own standard error.

    Unfortunately, several important statistical terms have similar names, and you need to be careful in using them. For instance, the terms "standard deviation," "standard error," and "margin of error" have different meanings.

Figure 10.3 summarizes the key features of the sampling distribution of $\hat{p}$.

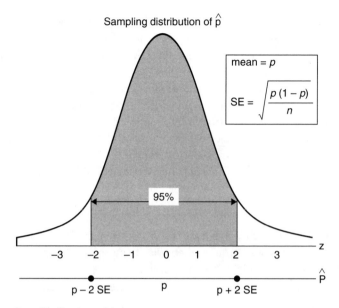

FIGURE 10.3 Sampling distribution of $\hat{p}$

If we interpret this figure according to the 68–95–99.7 rule, it tells us that about 95% of all the samples would give a value of $\hat{p}$ that is within 2 *SE*s of the true value.

We use this information to say we have "95% confidence" that the percentage we might get in any *one* particular survey is not off target by more than two *SE*s. We will discuss this idea further in Chapter 11.

Box 10.4

Margin of error based on the normal sampling distribution

By convention, we take the margin of error for a statistic with a normal sampling distribution to be 2*SE*, because a spread of two standard errors accounts for 95% of the distribution values. The risk of missing the value of the population parameter using this margin of error is no more than 5%, which is generally considered to be an acceptable risk of error.

In practice, in actual surveys, because we don't know p, we replace p in the formula for the standard error by $\hat{p}$ and use the formula:

$$SE = \sqrt{\frac{\hat{p}(1-\hat{p})}{n}}$$

This is an acceptable substitution because $\hat{p}$ is an unbiased estimator of p. And that's why the margin of error formula on page 92 is:

$$\text{Margin of error} = 2SE = 2\sqrt{\frac{\hat{p}(1-\hat{p})}{n}}.$$

Math note about the SE formula: You may have spotted a relationship between the standard deviation formulas for $\hat{p}$ and for S, the number of successes in a binomial experiment. The first formula is simply the second one divided by n. That is because S is the *number* of successes and $\hat{p}$ is the *percentage* of successes. If you divide the numbers in a distribution by n you divide the standard deviation by n also. The percentage of success in n trials is just the number of successes divided by the total number of trials.

Standard deviation of S: $\sigma = \sqrt{np(1-p)}$

Standard deviation of $\hat{p}$: $\sigma = \dfrac{\sqrt{np(1-p)}}{n} = \sqrt{\dfrac{np(1-p)}{n^2}} = \sqrt{\dfrac{p(1-p)}{n}}$

Making Use of a Sampling Distribution

You can see from the formulas in Figure 10.3 that in order to describe the sampling distribution of $\hat{p}$ we have to know p, the exact proportion of people in the population who have some characteristic. But in the world of real surveys it is not possible to know p, because we do not have data on every member of the population. If we did there would be no need for the survey in the first place. The whole point of the survey is to estimate p.

Not all is lost, however, because as we show in the next example we can use what we know about the sampling distributions of $\hat{p}$ to gain useful information.

Example: Sampling Distributions and School Data

Suppose it is true that all together 50% of the 4th grade students in a large state met the standards according to a certain test. Suppose also that in School A 60 of their 100 4th grade students met the standards.

Does it seem likely that the students of School A are a typical bunch of students, or are these exceptional results? We make this question specific by asking, "What is the probability that a random sample of 100 students from this statewide population would have at least 60% meeting the standards?" "At least 60%" means 60% or more.

Solution

This is a question about a sample statistic, $\hat{p}$. From the given data, $\hat{p} = 60/100 = .60$.

The sampling distribution for $\hat{p}$ tells us which values of $\hat{p}$ are likely and which are unlikely.

What do we know about this sampling distribution?

1. The sampling distribution is normal.
2. The mean is p, the true percentage of all students who met the standards. So $p = .50$.
3. The standard error is $SE = \sqrt{\dfrac{p(1-p)}{n}}$.

So, $SE = \sqrt{\dfrac{.50(1-.50)}{100}} = .05$.

The curve is shown in Figure 10.4.

This distribution tells us that the results found in School A are not likely to occur in a random sample

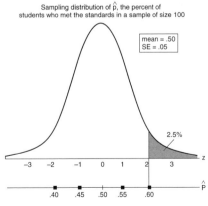

Sampling distribution of $\hat{p}$, the percent of students who met the standards in a sample of size 100

mean = .50
SE = .05

2.5%

FIGURE 10.4 Sampling distribution of $\hat{p}$ for $n = 100$ and $p = .50$

of 100 students. There is only about a 2.5% chance for a percentage that far out in the tail of a normal distribution. (That is the proportion of area to the right of $z = 2$.) There is evidence to support the conclusion that School A is exceptional.

Exercises about the Sampling Distribution of a Percentage

1. Suppose it is true that 20% of the students in a large state exceed the standards in reading. In School B, 13 of their 100 students met the standards. That's only 13%. Does it seem that the students of School B are a typical bunch of students? What is the probability that a random sample of 100 students from this statewide population would have a percentage of successful students with so few meeting the standards? "So few" means 13% or less, and so it is given by a tail area under the normal curve.

2. Suppose it is true for a major advertising campaign that 25% of the "scratch out" rewards are actually valuable. (Assume there are many thousands of these scratch outs produced.) We can say that p is .25, where p represents the percentage of scratch outs that are valuable.

    a. Draw and label a normal curve that describes the sampling distribution for the percentage of valuable rewards you will obtain if you try 80 randomly chosen scratch outs. The sketch is started here. The graph has two horizontal axes with corresponding values for the *percentage* of valuable rewards and the *number* of valuable rewards. Calculate *SE* and then fill in the missing axis values. (Round off *SE* to the third decimal place.)

    b. What is the probability that any one of the sets of 80 scratch outs will contain more than 30% valuable rewards? Between 20% and 30% valuable rewards?

    c. What is the probability that any one of the sets of 80 scratch outs will contain more than 26 valuable rewards?

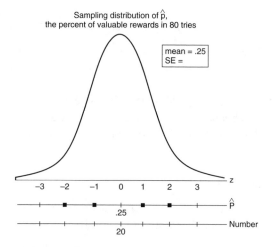

Sampling distribution of $\hat{p}$, the percent of valuable rewards in 80 tries

mean = .25
SE =

Simulation of the Sampling Distribution of a Statistic

It takes quite a bit of mathematics and knowledge of statistical theory to determine the correct formula for a sampling distribution. If you look in an advanced textbook you can find a mathematical derivation for the sampling distribution of the percentage statistic, $\hat{p}$. That approach is beyond what we can cope with here, but we can do some simple simulation experiments that may give you insight into the nature of sampling distributions.

Note: The following experiment is a hands-on simulation that is time consuming but valuable for getting a gut sense of what a sampling distribution is. You may want to supplement it or replace it by a computer-based simulation. Many applets are available for this on the Internet.

Experiment 1: Simulating the Sampling Distribution for a Percentage Statistic

(Best to do this with a partner.) The purpose of this experiment is to give you a concrete example of a sampling distribution.

We have a big bag containing about 2,000 beans, some of which are red. The entire bag of beans is called the population for the experiment. We want to estimate the percentage of the population that is red by looking at a *sample* of beans taken randomly from the population.

In Table 10.1 the population of beans is cleverly disguised as numbers. All the 1s represent red beans. The other numbers represent different color beans.

TABLE 10.1 Table representing the population of colored beans

	1	2	3	4	5	6	7	8	9	10	11	12	13	14	15	16	17	18	19	20
1	1	4	2	3	4	1	2	2	1	3	2	3	4	3	2	1	1	4	3	1
2	1	1	1	3	1	3	2	2	3	1	2	4	4	1	1	2	2	3	2	3
3	2	3	4	2	3	4	1	3	2	3	3	4	3	3	4	3	4	3	2	4
4	2	4	4	2	2	1	1	2	4	1	3	2	1	2	1	3	1	3	1	2
5	1	3	2	1	1	4	2	2	1	3	3	2	1	3	1	2	1	2	4	2
6	1	2	4	2	3	4	2	1	3	4	3	4	3	2	3	2	4	3	3	1
7	4	1	3	2	1	2	2	3	1	1	1	4	2	1	2	4	1	3	4	4
8	1	3	2	1	3	2	1	1	1	2	2	3	4	4	2	1	3	4	1	1
9	2	3	1	4	4	2	2	1	3	1	4	1	4	1	1	2	3	2	2	2
10	4	3	2	2	1	4	1	1	4	1	3	2	2	1	4	2	2	1	4	2
11	3	2	1	2	3	2	4	4	4	1	2	2	4	4	2	2	3	2	3	3
12	3	2	1	1	2	1	4	2	1	1	1	2	3	3	2	3	1	4	1	2
13	1	3	2	1	3	3	1	1	1	3	1	3	1	1	4	1	4	1	4	3
14	4	3	3	3	2	3	2	3	3	4	4	1	2	2	2	2	1	2	4	2
15	2	4	4	1	3	2	2	3	2	4	1	1	2	4	2	1	2	1	3	2
16	2	4	3	4	2	2	3	2	2	1	1	2	4	1	2	4	2	3	2	1
17	1	3	2	1	1	2	3	4	1	3	1	2	1	3	2	2	1	2	2	2
18	1	2	1	4	1	2	2	3	4	1	3	1	2	2	3	4	1	2	3	2
19	3	1	1	2	1	1	3	2	2	3	1	3	1	3	4	2	3	4	4	1
20	4	1	2	1	4	2	3	4	1	1	2	1	2	1	2	1	2	2	3	1
21	2	1	3	4	3	2	1	1	1	1	3	4	1	1	1	3	4	1	1	3
22	3	4	2	3	3	1	3	4	4	1	1	2	3	2	2	4	2	4	3	2
23	1	1	3	4	1	3	3	2	4	4	1	2	1	2	3	2	1	2	3	4
24	3	1	1	4	3	4	4	4	2	2	1	3	4	2	2	1	3	3	3	4
25	4	1	3	3	2	2	2	4	2	2	4	4	1	1	1	4	3	2	3	3
26	4	4	2	1	4	2	4	1	4	1	1	3	1	4	2	2	2	4	1	3
27	2	2	2	2	2	3	4	3	3	2	4	2	2	1	2	4	4	2	2	4
28	3	4	2	2	3	2	3	3	2	3	1	2	1	1	2	1	3	2	2	1
29	2	1	3	4	2	2	1	2	4	2	3	4	1	1	3	2	4	2	3	3
30	2	2	4	1	1	1	2	1	2	1	4	2	2	4	4	3	4	2	2	3
31	2	3	1	3	3	3	2	2	1	2	4	3	2	2	1	3	3	2	2	1
32	3	4	1	4	1	2	2	1	1	3	3	3	2	4	2	2	4	2	1	4
33	1	2	3	1	1	2	4	1	2	1	1	2	4	1	4	2	2	2	2	2
34	4	4	1	2	4	2	1	1	1	1	3	2	1	3	2	1	4	2	2	1
35	1	2	2	1	1	2	1	4	3	1	4	1	1	1	1	1	3	1	1	2
36	2	1	1	3	4	1	4	3	2	1	4	1	3	2	3	2	4	1	4	3
37	2	3	3	1	4	3	1	1	3	4	2	1	1	2	3	3	4	4	1	4
38	3	3	1	1	3	2	1	2	2	2	3	1	4	1	3	2	3	1	3	2
39	3	2	3	2	2	4	2	1	2	2	4	4	2	4	4	2	1	2	2	4
40	3	1	2	3	2	2	1	4	1	3	2	1	1	4	1	3	1	4	3	2

TABLE 10.1 *Continued*

	1	2	3	4	5	6	7	8	9	10	11	12	13	14	15	16	17	18	19	20
41	3	2	2	4	1	4	2	4	4	3	2	3	4	2	2	1	2	3	2	1
42	3	1	2	1	1	2	4	2	1	2	1	4	1	2	2	4	4	3	1	4
43	2	1	2	3	3	4	3	1	1	2	4	3	1	2	1	4	4	3	3	3
44	2	1	4	2	4	3	3	2	2	3	2	1	4	1	3	1	2	1	3	1
45	2	3	3	4	2	1	2	4	3	3	4	2	3	3	1	2	4	3	4	1
46	3	3	1	1	4	2	3	3	2	1	4	3	4	4	1	2	1	1	4	3
47	3	1	4	1	4	2	4	2	2	2	3	4	1	2	2	1	4	2	3	2
48	4	2	3	4	2	2	2	1	3	3	1	4	2	2	2	1	3	2	2	2
49	4	4	1	1	4	4	3	1	4	4	3	3	2	3	4	1	2	4	4	1
50	1	1	4	2	3	2	2	2	1	2	3	1	2	1	1	2	1	2	2	1
51	4	4	3	4	1	4	3	3	2	3	3	2	1	4	1	1	1	2	3	1
52	3	2	4	1	4	3	4	3	4	1	4	1	4	1	1	2	2	3	2	3
53	3	3	2	1	2	1	1	4	2	4	1	4	4	1	4	3	2	3	1	4
54	1	2	1	3	3	2	4	2	4	2	3	4	4	4	2	4	1	2	1	1
55	2	2	1	3	2	4	3	3	3	2	2	1	2	1	3	3	1	1	3	4
56	4	3	1	4	4	2	1	3	3	3	1	1	3	3	1	3	4	1	1	3
57	4	2	4	1	4	1	4	3	4	2	2	3	1	2	1	2	1	2	4	1
58	2	1	3	2	3	3	1	2	1	3	2	2	3	3	1	2	1	3	3	1
59	1	3	1	4	3	2	1	4	4	3	3	3	2	2	4	4	4	4	1	3
60	1	1	2	1	4	2	3	4	1	3	1	4	2	4	1	3	4	4	3	1
61	1	3	4	4	1	3	1	2	1	4	4	4	1	4	2	3	2	3	3	4
62	2	2	3	3	2	1	2	2	2	2	1	2	3	2	3	3	4	1	1	2
63	1	3	4	2	4	3	2	2	2	3	2	1	1	1	1	4	1	3	4	3
64	3	1	1	3	1	1	1	2	4	2	4	3	2	1	1	1	3	4	3	1
65	3	3	3	3	2	1	2	3	1	3	2	2	2	2	2	3	2	1	3	2
66	2	2	3	3	3	4	4	2	1	3	2	3	2	1	3	4	1	4	3	2
67	1	2	3	1	2	4	2	4	3	4	2	2	3	1	2	3	2	3	2	1
68	1	3	2	1	3	2	4	2	1	4	2	3	1	4	2	4	3	1	2	4
69	4	3	3	4	1	3	3	4	3	3	3	1	2	2	3	3	3	2	1	2
70	2	3	3	2	2	2	1	1	2	3	2	4	1	3	3	2	2	3	4	4
71	2	2	1	3	1	2	2	4	4	1	4	1	2	1	3	3	3	2	2	3
72	1	4	4	4	2	1	2	1	4	2	2	1	2	1	1	2	1	2	4	1
73	4	2	2	3	3	4	2	1	2	2	1	4	3	4	4	4	4	2	4	2
74	3	4	3	1	4	4	2	3	1	2	3	2	2	4	3	3	3	1	2	1
75	2	1	1	3	4	2	2	4	4	2	4	3	2	2	4	1	3	4	2	3
76	1	3	4	4	2	4	4	2	4	4	4	1	4	2	2	3	1	2	4	2
77	1	1	4	2	3	1	3	1	1	3	2	4	1	3	4	3	3	1	1	4
78	1	1	2	2	2	3	3	2	2	2	2	2	2	3	3	1	1	1	2	2
79	3	4	1	1	3	1	1	3	2	3	1	3	1	2	4	3	1	1	1	2
80	2	2	1	2	2	1	4	3	1	3	2	4	1	1	1	3	2	4	4	1
81	3	2	1	2	1	3	2	3	1	1	1	2	4	1	2	1	3	3	4	2
82	2	3	1	2	2	3	1	2	1	1	1	2	1	2	2	2	1	1	2	2
83	3	4	1	4	1	2	4	4	1	1	1	1	2	1	2	1	2	2	3	3
84	3	2	3	3	4	1	3	3	1	2	3	3	4	2	2	4	2	2	4	2
85	4	1	3	3	1	3	3	3	1	1	2	2	2	4	3	3	1	3	4	4
86	1	1	3	1	3	2	3	3	1	2	4	1	4	2	1	2	1	2	3	2
87	2	1	4	1	1	2	3	2	1	1	3	4	1	2	4	4	4	2	2	1
88	3	1	4	2	4	2	2	1	2	2	2	4	2	3	2	4	3	3	2	2
89	1	2	1	3	2	4	1	1	3	1	2	4	4	4	2	3	2	2	1	1
90	3	4	1	4	2	2	4	3	4	2	1	2	2	1	1	4	1	1	2	1
91	4	2	4	1	4	4	2	2	3	1	1	4	2	4	1	2	1	3	4	2

92	3	2	1	3	3	3	4	1	4	3	1	3	2	2	4	2	1	3	4	3
93	2	3	3	1	3	2	2	2	2	2	1	3	1	2	1	1	2	2	1	4
94	1	4	3	1	3	2	2	1	4	3	2	2	4	1	4	2	1	3	4	4
95	1	3	4	3	3	2	3	2	1	4	1	2	2	3	2	1	2	2	3	3
96	3	4	1	2	2	2	3	2	4	1	2	4	1	2	2	1	2	1	2	4
97	1	4	1	4	2	1	3	1	2	3	4	4	3	1	4	3	4	2	2	1
98	2	2	2	3	2	3	2	4	2	3	3	1	2	4	4	2	2	3	3	1
99	1	3	2	2	4	1	4	4	1	3	1	1	2	4	4	3	4	3	2	1
100	1	4	1	3	1	3	3	2	3	3	2	2	2	3	3	4	2	4	4	4

Each person should now pick 25 numbers ("beans") at random from this table. This is your sample. A suggestion for how to do this is to pick a row from 1 to 100, and a column from 1 to 20. That's the location of the first "bean" you draw. Then just move along to the right picking beans. When you get to the end of a row continue at the start of the next row.

Here's one way to get your very own personal starting row and column:

1. Write down the last four digits of your social security number. Using long division, divide it by 100. Write down the remainder. Add 1. This is the *row* of the table to start picking "beans."
2. Write down the last four digits of your social security number. Using long division, divide it by 20. Write down the remainder. Add 1. This is the *column* of the table to start picking "beans."

(Can you explain how this system works?)

After you have your 25 beans, calculate the percentage that is red. That's your $\hat{p}$. Each person in the class should select a sample and get a value for $\hat{p}$. Collect all of the $\hat{p}$s for the class and draw a histogram for the whole collection. *This histogram approximates the sampling distribution of the percentage statistic.* If it were possible to repeat this experiment forever, building a larger and larger collection of $\hat{p}$s, the collection would approach the true sampling distribution.

In principle, if you had built the histogram from enough samples, it would appear to be bell-shaped with a predictable mean and standard deviation, namely mean = p and $SE = \sqrt{\frac{p(1-p)}{n}}$.

(Be warned. A single classroom experiment with not very many samples may fail miserably to achieve this just by the luck of the draw.)

Exercises for the Simulation Experiment (1)

1. For the histogram that the class produced, find the mean and standard deviation for the list of $\hat{p}$s. You can use the regular formulas for the mean and standard deviation of any list of numbers.
2. On the basis of the class data, estimate p, the actual percentage of red beans in the entire population. How close do you think you are to the true value? How can you use the value of the standard deviation to help you think about how good your estimate is?

Experiment 2: The Sampling Distribution for a Range Statistic

The purpose of this experiment is simply to show that not all sampling distributions are like normal curves. The shape of a sampling distribution is affected by both the choice of statistic and the shape of the population itself.

Table 10.2 shows 1,000 entries consisting of 1s, 2s, and 3s. In an actual survey, this could perhaps be a coded representation of a town of 1,000 households where the numbers represent the number of TVs in a household.

TABLE 10.2 Table representing the number of TVs per household

	1	2	3	4	5	6	7	8	9	10	11	12	13	14	15	16	17	18	19	20
1	2	1	3	3	3	3	1	2	3	1	1	1	1	1	1	1	2	2	3	2
2	2	2	3	2	2	2	3	3	3	2	3	1	3	3	3	2	2	3	2	3
3	1	1	1	2	2	2	2	3	1	1	1	3	1	2	3	3	3	3	1	1
4	3	3	1	2	3	3	3	1	3	3	2	3	3	2	1	3	1	1	3	3
5	3	3	3	2	2	3	2	1	1	3	3	3	3	1	3	2	1	1	2	2
6	2	3	3	2	3	1	3	2	2	2	2	3	3	3	3	3	3	3	3	2
7	3	3	3	2	1	3	2	3	3	2	2	1	3	2	2	2	3	3	3	3
8	3	3	2	1	3	2	1	3	3	3	3	2	3	3	3	1	3	3	1	2
9	3	3	3	3	3	2	2	3	2	3	3	3	2	2	2	1	2	3	2	3
10	3	3	2	2	1	3	3	1	2	3	2	2	2	2	2	3	2	3	3	2
11	3	3	2	2	3	3	3	1	3	3	2	3	3	2	1	3	3	1	1	1
12	3	3	1	1	3	2	2	2	1	1	3	3	2	2	2	3	3	3	3	3
13	2	1	3	3	1	3	2	1	2	1	3	3	2	2	3	2	3	2	3	3
14	3	1	3	3	1	2	1	3	3	3	2	3	3	3	1	3	2	1	1	3
15	2	3	1	2	1	3	2	3	3	3	2	1	2	3	3	3	1	1	2	2
16	2	3	1	2	2	3	1	1	2	1	1	1	3	2	3	1	3	1	2	1
17	2	2	2	2	1	1	3	3	1	3	3	2	2	1	3	3	2	1	2	3
18	2	3	1	3	3	1	3	1	2	3	3	2	1	3	3	3	1	3	3	3
19	2	3	3	1	2	2	3	3	3	1	3	3	3	3	2	3	3	2	2	2
20	1	3	3	3	2	3	3	3	1	3	2	1	3	3	3	3	2	2	1	2
21	2	3	1	3	3	1	3	3	3	2	3	2	3	3	2	1	1	3	3	2
22	1	3	3	3	3	2	1	3	2	1	3	1	2	1	1	3	2	1	3	3
23	3	2	2	2	1	1	3	3	2	2	1	3	3	3	2	1	2	2	2	3
24	2	3	3	3	1	2	3	2	1	1	1	3	2	3	2	3	3	2	1	1
25	2	3	3	1	1	3	3	2	2	3	3	1	2	2	1	2	3	1	3	2
26	3	1	3	1	3	3	1	3	2	1	2	3	1	3	2	3	1	1	3	3
27	3	1	1	2	2	3	3	2	2	2	1	1	2	3	1	3	3	2	1	2
28	3	3	3	3	3	1	2	2	3	3	1	1	2	3	3	2	2	3	1	3
29	1	3	3	2	3	3	3	1	3	2	3	1	1	3	2	2	3	2	1	2
30	3	3	2	3	3	3	2	2	3	2	3	3	1	3	3	3	3	3	3	2
31	1	1	1	1	1	3	3	3	2	1	1	2	2	3	2	3	3	3	3	3
32	3	2	3	2	3	2	1	1	3	3	2	3	1	2	2	3	3	2	3	3
33	3	3	3	3	2	2	3	2	3	1	2	3	3	2	1	1	2	1	3	2
34	3	3	3	3	3	3	2	2	2	2	3	2	3	1	3	1	3	3	1	3
35	3	1	1	1	2	1	1	1	1	2	3	3	2	2	1	3	3	2	3	1
36	3	3	3	1	2	3	1	1	3	2	1	3	3	1	2	1	3	2	2	3
37	1	1	2	3	1	2	3	3	3	1	3	1	3	3	1	2	2	1	3	3
38	2	3	3	3	1	3	1	2	3	1	2	2	2	3	2	3	2	1	3	2
39	2	1	1	2	1	1	2	3	2	2	2	3	2	3	1	2	1	2	3	3
40	2	1	2	1	3	2	2	2	2	3	2	2	2	1	2	2	1	1	3	3
41	3	3	1	3	1	3	1	3	3	3	3	3	1	1	3	3	3	2	1	2
42	1	1	3	1	3	3	2	2	2	3	3	1	1	2	2	3	2	3	1	1
43	1	3	3	1	3	1	3	1	1	2	1	3	2	3	1	2	3	1	3	3
44	3	3	2	2	1	2	1	1	2	2	2	1	2	3	1	3	2	2	2	1
45	3	1	3	3	3	3	3	1	3	3	2	1	3	3	3	3	3	1	3	1
46	3	3	3	3	1	2	1	1	1	1	2	3	1	2	3	2	2	3	3	2
47	1	2	1	1	3	3	2	3	3	2	2	1	3	1	2	3	2	3	3	2
48	3	1	2	3	3	3	2	3	3	2	3	1	2	1	1	1	1	3	1	2
49	2	3	3	3	1	3	1	3	1	3	1	2	1	1	3	2	3	3	3	2
50	2	2	1	3	2	2	1	2	2	1	2	1	3	1	2	3	2	3	3	3

What is the sampling distribution of the range statistic in this context?

To simulate a sampling distribution we first specify a sample size and then we take more and more samples of that size from the population. For each sample we compute the range. The entire collection of these sample ranges is the desired sampling distribution.

For the sake of this experiment let us take $n = 25$. Pick 25 numbers at random from the table and compute the range of your sample. Call it $\widehat{range}$, "range-hat," to emphasize that it is a statistic based on sample data.

Each person in the class will supply a value for $\widehat{range}$. Draw a histogram for the whole collection of $\widehat{range}$s. This histogram represents the sampling distribution of the range statistic.

Exercises for the Simulation Experiment (2)

1. It should be evident that the class histogram is not even close to a normal distribution. Why did that happen? Could you have predicted the shape of this histogram before the experiment was carried out?

2. This is just a brainteaser, not vital at this time, but it may help you visualize a sampling distribution. A class of 50 students carried out a sampling experiment just like Experiment 2 above, also with $n = 25$, but on a different population.

    Here is the list of 50 sample ranges they found. On the basis of this data, can you say anything about the range of the population?

Table of sample ranges

27, 29, 31, 32, 33, 33, 33, 34, 34, 34, 34, 35, 35, 36, 36, 37, 38, 39, 39, 39, 39, 39, 39, 40, 40, 40, 40, 41, 41, 41, 41, 41, 42, 42, 43, 43, 43, 43, 44, 44, 44, 44, 45, 45, 47, 50, 52, 53, 55

Conclusion from Simulation Experiments

Different statistics may have different sampling distributions. The sampling distribution for many statistics is symmetric and mound shaped, as in Experiment 1, but this is not always the case, as demonstrated by Experiment 2. This matters because you need to know the sampling distribution in order to determine the margin of error for that statistic.

Determining the mathematical function for the sampling distribution of a statistic is one of the jobs of mathematicians who work in statistics. The sampling distribution is affected both by the particular statistic you choose and by the underlying population distribution. This can be a tough mathematical problem.

Exercise: The Role of Sample Size in Sampling Distributions

1. This exercise shows how a sampling distribution is affected by the sample size. You will see that with larger samples the histogram in this exercise approaches a normal curve. Very often it is easier to say what the sampling distribution shape is when samples are large. This is why many statistical formulas are more accurate when the studies have large samples.

    Suppose that a survey was designed to estimate the percentage of people in a large population who would answer yes to the question, "Did you watch television last night?"

    Suppose further that, in truth, 70% of the population did watch TV and would have answered "yes" if we had asked all of them.

a. We simulate what might happen in a survey that interviews a very small sample from this population. Suppose we interview only two people ($n = 2$) and record the percentage of yeses we get. We repeat this process many times (about 500 times in this illustration) to see the overall pattern of results that can occur in such interviews. Figure 10.5 is the resulting histogram. Look at this graph and explain what it means. For example, what does the first bar tell you? Why are there only three bars?

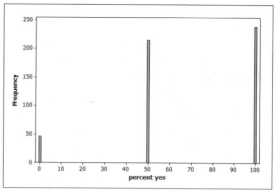

FIGURE 10.5 Sampling distribution for $n = 2$ from a population where $p = .70$

b. Figure 10.6 shows the histogram resulting from another simulation based on the same population but this time each sample has $n = 20$. Look at this graph and explain what it means. For example, what does the first bar tell you? Why are there more than three bars? Why is there no bar for 0%? Why are the bars shorter in this graph than the previous one?

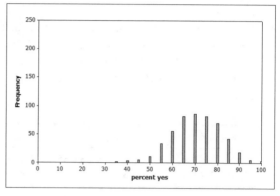

FIGURE 10.6 Sampling distribution for $n = 20$ from a population where $p = .70$

c. Figure 10.7 shows the histogram resulting from another simulation based on the same population but this time each sample has $n = 200$. Why are there so many bars? Why is there no bar at 90%? Why are the bars shorter in this graph than the previous one?

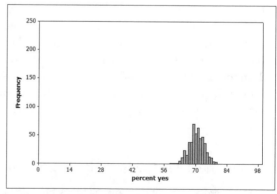

FIGURE 10.7 Sampling distribution for $n = 200$ from a population where $p = .70$

d. In a., b., and c. above we said the population was "large." Suppose in b. above the population consisted of 1,000 people, and in c. above it consisted of 10,000 people. How do the histograms shed light on the question, "Is polling 20 people in a population of 1,000 just as reasonable as polling 200 people in a population of 10,000?" After all, in both cases we poll 2% of the population. What difference does it make?

e. If you take one sample of size 200 from this population (as was done in c. above), how far off would you expect the percentage in your sample to be from 70%, which is the actual population percentage?

11

CONFIDENCE INTERVALS

There are two distinct ways by which we use statistics to estimate parameters: point estimates and interval estimates. A **point estimate** is *one* number used to estimate a parameter. For example, the statistic $\hat{p}$ is a point estimate of the parameter p. It is the best one number based on sample data by which to estimate p. A point estimate will often be very close to the target parameter, but it is not necessarily precisely correct.

We use the margin of error to decide how precise a point estimate is. By attaching a margin of error to a point statistic you get an interval of values called a **confidence interval estimate**. This gives an interval of values that is likely to capture the parameter of interest.

For statistics that have a normal sampling distribution we usually add and subtract two standard errors to get the endpoints of the interval. Because 95% of the area under a normal curve is within 2 standard deviations of the mean, we expect this interval to capture the parameter about 95% of the time. That is why we call the final interval a *95% confidence interval*. The formula is given in Box 11.1.

Box 11.1

95% confidence interval estimate of a population percentage (based on a sample percentage)

Sample percentage ± Margin of error
Sample percentage ± 2 SE

$$\hat{p} \pm 2\sqrt{\frac{\hat{p}(1-\hat{p})}{n}},$$

where $\sqrt{\frac{\hat{p}(1-\hat{p})}{n}}$ estimates the SE for the percentage statistic

This formula is most accurate with large samples. As a rule of thumb, "large" means that both $n\hat{p}$ and $n(1-\hat{p})$ are greater than 5. (That is, we should have at least five "yeses" and five "nos" in the survey data.)

If either $n\hat{p}$ or $n(1-\hat{p})$ is too small the normal curve may not fit the sampling distribution well enough for us to say with 95% confidence that the interval given by this formula will capture the parameter.

Illustration of a Confidence Interval Calculation

In an earlier example involving opinions about climate change, a survey of 500 people found 400 who thought that climate change was an important issue.

That gives $n = 500$, $\hat{p} = \frac{400}{500} = .80$, and $(1 - \hat{p}) = .20$

The 95% confidence interval is:

$$\hat{p} \pm 2\sqrt{\frac{\hat{p}(1-\hat{p})}{n}}$$

$$.80 \pm 2\sqrt{\frac{.80(1-.80)}{500}}$$

$.80 \pm .035$

$.765$ to $.835$

On the basis of our random sample, we can be confident (but not totally sure) that the percentage of people in the population who think climate change is a crucial issue is some value between 76.5% and 83.5%. In the popular media this would probably be reported as 76% to 84%; decimals are rarely given. In more formal research this might be shown as 95%CI: 76.5% – 83.5%.

Graphical Depiction of Confidence Intervals (Error Bars)

A confidence interval may be represented graphically by an **error bar** as shown in Figure 11.1. The meaning of an error bar in a graph must be explicitly stated. Do not assume that anytime you see a graph with an error bar it represents a 95% confidence interval. In many graphs an error bar represents 1 standard deviation or 1 standard error. Different choices are commonly made in different fields of research. In each case they do indicate a measure of uncertainty, but there's no one standard way to do this. In accordance with our formula for a 95% interval, the length of the error bar on each side of the point estimate should be equal to the margin of error, namely 2 standard errors. In Figure 11.1 that came to about 3.5%.

It is quite common to see graphs like the one on the left, but it is increasingly popular in technical reports to use the style on the right. They carry the same information. The bar adds no information.

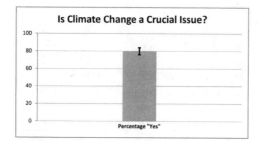 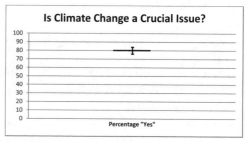

FIGURE 11.1 Survey percentage saying "yes," with 95% confidence interval shown as an error bar

Exercises for Confidence Intervals (Percentages)

1. You want to estimate the percentage of public school teachers in your state who have been employed in their current school more than five years. You get a random sample of 144 public school teachers in your state and you find that 90 of them have been employed in their current school more than five years.

    a. Find the 95% confidence interval estimate based on this data and explain what it means.
    b. Show a bar graph with an error bar to represent this confidence interval.
    c. Identify the groups that are the sample and the population in this survey. Is n the number of people in the sample or the number of people in the population?
    d. In the context of this exercise, distinguish what p and $\hat{p}$ represent.

2. The results of a published study stated that only 18 of 46 American elementary school teachers solved $1\frac{3}{4} \div \frac{1}{2}$ correctly. Assume the study was based on a random sample of K-6 teachers in your state.

    a. Estimate the percentage of all the K-6 teachers in your state who could do this problem correctly. Give both a point estimate and a 95% confidence interval estimate.
    b. How would your answers in a. above change if the numbers were 180 and 460 instead of 18 and 46?

3. When you are estimating a population percentage, if you can increase the size of the sample will the confidence interval become shorter or longer? Why would you want to use as large a sample as possible in a study?

4. A tiny class consists of four students. After a brilliant intervention by their teacher, two of them can do multiplication at the speed of light. Find the margin of error and the 95% confidence interval for the percentage of similar students who will be able to multiply at the speed of light after such an intervention. Do you like the result?

5. A Gallup poll about people's fears, taken in February 2001, found that snakes were the number one object of fear: 51% of those interviewed said they were afraid of snakes. Second and third in the list were public speaking (40%) and heights (36%). The sample size was 1,016. Calculate a margin of error for these estimates. For each case use the formula in Box 11.1. Then see how much difference it would have made if you had just used $\dfrac{1}{\sqrt{n}}$ for the margin of error. (Assume the samples are random samples from the adult population of America.)

6. In a recent poll of 900 adults chosen at random in one city, 513 people agreed with the statement that "The country would be governed better if there were more women in politics."

    a. Find a point estimate for the percentage of *all* adults in that city who agree with that statement, and calculate the margin of error for the estimate.
    b. Calculate a 95% confidence interval for the percentage of all adults who agree with the statement. Does it seem likely that a majority of all the adults in the city agree that the country would be governed better if there were more women in politics?

7. The figure shows some results of a statewide administration of a standardized test.

    a. Give a likely reason that the error bar on "State" is so much smaller than the one on "School 1."
    b. Why might there be no error bar shown on the bar for School 2? Isn't it about the same size as School 2?

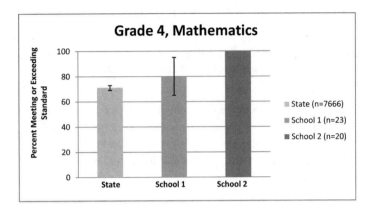

Estimating a Population Mean

Notation: Just as in the case of estimation of percentages, we need symbols to distinguish the mean of a sample from the mean of a population. The most common choice is $\bar{x}$ for the mean of a sample and μ for the mean of a population. The statistic $\bar{x}$ is used to estimate the parameter μ (μ is lower-case Greek "m," pronounced "mew" and spelled "mu").

Similarly, it is common to use s for the standard deviation of a sample and σ for the standard deviation of a population. In statistical inference, where we use s to estimate σ, you should calculate s using $n - 1$ as the divisor instead of n. This compensates for the tendency of variability within a sample to be smaller than variability within the population. As noted earlier, the two formulas give very similar results except when n is small. Calculators usually have two separate keys so that you can choose the divisor you want. Statistical programs on computers tend to use the $n - 1$ formula as the default choice.

Symbols associated with statistical inference

	Statistic	*Parameter it estimates*
Percentage	$\hat{p}$ (p-hat)	p
Mean	$\bar{x}$ (x-bar)	μ (mu)
Standard deviation	s	σ (sigma)

Confidence Interval Estimate of a Population Mean (μ)

We said earlier that every statistic has its own sampling distribution and that we depend on statisticians to determine their properties. We use the statistic $\bar{x}$, the mean of a random sample, to estimate μ, the mean of the population. In order to establish a margin of error and a confidence interval for $\bar{x}$ we need to know the sampling distribution for $\bar{x}$. Statisticians have shown that under some fairly common conditions $\bar{x}$ has a sampling distribution very close to a normal distribution with mean μ and standard deviation $\frac{\sigma}{\sqrt{n}}$, where σ is the standard deviation of the population.

Based on this information, we can construct a confidence interval for μ, but because both μ and σ are not known we replace them in the formulas by their point estimates, $\bar{x}$ and s.

The fraction $\frac{\sigma}{\sqrt{n}}$, because it is the standard deviation of a sampling distribution, is called the **standard error of the mean (SE)**. The denominator, $\sqrt{n}$, implies that larger samples give estimates with greater precision and narrower confidence intervals.

Notice that the formulas for the SE of $\hat{p}$ and the SE of $\bar{x}$ both have $\sqrt{n}$ in the denominator. This means that the precision of these estimates is inversely proportional to the *square root* of the sample size, not the sample size itself. Doubling the sample size will not make your estimate twice as precise.

Box 11.2

95% confidence interval estimate of a population mean (based on a sample mean)

Sample mean ± Margin of error
Sample mean ± 2 SE

$$\bar{x} \pm 2 \frac{s}{\sqrt{n}} \ , \ (n \geq 30)$$

For samples with $n < 30$, the sampling distribution of $\bar{x}$ may differ somewhat from the normal distribution. You can often compensate by increasing the coefficient from 2 to a higher value given in a t-table. See Table A.2 in the Appendix.

Math sidelight about SE formulas: You may have wondered if there is a relationship between the two SE formulas, $\sqrt{\frac{\hat{p}(1-\hat{p})}{n}}$ and $\frac{s}{\sqrt{n}}$. In fact, they are identical. To see that, recall that the formula with the $\hat{p}$s is based on binomial experiments, where each trial results in either success or failure. Success and failure can be given the values 1 and 0. Then the result of a binomial experiment is a data set consisting of 1s and 0s.

For example, if $n = 5$ trials, you might end up with three 1s and two 0s. You can check that the mean will be 3/5, which is exactly $\hat{p}$, and the variance will be 6/25, which is exactly $\hat{p}(1-\hat{p})$.

So both SE formulas boil down to $SE = \sqrt{\dfrac{\text{variance}}{n}}$.

Precision and Accuracy of Estimates

We make a distinction between precision and accuracy in the context of estimation. Why do we use the sample mean, $\bar{x}$, as the point estimate of the population mean? One reason is that it is accurate: if we use random samples, then the sample mean is no more likely to produce an estimate that is too high than one that is too low. We say that $\bar{x}$ is an *unbiased* estimator of the population mean.

We control the precision of an estimate by its standard error. When an estimate has a small standard error, it means that in repeated sampling it gives practically the same value each time. An estimate with a smaller standard error is more precise. Ideally we want estimates to be both accurate and precise. A major contribution of theoretical statistics is the determination of such properties of estimators.

The distinction between precision and accuracy is often portrayed in a sketch such as that shown in Figure 11.2.

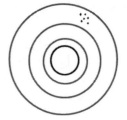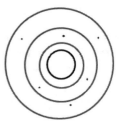

Good precision, good accuracy   Good precision, poor accuracy   Poor precision, good sccuracy

FIGURE 11.2 Precision and accuracy

Exercises for Confidence Intervals (Means)

1. You want to estimate the mean salary of public school teachers in your state. You get a random sample of 144 such teachers. You find that their mean salary is $48,250 with a standard deviation of $12,000.

    a. Find the 95% confidence interval estimate and explain what it means.

    b. Show this result in a graph with an error bar. For a 95% confidence interval, the error bar extends $2SE$ in each direction, where $SE = \frac{s}{\sqrt{n}}$.

2. Below is a set of 36 fictional scores for a 4th grade class on a standardized test. Test scores such as these are often the result of some algorithm based on the students' responses and are called *scaled scores*. For example, a score on PSAT may be 560. That doesn't mean the student got 560 questions right, but rather that the combination of the student's responses was converted to 560 on an artificial scale.

Fictional scaled scores on a standardized test

410	411	418	418	419	420	421	422	424	424	427	428
428	430	432	433	435	438	439	439	442	443	443	445
445	446	451	451	452	454	456	458	463	463	465	466

    a. The mean and standard deviation for the 36 scaled scores shown are $\bar{x} = 437.75$ and $s = 15.94$. Confirm that the standard error (SE) of the mean is 2.66.

    b. Construct a 95% confidence interval for the true mean scaled score of the population these children represent.

    c. Draw two graphs similar to those in Figure 11.1 (page 108). In the first graph the length of the error bar should be the SE and on the other it should be the margin of error ($2SE$). Include legends so that the nature of the error bar is evident. This exercise is a reminder that you cannot interpret error bars just by looking at them. A legend must explain what they represent.

    d. Confirm that the values given in a. above are correct.

3. Every three years the Federal Reserve Board issues statistics on family income in the United States. In 2007, based on a random sample of 4,422 families, it estimated the mean before-tax

income of all American families at about $84,000 with a standard error (*SE*) of about $1,300. (*Source: Federal Reserve Bulletin*, February 2009.)

    a.   Use this information to compute a 95% confidence interval for the mean family income for all American families that year.

    b.   That same year the median income was about $47,000. Why do you think the mean and median are so different? What might the frequency histogram of family incomes look like?

    c.   Assume it is reasonable that $SE \approx \frac{s}{\sqrt{n}}$ for these data, and estimate *s*. For this survey explain the distinction between what *s* measures and what *SE* measures.

4.   These data appeared in a recent report on student mobility:

Grade 4, Language arts

	Mean SAT-9	95% confidence interval
Stable students	663	[662.5, 664.1]
Mobile students	652	[649.9, 654.2]

    a.   What is the basic implication of these statistics?

    b.   Using the data from the confidence intervals estimate *SE*, the standard error of the mean. (There will be some rounding error because the means 663 and 652 have been rounded to integers.)

    c.   The *SE* in both cases is very small. Give a possible reason for this.

Confidence Intervals and School Assessment

The idea of imperfect measurement is rooted in the physical sciences. For example, in a physics experiment you may need to find the time it takes a ball to fall from a given height to the floor. You repeat the procedure, but you don't get precisely the same value each time. In psychology you might measure the response time of a subject to some stimulus. Similarly, you don't get precisely the same result each time. In both cases, however, the assumption is that there is a true value that you are trying to determine. It's just that you can't quite know if you've got it.

It is always the case that if you make just one observation you cannot be confident you have found the true value. Like a single observation in a science lab experiment, the score a student gets on a test can be considered just one point estimate of the student's "true" ability to answer those test questions. Any number of factors can cause a particular test score to be not quite true, such as the student's mood or health at test time, or the noise level in the room. On top of that we also need to acknowledge that the test questions themselves may not be perfect for capturing true ability in a particular subject area. In fact, "true ability" in a subject area is a tough idea to quantify.

From the point of view of the statistician, a score on a test is a single estimate of some true ability. The score is considered to represent a student's "true" ability plus or minus an "error" amount. So, when a student gets a 75, we interpret that to mean that the student's true ability is "around" 75. You must accept that you will never know the exact value of the true score. By creating a confidence interval around this particular test score we can compute an interval that probably contains the student's true ability. We hope that the interval is small enough to be meaningful.

Similarly, the percentage of students in a school who achieve the standards on one administration of a standardized test is only one point estimate of the school's true percentage. We can create a confidence interval around a school-wide assessment to provide an interval which contains the school's true score. Many AYP decisions are based on such confidence intervals, as shown next. This approach has generated controversy, and not all states continue to use it.

Application of Confidence Intervals to Adequate Yearly Progress (AYP)

This excerpt was taken from the FAQ section of the website of the Colorado Department of Education (CDE) (*source:* http://www.cde.state.co.us/FedPrograms/danda/aypfaq.asp; accessed September 5, 2011). Note how AYP decisions depend on the confidence interval, and note, particularly, the influence of school size.

> **CDE incorporates the use of "confidence intervals" and upper "confidence limits" in making AYP determinations. What does this mean?**
> Confidence intervals have important and positive implications for a school's or district's opportunity to make AYP. CDE uses a specific formula (developed by Ghosh) to calculate confidence intervals around a proportion or percentage (see Glass & Hopkins, 3rd Edition, 1996, p. 326). When using confidence intervals, upper and lower limits around the percent proficient are calculated, creating a range of values within which there is "confidence" that the true percentage lies. CDE will use a 95 percent confidence level, meaning that we are 95 percent confident that the percent proficient for a school or district falls within the limits determined by the confidence interval formula.
>
> For example, let's say the percent of AYP proficient students in reading at an elementary school is 82.68 and the upper and lower limits of the 95 percent confidence interval are 89.54 and 75.82, respectively. Given that the proficiency target for elementary reading is 88.46 percent, the school would be considered to have reached the target because the upper limit of the 95 percent confidence interval (89.54) is higher than the target (88.46).
> . . .
>
> **Does this mean that one school with a given proficiency rate might make AYP while another school with the same proficiency rate would not?**
> Yes. Sample size directly affects the ranges of confidence intervals—the larger the sample size, the narrower the range. Large disaggregated groups will have relatively narrow confidence intervals compared to small disaggregated groups, which will have wider confidence intervals.

12

STATISTICAL SIGNIFICANCE

Introductory Investigation

Statistically Significant Difference?

This table appeared in a press release from the Survey Center at the University of Wisconsin. What is the main point of the table? Why would the phrase "statistically significant" be used?

Same sex marriage, unions, and referendum

When asked about laws allowing same-sex couples to marry, 40% of the Wisconsin public said they support such laws. However, people are more likely to approve of civil unions than to approve of laws allowing people of the same sex to marry. Overall, close to 60% of the Wisconsin public approves of civil unions.

   However there are differences by gender. Gender differences in support for same-sex marriage are statistically significant at conventional levels.

	Approval, by gender	
	Men	Women
Approval of same-sex marriage	33.5	45.2
Approval of civil unions	55.8	61.5

Source: Badger Poll™ 22, Release 3, University of Wisconsin Survey Center, July 17, 2006.

Using Statistics to Make Comparisons

What Does "Statistically Significant" Mean?

The phrase "statistically significant" has meaning only in the context of statistical inference, that is, when you make a statement about populations based on sample data. Basically, it means you have confidence that something you found in the sample data truly reflects something in the populations. For example, one may say that a difference between two groups is statistically significant.

This means that the difference you found in the sample data leads you to conclude that a similar difference exists between the two populations from which the samples were taken. The difference in attitude between the men and women in the Wisconsin survey was strong enough for the researchers to announce that it reflected a true difference between men and women in the general Wisconsin public.

If a difference in the sample data is *not* statistically significant then you are less confident you would have found any difference at all if you had the data from all members of the populations. You might or might not have found a difference if you had polled everyone, but the limited sample data is not conclusive.

What Does "Statistically Significant Difference" Not Mean?

It does not mean that the difference is necessarily *important*. The importance (or "real world" significance) of a difference between two populations is another matter that cannot be decided by statistical calculations alone. We will say more about this as we go, but meanwhile beware of confusing the word "significant" as it is used in ordinary conversation with "statistical significance," which is a technical term in inferential statistics.

Comparing Two Proportions or Percentages

How Do You Determine if a Difference Is Statistically Significant?

One way to determine statistical significance is to construct a confidence interval around the difference you find in your particular study. We specifically mean by "difference" a value obtained by subtraction.

A difference is statistically significant if its confidence interval does *not* include zero.

BOX 12.1

95% confidence interval estimate of the difference of two percentages

Sample difference ± Margin of error
Sample difference ± 2 *SE*

$$(\hat{p}_1 - \hat{p}_2) \pm 2\sqrt{\frac{\hat{p}_1(1-\hat{p}_1)}{n_1} + \frac{\hat{p}_2(1-\hat{p}_2)}{n_2}} \qquad \text{(when the } ns \text{ are large)}$$

This formula is correct because the sampling distribution for differences of percentages has approximately the shape of a normal curve when the samples are large enough. A rule of thumb for "large enough" is that both samples should contain at least five "yeses" and five "nos."

Gender Gap Example

Suppose that in your school district all 4th grade students were tested and 70% of the girls and 50% of the boys achieved the standards in Subject A. Is this difference statistically significant?

The answer is, "It depends." Here are two possible scenarios. You will see that the answer depends on the margin of error for your estimate of the difference.

Case 1: Difference Is *Not* Statistically Significant (Large Margin of Error)

The difference in the success rates is .70 − .50 = .20. That is our basic summary statistic. The confidence interval for this difference is therefore .20 +/− margin of error.

Suppose that in this study the margin of error is .25. Then the confidence interval covers values from .20 − .25 to .20 + .25, that is, from −5% to +45%. Note the negative 5% and the positive 45%.

Because 0% is in this interval, the data we have are consistent with two populations that do not actually differ. The difference in the sample data is not statistically significant.

Case 2: Difference *Is* Statistically Significant (Small Margin of Error)

Suppose the margin of error is .12. Then the confidence interval estimate of the true difference covers values from .20 − .12 to .20 + .12, that is, from +8% to +32%. Both percentages are positive.

Because 0% is not in this interval, the data we have are consistent with two populations that *do* differ. Evidently, girls do better. In the larger populations we don't know precisely how much better the girls are, but our single best guess is that the gap is about 20%, and we are quite confident that the gap is at least 8%. The difference is statistically significant.

Illustration of Calculations for the Gender Gap Example

In one study, 105 out of 150 girls met the 4th grade standards, while 50 out of 100 boys did so. Is the difference in success percentages statistically significant? Note that both samples are relatively large, which will cause the margin of error to be relatively small.

Let subscripts 1 and 2 represent girls and boys respectively.

Girls	*Boys*
$n_1 = 150$	$n_2 = 100$
$\hat{p}_1 = 105/150 = .70$	$\hat{p}_2 = 50/100 = .50$
$SE_1 = \sqrt{\dfrac{70(30)}{150}}$	$SE_2 = \sqrt{\dfrac{50(50)}{100}}$

95% confidence interval for the true difference:
Observed difference $\pm 2\ SE$

$$(.70 - .50) \pm 2\sqrt{\frac{.70(.30)}{150} + \frac{.50(.50)}{100}}$$

.20 $\pm$ .122 = .078 to .322 or 7.8% to 32.2%, which does not include zero.

The difference is statistically significant.

You can also recognize statistical significance by the non-overlap of the 95% confidence error bars as shown in Figure 12.1. *Watch out!* If the error bars do not overlap the difference is statistically significant, but if they do overlap you need to check by the formal calculations because the difference may still be statistically significant. Remember in the first place to check that the error bars shown represent a 95% confidence interval.

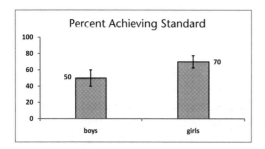 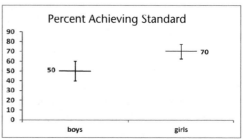

FIGURE 12.1 Difference in percentages is statistically significant because 95% confidence interval error bars do not overlap. Error bars are for 95% confidence intervals.

Exercises about Differences in Percentages

1. In a gender gap study, 14 out of 20 girls met the 4th grade standards, while 10 out of 20 boys did so. Show that the difference in success percentages is not statistically significant. The percentages who achieved the standards are the same as in the previous gender gap illustration. Why is the conclusion about statistical significance not the same?

2. This is the kind of data you might see in an action research study. Do these data imply that the difference in male and female success rates is statistically significant at the 95% confidence level? Draw a graph similar to Figure 12.1 above (with error bars). Summarize the data in a 2×2 table as shown. (*Hint:* Read the caution given along with Figure 12.1.)

ID	Sex	Achieved standard	ID	Sex	Achieved standard	ID	Sex	Achieved standard
01	M	Yes	13	M	No	25	M	Yes
02	F	No	14	M	No	26	M	No
03	F	Yes	15	M	No	27	M	No
04	M	No	16	F	No	28	M	Yes
05	F	Yes	17	F	Yes	29	M	No
06	F	No	18	M	No	30	F	Yes
07	F	Yes	19	F	No	31	M	Yes
08	F	Yes	20	F	Yes	32	F	No
09	F	Yes	21	F	Yes	33	M	No
10	F	Yes	22	F	Yes	34	F	Yes
11	F	Yes	23	M	No	35	M	Yes
12	M	No	24	M	No	36	F	No

	Achieved standard	
	Yes	No
Male		
Female		

3. This table shows scaled scores for 28 students who took a standardized test. The scores were recorded before their teacher began an intervention. Data at the beginning of a study before any intervention are called *baseline* data.

Control group		Intervention group	
Student	Scaled score	Student	Scaled score
A	449	Aa	446
B	447	Bb	441
C	433	Cc	456
D	441	Dd	425
E	427	Ee	458
F	452	Ff	461
G	435	Gg	447
H	452	Hh	451
I	430	Ii	444
J	457	Jj	424
K	457	Kk	460
L	458	Ll	444
M	458	Mm	437
N	419	Nn	437

As part of her analysis of the study she wanted to claim that the two groups were similar at the start of her study. She did this by showing that the difference in the percentages who achieved the standards in both classes (scaled score 440 or more) was not statistically significant. Confirm her calculation.

4. Suppose your own class has 15 boys and 12 girls. Of the boys 10 meet the standards in Subject X, and of the girls 6 do. Is this difference statistically significant according to a 95% confidence interval? Discuss why you may want to know more than just whether or not a difference is statistically significant if you are concerned about gender differences.

5. The following quotation is excerpted from the website mediamatters.org. It appeared in July 2008.

> **MSNBC's *Hardball* falsely suggested McCain holds statistically significant lead over Obama among white suburban women**
>
> Summary: On-screen graphics based on an NBC News/*Wall Street Journal* poll that aired during MSNBC's *Hardball* falsely suggested that Sen. John McCain's lead over Sen. Barack Obama among white suburban women is statistically significant because it provided only the poll's margin of error for the overall poll – not the higher margin of error for the crosstab of white suburban women.
>
> On June 12, *Hardball* host Chris Matthews aired two separate on-screen graphics, based on an NBC News/*Wall Street Journal* poll conducted June 6–9, that falsely suggested that Sen. John McCain's lead of 44 percent to 38 percent over Sen. Barack Obama among white suburban women is statistically significant. Specifically, the charts provided only the margin of error for the survey as a whole – 3.1 percentage points – and not the margin of error of 9.34 percentage points for the crosstab of white suburban women.
>
> (*Source:* http://mediamatters.org/items/printable/200806130003;
> accessed September 5, 2011)

a. What is the math behind the controversy? Why isn't the margin of error for suburban women 3.1 percentage points?

b. Based on the 9.34 figure, estimate the number of suburban women who participated in the poll.

c. The margin of error for the whole poll is about three times smaller than the margin of error for the subgroup of suburban white women. Does that mean the whole group was about three times as large as the subgroup? If not, how many times larger was it?

6. Analyze and compare these findings by a 95% confidence interval. Include a comparison of the pass rates in your discussion. What is the point of this exercise?

TABLE A	Pass	Fail
Boys	10	5
Girls	6	4

TABLE B	Pass	Fail
Boys	100	50
Girls	60	40

7. a. Analyze these differences by calculating first a 95% confidence interval and then an 85% confidence interval. Compare and contrast your conclusions. Check by referring to the normal curve table that you should add and subtract 1.44 standard deviations for an 85% confidence interval.

2004, Grade 4, Math skills

	Percentage meeting or exceeding standards
Barre City ($n = 104$)	61%
Barre Town ($n = 94$)	73%

b. True or false? If a finding is statistically significant at the 95% level then it will be significant at the 85% level. Explain why this makes sense.

c. True or false? If a finding is statistically significant at the 85% level then it will be significant at the 95% level.

8. Once again, we stress that statistical significance is not synonymous with educational significance. This is an unrealistic example, but it makes the point that if samples are large enough even a small difference can be statistically significant.

A test was given to see if a certain mathematics standard was being met. The test was given to n boys and n girls: 60.1% of the boys met the standards; 60.2% of the girls met the standards. Almost certainly this difference is of no educational importance. But for what values of n would this difference be statistically significant?

9. (Activity) At your table, come up with some characteristic on which to compare two groups in the class. The comparison should be based on percentages. Conduct a quick survey among your classmates. Then double the numbers as if there had been twice as many people. Make tables and graphs, and test for statistical significance. Make a formal report with a brilliant interpretation.

10. (Activity) Make up a scenario with fake data to be analyzed by a confidence interval for the difference of two percentages. Analyze your fake data and report clearly what they imply.

Comparing Two Means

In many studies the difference between two *means*, not the difference between two percentages, is the statistic used to compare two groups. The general approach is the same for both comparisons, but the details of the computation differ.

BOX 12.2

95% confidence interval estimate of the difference of two means

Sample difference ± Margin of error
Sample difference ± 2 *SE*

$$(\bar{x}_1 - \bar{x}_2) \pm 2\sqrt{\frac{s_1^2}{n_1} + \frac{s_2^2}{n_2}} \text{ (where both } ns \text{ are large)}$$

This formula is correct when the sampling distribution for differences of means has approximately the shape of a normal curve. This happens if the samples are large enough. A rule of thumb for "large enough" is that the size of both samples should be at least 30.

When the samples are small, adjustments need to be made in the formula. That's because the sampling distribution of differences is often not normal, but is a related shape called a *t*-distribution. These adjustments are made automatically by statistical calculators or software. The effect of these adjustments is to change the 2 in the formula slightly.

Example: Comparing Scaled Scores

Below are fictional scaled scores on a standardized test for two 4th grade classes. Is the difference in their mean scores statistically significant?

X1: Fictional 4th grade scores (Class 1)

410	411	418	418	419	420	421	422	424	424	427	428
428	430	432	433	435	438	439	439	442	443	443	445
445	446	451	451	452	454	456	458	463	463	465	466

X2: Fictional 4th grade scores (Class 2)

400	445	430	438	426	444	408	402	434	402
442	431	409	416	406	415	422	436	416	420
403	411	421	440	428	403	428	425	438	405
427	419	417	416	424	419	408	433	446	412

First we look at the two distributions to see if there is anything unusual. There is not, and we see that the Class 1 scores tend to be higher.

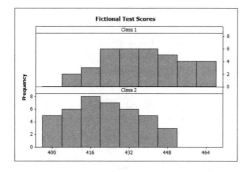

Here are the summary statistics for both classes. Construct the 95% confidence interval for the mean difference in the scaled scores.

	n	$\bar{x}$	s
Class 1	36	437.8	15.9
Class 2	40	421.6	13.5

$$(\bar{x}_1 - \bar{x}_2) \pm 2\sqrt{\frac{s_1^2}{n_1} + \frac{s_2^2}{n_2}} = (437.8 - 421.6) \pm 2\sqrt{\frac{15.9^2}{36} + \frac{13.5^2}{40}} = 16.2 \pm 6.8 = 9.4 \text{ to } 23.0$$

(More roughly, 95% CI: 9 to 23 points.)

The confidence interval does not include 0, so the difference is statistically significant. We can be confident that the true mean score for Class 1 is at least 9 points higher.

You can also recognize statistical significance by the non-overlap of the 95% confidence error bars, as shown in Figure 12.2.

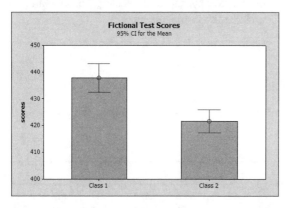

Reminder: If the error bars do not overlap, the difference is statistically significant, but if they do overlap you need to check by the formal calculations because the difference may still be statistically significant.

FIGURE 12.2   Difference in means is statistically significant because error bars do not overlap

Change within a Group: Matched Pairs Confidence Interval

Example: Difference between Pre-test and Post-test Scores

In many intervention studies we want to describe how big a change the intervention made. Commonly this includes comparing the mean scores of a group before and after the intervention.

Figure 12.3 shows the data and a plot for such a situation. The data in such a study are called **matched pairs** because the pre-test score and the post-test score are linked for each student. Each post–test score is matched to a particular pre–test score.

Student	Pre-test	Post-test	Change
A	433	435	2
B	432	441	9
C	428	432	4
D	445	447	2
E	450	456	6
F	445	446	1
G	433	440	7
H	431	436	5
I	445	450	5
J	419	425	6
K	450	452	2
L	433	434	1
M	448	455	7
N	460	469	9
Mean	439.4	444.1	4.7
SD	11.1	11.7	2.8

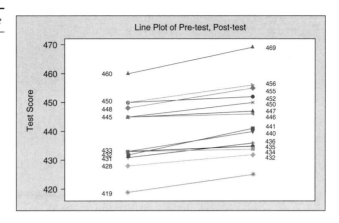

FIGURE 12.3   Matched data from pre-test and post-test

It is clear from Figure 12.3 that every student experienced a positive change. Such data support the effectiveness of the intervention. The consistency of the change is notable. If we evaluate the difference between the two means according to the method we have previously used we will throw away the knowledge we have about each child's individual improvement. By ignoring the individual changes we would be using an analysis that is weaker than necessary. A stronger method, which makes use of all the information in the data, is to use the change column itself and construct a confidence interval around its mean. That approach will provide a more precise estimate of the mean amount of change due to the intervention. Box 12.3 gives the formula.

BOX 12.3

95% confidence interval for the mean change from pre-test to post-test using matched pairs

$\bar{x} \pm 2\sqrt{\dfrac{s^2}{n}}$, where $\bar{x}$ and s are the mean and standard deviation for the list of changes

This is very similar to the previous formula but simplified to deal with one set of values instead of two.

The computation is:

$$\bar{x} \pm 2\sqrt{\frac{s^2}{n}} = 4.7 \pm 2\sqrt{\frac{2.8^2}{14}} = 4.7 \pm 1.5 = (3.2, 6.2)$$

This interval does not contain zero. The change is statistically significant.

The computation indicates that we can have 95% confidence that the mean change from pre-test to post-test is positive. This is clear evidence of growth.

Note: If you construct the confidence interval as we had done previously using the means and standard deviation of the two groups but not matching the pre- and post-test scores for each child, you will find the difference between the two means is *not* statistically significant. That analysis is less precise than the one we just showed. The fact that the two approaches reach different conclusions is a reminder that the statistical analysis you do should be appropriate to the way the research was conducted.

Exercises about Differences between Means

1. These data were taken from a 1995 study about gender differences:

Grade	Mean score (standard deviation)	
	Female (n = 32)	Male (n = 28)
6	23.94 (7.89)	25.61 (5.19)
8	37.47 (6.45)	41.82 (5.19)

Source: Lindsay Anne Tartre and Elizabeth Fennema, Mathematics Achievement and Gender: A Longitudinal Study of Selected Cognitive and Affective Variables (Grades 6–12), *Educational Studies in Mathematics*, 1995, 28: 199–217.

    a.   Find the 95% confidence intervals for the difference between male and female scores in each grade level. Is the difference statistically significant in either grade?

    b.   Show the results in graphs with appropriate error bars.

2. Data are collected in a large school district to compare scores on a reading test for children in two different SES categories. The data are summarized as shown:

Summary statistics for reading test

	n	$\bar{x}$	s
Lower SES	400	335.4	20.1
Higher SES	600	380.1	21.5

    a.   Construct a 95% confidence interval for the difference in mean scores and decide if the difference is statistically significant.

    b.   Would the conclusion about statistical significance change if you constructed a 90% confidence interval? That is, is the difference significant at the 90% level of confidence? *Note:* The multiplier 2 in the formula would change to 1.645. (Why? Refer to Table A.1 in the Appendix.)

3. This graph compares grades in mathematics on several campuses of a university system. Do any differences appear to be statistically significant?

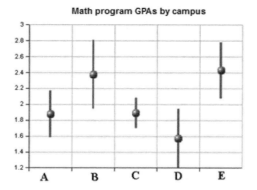

Math program GPAs by campus

Bars represent 95% confidence intervals

Note: Graph adapted from www.comfsm.fm/~dleeling/training/openoffice/ci.html

4. Here are some (totally fake) IQ data from random samples of American adults by Dr. Belle Kerve (also totally made up). Dr. Kerve concluded that the difference in mean IQ for the sexes is statistically significant. Is she correct? What is the point of this exercise?

	Male	Female
n	10,000	10,000
$\bar{x}$	100.3	99.9
s	10.3	10.2

5. In an earlier exercise we compared these two sets of data by showing that the difference in the *proportion* of students in each class who scored 440 or higher was not statistically significant. Now show that the difference in *mean* scaled scores is not statistically significant. Both comparisons were used to support the claim that these two groups of students had similar abilities at the start of a research project.

Control group	
Student	Scaled score
A	449
B	447
C	433
D	441
E	427
F	452
G	435
H	452
I	430
J	457
K	457
L	458
M	458
N	419

Intervention group	
Student	Scaled score
Aa	446
Bb	441
Cc	456
Dd	425
Ee	458
Ff	461
Gg	447
Hh	451
Ii	444
Jj	424
Kk	460
Ll	444
Mm	437
Nn	437

Note: In this example the sample sizes are small, but for the sake of practice assume that the 95% confidence interval algorithm from page 121 is reasonable. (It is.)

6. (Activity) Make up a scenario with fake data to be analyzed by a confidence interval for the difference of means. Analyze your fake data and report clearly what they imply.

Deciding if a Difference Is Important

A finding that a difference is statistically significant is a *mathematical* result. *It is important to note that statistical significance does not say anything at all about the practical importance of that difference.*

For instance, suppose you compute a confidence interval for the difference between the mean score on a test between 20 boys and 20 girls who represent larger populations. The mean score for the girls is 275, and the mean score for the boys is 272. You find that the 95% confidence interval for the difference is 3 ± 1. The interval is therefore 2 to 4. The difference is statistically significant because the interval does not include 0. You can announce that you have a gender gap: On average it seems that girls do at least 2 points better than boys.

But is the magnitude of the average difference, 2 or 3 or 4 points, educationally important? The calculation does not tell you the answer. The educational importance of such a result is a decision to be made by concerned citizens and educators. Such a decision should be supported by statistical evidence, but other considerations are needed too.

In short, you can't use statistics as a substitute for responsible decision making. Very often a finding of statistical significance is a flag that means some action should be taken to change the status quo. But not always. You may have discovered a situation that is not worth spending resources on. On the other hand, a finding that is not statistically significant but potentially consequential may justify further study or even some preliminary action.

Because calculations for confidence intervals involve the sample sizes, a potentially important finding based on small samples may fail to be statistically significant. Conversely, if you use very large samples a small difference of little practical importance may be statistically significant.

In most published research, statistical significance is associated with confidence intervals set at the 95% level. However, this is not a law. You should always check to see if someone is using an unconventional level. If you use a level of confidence lower than 95% you will get a smaller margin of error and you are more likely to find statistical significance (at this lower level of confidence), *but you pay a penalty.* Because you use a lower confidence level, you increase the chance that you are announcing a difference that may not hold up in further testing. You are using weaker evidence from samples to support the claim of a difference in the populations they represent.

Confidence Intervals and School Research

The children who are the subjects in a school research project may often be thought of as a sample of a larger population of "similar" children. For example, this year's 4th graders may be thought to represent the 4th graders who will be coming along in the next few years. So you can legitimately attach a margin of error to your findings. This interval allows you to generalize your findings to the larger population of 4th graders. You may sum up by saying something like: As a result of this intervention, 70% of my class achieved the standard. I conclude that (for students like mine) between 67% and 73% will achieve the standards after this intervention. That conclusion can support your decision to keep using (or to abandon) this intervention in the future.

Now for the bad news. Many school research projects involve a small number of children. This may result in an unhelpfully large margin of error – something like: "The 95% confidence interval for the percentage of children who would be helped by my fabulous intervention is between 2%

and 97%." In the end, a sensible conclusion is likely to be more like: "This is what happened in my classroom. I believe in my heart of hearts that it is a genuine finding, but my statistical evidence is not strong enough to make a dependable generalization. I can also support my belief by the following anecdotal evidence. . . ." In more formal research a result like this may suggest that time and money be spent studying the issue further.

Effect Size for a Difference of Two Means

Even though there is no mathematical way to decide if a difference has practical importance, researchers develop statistics that provide guidance for such a decision. One type of statistic that has become popular recently, especially in educational assessment research, is called **effect size**. There are different varieties of effect size statistics, several of which have been designed to compare two means. One popular effect size statistic, often symbolized by the letter d, is the **standardized mean difference**.

Suppose that an intervention raises the mean score of a class from 100 to 105 on some appropriate test. Assume that the standard deviation is 15 points both times. The effect size of the intervention is defined as the 5-point improvement divided by the average of the two standard deviations.

$$\text{Effect Size} = d = \frac{\text{change}}{\text{average standard deviation}} = \frac{\bar{x}_1 - \bar{x}_2}{s_{\text{average}}} = \frac{105 - 100}{15} = \frac{5}{15} = .33$$

The intervention raised scores one-third of a standard deviation.

(The statistic d is often referred to as Cohen's d. Jacob Cohen, who died in 1998, was an influential statistician at New York University.)

The statistic d expresses the magnitude of the mean change relative to the underlying amount of variability. So the change is re-expressed in units of standard deviations, much as z-scores give relative placement in terms of standard deviations.

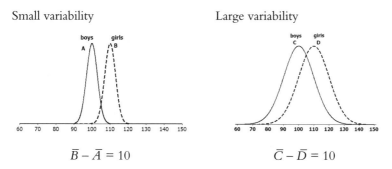

FIGURE 12.4 Underlying variability affects interpretation of a difference

Figure 12.4 shows why considering the variability of the distributions you want to compare is sensible. In both panels the mean of the distribution for girls is 10 points higher than the mean for boys. In the left panel, the skinny graphs mean there is small variability in each group. For these distributions a 10-point difference is substantial. Virtually all the girls exceed the average performance of the boys. In the right panel the difference of 10 points is not as dramatic. Because of the large variability there is a lot of overlap between the two groups. Consequently, the effect size shown in the right panel is smaller than the effect size for the left panel.

Here are some specific variability measures to make the point precisely:

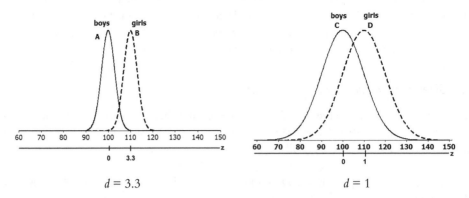

FIGURE 12.5 Underlying variability influences effect size

In the left panel of Figure 12.5 both curves have $SD = 3$, making the effect size $d = 10/3 = 3.3$. In the right panel both have $SD = 10$, making the effect size $d = 10/10 = 1$.

We can also see effect sizes in terms of z-scores. In the left panel $d = 3.3$ says that the girls' mean is at the same place as $z = 3.3$ in the boys' group; an average score for a girl is a very high score for a boy. In the right panel $d = 1$, which says that the average for a girl is higher than the average for a boy, but not as strikingly superior as in the left panel.

Here's an example of how this concept is expressed in some published research: "An effect size of 0.4 would mean that the average pupil involved in an innovation would record the same achievement as a pupil in the top 35% of those not so involved" (*source:* P. Black and D. Wiliam, Inside the Black Box: Raising Standards through Classroom Assessment, *Phi Delta Kappan*, 1998, 80, http://www.pdkintl.org/kappan/kbla9810.htm).

This means that on a normal curve if you move from a z-score of 0 (average) to a z-score of 0.4 you will change from a percentile rank of 50 to a percentile rank of 65, which is the dividing point for the top 35%.

Exercises about Effect Size

1. a. The test scores before and after an intervention are summarized in the table. Estimate the effect size.

   b. How would this be reported as a potential increase in percentile rank as was done in the

   Scores on standardized test

	Mean	Standard deviation
Pre-test	440	8
Post-test	444	8

   quote from Black and Wiliam above?

2. Two fairly similar interventions are tried in two similar schools. Let's suppose they both try a particular method of formative assessment while teaching something about fractions. However, suppose that the schools use different tests to measure change. Here are the results:

   a. Compare the effect sizes for the two interventions. How would you compare the effective-

	Pre-test		Post-test	
	Mean	Standard deviation	Mean	Standard deviation
School A (n = 36)	60	10	65	10
School B (n = 49)	380	15	390	15

    ness of the two interventions?

    b.   Compute the mean of the two effect sizes and use it to report out what these two studies together say about the impact of this type of formative assessment.

3.   An effect size of 0.8 or more is considered "large" in many areas of educational research. The rough categories, small, medium, and large, were made up by Jacob Cohen so that effect sizes (ES) for a variety of statistics could be compared easily:

> My intent was that medium ES represent an effect likely to be visible to the naked eye of a careful observer. . . . I set small ES to be noticeably smaller than medium but not so small as to be trivial, and I set large ES to be the same distance above medium as small was below it.
> (*Source:* Jacob Cohen, A Power Primer, *Psychological Bulletin*, 1992, 112 (1), July: 155–159)

    a.   Make up a table like the one in Exercise 1 that would yield a large effect size.

    b.   What would be the effect on percentile ranks for an effect size equal to 0.8?

4.   If the two standard deviations are not equal, some reasonable choice must be made for the denominator in the effect size formula. Two popular choices are: 1) use s from the pre-test (or control) group; and 2) use an appropriate weighted mean of the two standard deviations. Use the first approach to find the effect size that corresponds to the data in this table.

Scores on standardized test		
	Mean	Standard deviation
Control group	440	10
Intervention group	444	8

Aggregating Effect Sizes (Meta-analysis of Several Studies)

Because effect size is a standardized measurement, you can aggregate the results of several related but different studies:

- *Study 1:* Intervention A in a rural school consists of singing multiplication tables. It is shown to have an effect size of 0.40 when compared to regular teaching.
- *Study 2:* Intervention B in an urban school consists of singing multiplication tables. It is shown to have an effect size of 0.80 when compared to regular teaching.

The details of the intervention (the tunes, the amount of time spent, and so on) were not the same in both schools, nor were the pre- and post-tests. But in both cases it was possible to compute an effect size. Because effect sizes are standardized scores, we can combine them, and state that the mean effect size for these two interventions is 0.60. There is consistent evidence that singing the tables improves performance. Once again, you have to be sensible about what studies you combine. There must be a legitimate reason to claim they are studying the "same thing." You may also want to compute a weighted mean of the two effect sizes if the studies have different sample sizes so that studies based on larger samples carry more weight.

A popular kind of research paper is one that reviews several published studies that all looked at the same issue. In such a paper it is usual to see the mean or median effect size of the published studies given as a summary. A paper that aggregates the results of already published findings is called a **meta-analysis**.

In this next illustration the analysis is based on the results of NCLB standardized tests in various states. The main finding of this meta-analysis is that there is no gender gap in math achievement grades 2 to 11. All these effect sizes (*d*) are very small.

Gender and average performance. Effect sizes for gender differences, representing the testing of over 7 million students in state assessments, are uniformly < 0.10, representing trivial differences. . . . Of these effect sizes, 21 were positive, indicating better performance by males; 36 were negative, indicating better performance by females; and 9 were exactly 0. From this distribution of effect sizes, we calculate that the weighted mean is 0.0065, consistent with no gender difference. . . . In contrast to earlier findings, these very current data provide no evidence of a gender difference favoring males emerging in the high school years.

(*Source: Janet S. Hyde, Sara M. Lindberg, Marcia C. Linn, Amy B. Ellis, and Caroline C. Williams, Gender Similarities Characterize Math Performance, Science, July 25, 2008*)

Grade	Effect size (d)	SE for d
2	.06	.003
3	.04	.002
4	−.01	.002
5	−.01	.002
6	−.01	.002
7	−.02	.002
8	−.02	.002
9	−.01	.003
10	.04	.003
11	.06	.003

Graphs like the one shown here are often used in meta-analyses. They are called **forest plots**, and are useful for noticing patterns in the effects. Each entry in the graph is a confidence interval. They are all plotted against a horizontal axis centered on *d* = 0. If a confidence interval overlaps zero then the finding is not statistically significant. In that sense, all of the effect sizes shown are statistically significant. However, in many areas of the social sciences effect sizes smaller (in absolute value) than 0.2 are negligible. That is the case in this study, where all are smaller than 0.1.

The calculations for a 95% confidence interval for *d* are more complex than what we have been doing, so we will omit them from this text and emphasize the interpretation of the confidence interval rather than its calculation.

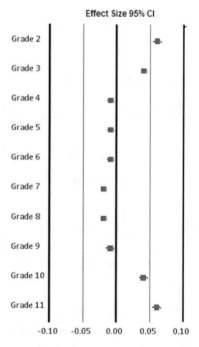

Exercises on Effect Size in Meta-analysis

1. a. In the table above in Hyde's study on gender difference what is the distinction between effect sizes with plus and minus signs? The forest plot makes this clearer.

    b. In Grade 2, the estimated effect size is .06. How would this be interpreted in terms of change in percentile rank? Does that agree with the claim that this is a "very small" effect size?

2. Here is an abstract of a research paper about distance education. We have also provided some statistics from the paper. Read the abstract; then describe how the table supports one of the conclusions of the abstract. Be sure to describe what two groups are being compared and what a positive effect size means. The particular effect size statistic the author uses is denoted g. This statistic is similar to Cohen's d. *Terminology:* In synchronous distance education all participants are online at the same time; in asynchronous distance education each participant logs on at his or her own convenience.

> A meta-analysis of the comparative distance education (DE) literature between 1985 and 2002 was conducted. In total, 232 studies containing 688 independent achievement, attitude, and retention outcomes were analyzed. Overall results indicated effect sizes of essentially zero on all three measures and wide variability. This suggests that many applications of DE outperform their classroom counterparts and that many perform more poorly. Dividing achievement outcomes into synchronous and asynchronous forms of DE produced a somewhat different impression. In general, mean achievement effect sizes for synchronous applications favored classroom instruction, while effect sizes for asynchronous applications favored DE. However, significant heterogeneity remained in each subset.
>
> (*Source:* Robert M. Bernard et al., How Does Distance Education Compare with Classroom Instruction? A Meta-Analysis of the Empirical Literature, *Review of Educational Research*, 2004, 74 (3): 379)

Confidence intervals for effect sizes

	95% confidence interval
Synchronous only	(−0.1485, −0.0559)
Asynchronous only	(0.0289, 0.0764)
Combined	(−0.0068, 0.0325)

Caution about Measuring Change Due to an Intervention

Comparing assessments at two points in time is a common research task. For such comparisons the issues we have mentioned about statistical significance are important, but some additional considerations are called for.

Take a look at Figure 12.6 taken from a recent action research project. Like those in many intervention studies it shows that the intervention had a greater impact on the students who scored the lowest to begin with.

There are several reasons this might have happened, and a good analysis would consider them all:

•   First, it might be that this intervention works superbly with low scorers and brings them up to the rest of the class.

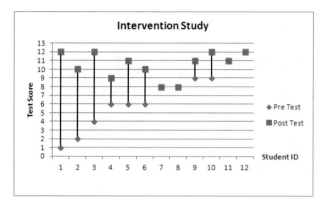

FIGURE 12.6 Individual change in an intervention study

- Second, there might be a **ceiling effect** with the test. There was no way for the top scorers on the pre-test to show the growth they made because of the intervention. The test was too easy for them.
- Third, we might be seeing the additional effect of **regression to the mean**. This simply means that a student who scored very low on the pre-test did so not just because he or she was a weak student, but also because random measurement error made his or her score even lower (maybe the student had a bad day). That student may very well improve on the post-test even if the intervention is ineffective. The part of the student's low pre-test score that was due to "bad luck" may vanish, or turn into good luck on the post-test, thereby raising the score even though the student really hasn't learned anything. A similar effect can cause the scores of the very highest pre-test students to drop on the post-test.

The main point is that you need to be careful when you claim that an intervention works extremely well for the lowest scoring students. Maybe doing nothing would have had the same effect.

Activity to Demonstrate Regression to the Mean

(*Note:* Before this activity begins, the instructor will need to make up two different sets of correct answers to a 20-question multiple choice test with choices a, b, c, and d for each question. It does not matter what these answers are, but they must be kept very secret so as not to spoil the fun.)

Total Guesswork

Part 1:
Here is a blank answer sheet for a 20-question multiple choice pre-test you must take:

Unfortunately, you know nothing about the subject of the test and will have to guess at every answer. In fact, there is no point in even showing you the questions. So go ahead and fill in the answers, choosing a, b, c, or d. The instructor will then read off the correct answers and you can grade your paper.

Some questions about this test are:

1. About what percentage of the class do you expect to get the correct answer to question 1? What about questions 2?
2. About what percentage of the class do you expect to get both questions 1 and 2 correct? And 1, 2, and 3 correct?

Pre-test

Question	Answer choice (a, b, c, or d)	Question	Answer choice (a, b, c, or d)
1		11	
2		12	
3		13	
4		14	
5		15	
6		16	
7		17	
8		18	
9		19	
10		20	

3. What is the probability someone will get all 20 questions correct? All 20 wrong?
4. Let's say you meet the standards if you get 60% or more correct. How many questions is that? The probability of that happening by random guessing is .0009. Did anyone pass?

Part 2:
We now execute an intervention. It consists of standing up, saying Go, Team, Go!, and then sitting back down.

Part 3:
An equivalent post-test is now administered where you fill out a new answer sheet and then score it.

Post-test

Question	Answer choice (a, b, c, or d)	Question	Answer choice (a, b, c, or d)
1		11	
2		12	
3		13	
4		14	
5		15	
6		16	
7		17	
8		18	
9		19	
10		20	

Get all the scores for the class and identify those people who were really helped by the intervention. Can you characterize them?

This activity may help shed light on the need always to consider the question, "What would we have expected to happen if we had done nothing?"

Additive versus Multiplicative Comparisons

Suppose an intervention raises the mean score on a standardized test for your students from 30 to 60. You can say that the intervention raised the mean score by 30 points, but you can also say that the intervention doubled the mean score. The first description of change is called an additive comparison; the second is called a multiplicative comparison. We noted in Chapter 2 ("Math connections and extensions," Exercise 3) that multiplicative comparisons make sense only when the value zero means "none." So we can compare probabilities multiplicatively, because zero means "no chance," but we cannot compare Fahrenheit temperatures this way, because zero degrees does not mean "no heat." Our earlier multiplicative comparison of test scores of 60 and 30 assumes that a zero on the test means "no correct answers."

There are formal statistical techniques for comparisons of both types. The comparisons we have already done by evaluating *differences*, which we calculated by subtracting one statistic from another, have been additive. The next section describes one kind of multiplicative comparison.

Relative Risk

Multiplicative comparisons are most often associated with *risk*. That's because of its heavy use in medicine. The classic comparison is smoking as a risk factor for lung cancer. You usually say that smoking increases the risk of lung cancer by some multiplicative factor. For example, a smoker is six times as likely to get lung cancer as a non-smoker. The basic statistic for multiplicative comparison is the **relative risk (RR)**. Relative risk is a ratio of probabilities or rates of occurrence.

$$RR = \frac{\text{probability of occurrence of some event in one group}}{\text{probability of occurrence in another group}}$$

Big idea: If $RR = 1$, the two risks are equal.

Table 12.1 illustrates a classic medical setting where researchers followed a group of smokers and a group of non-smokers for ten years to see who would develop cancer.

TABLE 12.1 Smoking and cancer

	Smoker	*Non-smoker*
Cancer	30	5
No cancer	10	35
Total	40	40

Note: The data are totally fictional.

Relative risk calculation:
For smokers the risk of cancer is $\hat{p}_1 = 30/40$.
For non-smokers the risk of cancer is $\hat{p}_2 = 5/40$.
The relative risk of cancer for smokers is $RR = \dfrac{\hat{p}_1}{\hat{p}_2} = \dfrac{30/40}{5/40} = 6.0$.
A smoker is six times as likely to get cancer.

This is all very nice, but what does it have to do with educational research?

The mathematical calculations do not care what variable you call a "risk factor," or what your outcome variable is. The analysis may have nothing at all to do with medicine. You could say that doing homework every day doubles the "risk" of getting a good grade. Just think of risk as "probability."

Relative risk is a statistic. Therefore it has an associated margin of error and confidence interval. We mention RR here because you may see it in research papers, but we won't present formulas for the confidence interval. The sampling distribution of RR is not a normal distribution, so we leave that for a more advanced text.

(Using a computer program we found that the 95% confidence interval for the $RR = 6$ above is [2.6, 13.9].)

If the confidence interval for relative risk contains the value 1, then the ratio is not statistically significant.

Another statistic that makes a multiplicative comparison of risk is called the **odds ratio (OR)**. Like the RR, $OR = 1$ implies equal risk. For the data in Table 12.1, $OR = \dfrac{30/10}{5/35} = 21$. This again implies that the risk of cancer is greater for smokers. (Using a computer program we found that the confidence interval for this OR is [6.5, 68.3].)

When you report RR or OR your words need to make clear which outcome was in the numerator. For example, though we said the relative risk of cancer for smokers is 6, we could have said the relative risk for non-smokers is $\frac{1}{6}$.

Exercises about Relative Risk

1. Why is 1 the number used to determine statistical significance for relative risk while 0 is the number used to determine the statistical significance of a difference of means?

2. This graph appeared in a meta-analysis of seven studies, each looking at the relationship between cannabis use and mental health outcomes. "Whether cannabis can cause psychotic or affective symptoms that persist beyond transient intoxication is unclear. We systematically reviewed the evidence pertaining to cannabis use and occurrence of psychotic or affective mental health outcomes." (*Source:* Theresa Moore et al., Cannabis Use and Risk of Psychotic or Affective Mental Health Outcomes: A Systematic Review, *The Lancet*, July 28, 2007. Reprinted from *The Lancet*, with permission from Elsevier.)

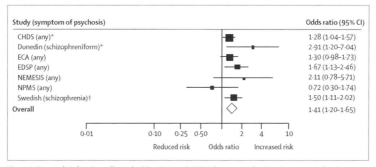

Figure 1: Forest plot showing adjusted odds ratios and 95% CI for any psychosis outcome according to ever use of cannabis in individual studies

Each of the seven studies produced its own odds ratio statistic. The sample sizes for the studies are represented by the areas of the squares. What is the general impression this graph makes? Of the seven studies, how many produced statistically significant findings? (*Note:* Studies that do not produce statistical significance are less likely to be published. This may produce bias in a meta-analysis, because it is a summarization of results of several published studies.)

3. a. Analyze these data using the relative risk statistic. Explain what the relative risk statistics tells you.

Divorce and school failure (fake data)

	Divorce	No divorce
Fail	4	15
Pass	16	85

    b.   It turns out that the 95% confidence interval for the relative risk of failure given divorce versus failure given no divorce is (0.5, 3.6). Is the finding in these data therefore statistically significant or not?

4.   In 2004 the US population was about 294 million. That year 843 people riding pedal cycles were accidently killed, as were 4,018 motorcyclists. (*Source:* National Safety Council, www.nsc. org/research/odds.aspx.)

    a.   What was the probability that a US citizen was killed while pedaling a cycle? Express this risk two ways: as a rate per million people, and in the form "1 out of *n*."

    b.   What was the probability that a US citizen was killed while motorcycling? Express this risk two ways: as a rate per million people, and in the form "1 out of *n*."

    c.   What was the relative risk of being killed while riding a motorcycle as compared to pedaling a cycle?

5.   Here is an abstract from an article that assessed risk by the odds ratio. What are the outcome and risk factor variables? What conclusion do they come to and what statistics do they give to support their conclusion?

The purpose of this study was to assess the impact of extreme prematurity on three global measures of school outcomes. Using a matched cohort design, exposed infants comprised all surviving singleton infants 28 weeks gestation born at one regional neonatal intensive care hospital between 1983 and 1986 (n = 132). Unexposed infants comprised randomly selected full-term infants (37 weeks gestation) frequency matched on date of birth, zip code and health insurance. All children were selected from a regional tertiary children's centre serving western New York population. Standardized telephone interviews elicited information on grade repetition, special education placement and use of school-based services. . . .

Extreme prematurity was associated with a significant increase in risk of grade repetition (OR = 3.22; 95% CI = 1.63, 6.34), special education placement (OR = 3.16; 95% CI = 1.14, 8.76) and use of school-based services (OR = 4.56; 95% CI = 1.82, 11.42) in comparison with children born at term, even after controlling for age, race, maternal education, foster care placement and the matching factors. These findings suggest that survivors of extreme prematurity remain at risk of educational underachievement.

(*Source:* G. M. Buck, M. E. Msall, E. F. Schisterman, N. R. Lyon, and B.T. Rogers, Extreme Prematurity and School Outcomes, *Paediatric and Perinatal Epidemiology*, 2000, 14, October: 324)

13
ASSESSMENT

Some Statistical Issues in the Interpretation of Standardized Tests

LINCOLN STANDARDIZED TEST CENTER
FORMERLY
LINCOLN HIGH SCHOOL

S. Harris

Assessment of Students, Teachers, and Programs

We are living in an era obsessed with assessment of student achievement and teaching effectiveness. We search for the fantastic insight that will reveal the long-hidden promise of perfect pedagogy. Claims of progress must be backed by hard evidence.

Student assessment is a big idea. It includes the collection and interpretation of every conceivable aspect of a student's work or behavior. You are assessing a student when you notice if she seems tired, when you chat with her about how she solved a math problem, when you give her a unit test, when you look at her results on a statewide standardized test.

Assessments are often categorized as **formative** or **summative**. A succinct distinction is that formative assessments are specifically intended to shape further instruction, to check in on how a student is doing, and to suggest what to do next to foster understanding, while summative assessments are snapshots at a fixed time that tell you what material or skill a student has mastered. Like many other educational bifurcations, the strict division of assessments into these two categories is a useful oversimplification. The split into formative versus summative is primarily about the *intention* of an assessment and less about its actual form.

Tests

You are most likely to use statistical language when you discuss the results of summative tests, particularly large-scale standardized tests that involve lots of data. Traditionally, the big tests, such as the SAT-10 or statewide achievement tests, are summative and are used to establish achievement level at a given time. It is risky to use the results of such tests for guidance in curriculum development or for critical analysis of teaching effectiveness. That's not what they are designed to reveal. If you have several years' worth of such tests you may be able to analyze them for trends that indicate strengths or weaknesses in curriculum or in the teaching, but one administration of the test, by itself, will not be very helpful. There may be pressure on administrators and teachers to over-interpret the results of a summative standardized test. The goal of this section of the text is to familiarize you with the elements of such tests so that you understand more precisely what the results mean and can be clear about their appropriate use.

Two major concerns of test makers and test users are the **reliability** and **validity** of a test. Roughly speaking, reliability and validity are analogous to precision and accuracy. A reliable test will give two children the same test score if they have the same knowledge. A valid test, or more correctly the valid use of a test, enables you to make good decisions based on the test results.

Reliability

A test is perfectly reliable if the same student taking it over and over (with no change in ability) will get the same score each time or if two students with the same ability get virtually the same score on a test. A perfectly reliable test gets a reliability score of 1. A totally unreliable test gets a score of 0. One common statistic for measuring reliability is called Cronbach's alpha (α). The closer alpha is to one, the more reliable the test is. In practice, tests such as the SAT usually have alpha in the ball park of .9. There are various ways to determine the reliability of a test, all of which involve trying the test out on a representative sample of test takers. By altering the questions or comparing different combinations of questions during this trial period, test designers finally arrive at an official version of the test that has high reliability.

Validity

If a test is unreliable you will have a very imprecise assessment of a student's ability. So you definitely want a test to have high reliability. But that's not all you need for a good test. High reliability is valuable only if the test questions themselves were sensible to begin with. If the test was constructed so that it asked irrelevant questions or omitted important questions, its reliability won't matter. You won't be getting the information you need. The quality of a test that describes how well we can use the information it gives us is called validity.

Validity can be hard to achieve because it is not simply a matter of what's on the test but it is ultimately connected with what people do with the results. It is perhaps more meaningful to talk about the valid use of a test than the validity of the test itself. Many controversies in educational policy boil down to a difference of opinion about what inference one can legitimately make from test scores. For example, it may be valid to use a senior's SAT score to predict her success at freshman math at a particular college, but it may not be valid to use that same score to judge how good her math teachers were. Outside the world of education, arguments about validity are common: Is the so-called "poverty rate" a good measure of how many people cannot afford their basic expenses? Is the usual "unemployment rate" a valid measure of how many people can't find jobs? Is "gross domestic product" a valid way to measure the health of our economy?

Validity is a complex topic; various aspects may have specific names and emphases, as indicated in Table 13.1. For our purposes we take a general simple approach and use "validity" to refer to the broad issue of the proper interpretation of the test for any reason. A valid test should have the right questions on it, and it should be used to draw appropriate conclusions.

TABLE 13.1 Two types of validity

Type	Definition	Example/non-example
Content validity	The extent to which the content of the test matches the instructional objectives.	A final semester exam that includes only content covered during the first four weeks is probably not a valid measure of the course's overall objectives and likely has very low content validity.
Concurrent validity	The extent to which scores on the test are in agreement with an established standard.	If scores on a new shorter test tend to agree with the scores on an established longer version, the new test has concurrent validity.

Here are a few examples that we subsume under the general heading of validity issues, whether with the test itself or its interpretation:

- An extreme case of destroyed validity is when a teacher or principal cheats by changing the answers on student test papers. You can no longer make a valid inference about what any student knows. And you certainly won't be able to rate the effectiveness of the school curriculum.
- Key questions were omitted. If the specific questions on a test for multiplicative reasoning omit some key concept, then it will be difficult to make a valid inference about a student's understanding of that concept. Omission or underrepresentation of key concepts can be a severe problem when the number of test items is limited. The issue of what specific questions, and how many of them, to put on a standardized test is a difficult one. You may hear complaints by teachers whose students do poorly on a standardized test that the questions did not cover the concepts she taught. She would be concerned that someone would make invalid inferences about her teaching or about her students' knowledge.

- The questions were just bad questions—ones that are not clearly enough related to the conceptual knowledge you hoped to learn about. If a question is very complex, a student can mess up on a part of the question that is not focused on the ability you care about. Then you may have trouble making a valid inference about the student's understanding.
- Attitude surveys with young children. They may be more concerned about pleasing the teacher than holding fast to an attitude. You cannot properly infer their true attitudes from their survey responses.

Standardized Tests

The phrase **standardized test** refers to the manner in which a test is given and scored. It does not refer to the format or content of the questions. Its simplest meaning is that such tests are administered and scored under uniform conditions. Without standardization you cannot make accurate test-based comparisons. Achievement of perfectly comparable testing conditions may not be possible, but that should be the goal. You are probably most familiar with this attempt in the administration of large-scale professionally developed tests such as statewide achievement tests. But, even in class-based action research, you should do assessments under similar conditions if you are going to compare them later. It is hard to measure change due to an intervention, for example, if a pre-test is given on a quiet "normal" afternoon and the post-test is given on the first morning back after a holiday or in the middle of a flu epidemic.

Two distinct types of standardized tests are common in educational assessment: **norm-referenced** and **criterion-referenced** (or **standards-based**). The essential goal of a norm-referenced evaluation is to describe relative placement—how does this student compare to others? The essential goal of a criterion-referenced evaluation is to describe what the student actually knows and how the student's competence compares to an established standard. In practice, tests you make for your students may serve both purposes, so it may be more precise to talk about the *use* of a test rather than its inherent nature. But only the large professionally developed tests allow you to compare your students to national or state norms. Whether from multiple interpretations of the same test or from the use of several different kinds of tests, a good assessment system makes use of both approaches.

Historical note: Robert Glaser, a psychologist whose area of research was assessment, originally coined both terms, "norm-referenced" and "criterion-referenced," in about 1963.

Norm-referenced Tests

The results of a norm-referenced test tell you how well a person did in comparison to others. Those "others" are called the norming group. In major tests such as TerraNova or SAT-10, the norming group is a nationally selected representative sample of students similar to the ones who will be taking the test. Potential questions for the final version of the test are tested on the norming group, and the test is considered finally developed when their scores meet certain criteria. One of those criteria is likely to be that the entire collection of their scores form a normal distribution.

After the final version of the test is determined, it is released to the public. If one of your students takes the test, her results can then be compared to the national norming group. For instance, if 60% of the norming group scored less than 200 points on the test, and your student scores 200, then she will get a percentile rank of 60. For clarity this is sometimes called the student's *national* percentile score (NP). This student did better than 60% of the students in the norming group. It does not mean she did better than 60% of the students in your school or district. It could happen, for example, that, if you had a brilliant class, all of your students could score NP = 90.

A typical norm-referenced test usually reports several measures of achievement. Besides a student's percentile score of 60, you may also see that her **scaled score** was, say, 105. This 105 is a point assignment based on her answers. Psychometricians, statisticians with special expertise in assessment who help construct the test, develop an algorithm for determining scaled scores from the number and types of correct answers. The major purpose of scaled scores is to allow comparisons from one test administration to another. If the number of questions changes, or the difficulty of one version does not quite match that of another, the scores can be recoded into the same scale. So the scaled score is a type of standardized score analogous to a z-score.

If the scaled scores and the test questions are developed properly they can also be used to measure a student's growth from one year to the next. The adjective *vertical* is associated with test scores that can be compared from one grade to the next. You may see that a certain sequence of tests are vertically *aligned* or vertically *equated*. There are technical differences between these two labels, having to do with whether or not any of the same items appear on tests for two consecutive grade levels, but the key point is that in either case you learn something about student growth by comparing a child's score in 4th grade to her score in 3rd grade. Conversely, if tests are *not* vertically aligned or equated then it is not possible to measure growth from one year to the next from a child's test scores. The same issues of vertical scaling occur in criterion-referenced tests. It is tough to design tests and scaling that will allow for this kind of comparison.

The specific scaled scores on various national tests differ. Each test creates its own, and you often then can't compare one to the other. You have to find out what you can do with the scaled scores by reading their descriptions carefully. For instance, NAEP mathematics results are reported on a 0–500 scale, but NAEP science results are on a 0–300 scale, and so math and science scores cannot be compared. Some reading achievement tests report Lexile scores, which have been specifically developed to assess reading level. Lexile scores range from 200L to over 1700L. On the other hand, some tests are purposely designed to have similar scaled scores so that scores are easy to interpret. Most IQ tests, for example, are designed with a scale that has mean 100 and standard deviation 15.

A norm-referenced test does not necessarily tell you anything about the individual's level of knowledge of a subject except how it compares to others. For example, it is possible to get a high percentile rank on a norm-referenced geometry test even if you don't know much geometry as long as you know more than most of the people in the norming group. (Of course, if the test was well designed in the first place, this should not happen.)

Terminology note: The word "norm" in norm-referenced refers to the national sample of students whose work was used to construct the final version of the test. It does not refer to "normal" curve. That's just an accident of vocabulary.

Exercises on Norm-referenced Test Scores

1. (Devious question) Your class of 20 students takes a national norm-referenced test. What is the maximum number of students in your class who could receive a national percentile score of 70?
2. (Devious question) The scores on a norm-referenced algebra achievement test come in for your class. Jane scores at the 50th percentile and John scores at the 60th percentile. How much better is John than Jane?

3. The graph shows some made-up test scores for 100 people.

    a. Find the percentile ranks for test scores of 130, 140, 170, and 180.

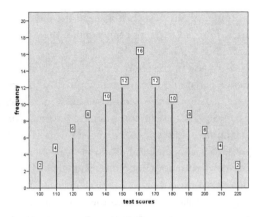

$$PR = \frac{\text{(number of values less than x)} + \text{(half the number of values equals to x)}}{\text{total number of values}} \times 100$$

    b. Compare the change in percentile rank for a student who raised her score from 130 to 140 with that of a student who raised his score from 170 to 180.

4. The graph shows some made up test scores for 100 people.

    a. Find the percentile ranks for test scores of 130, 140, 170, and 180.
    b. Compare the change in percentile rank for a student who raised her score from 130 to 140 with that of a student who raised his score from 170 to 180.

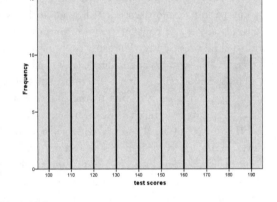

    c. Why are the answers to this exercise and the previous one not the same?

5. Most norm-referenced tests report results in percentiles. A student or parent will probably prefer to know that the child scored at the 80th percentile on the test rather than that her scaled score was 216. On the other hand, a teacher involved in curriculum development may find the scaled score more informative.

    Suppose a set of test scores has a normal distribution with mean 500 and standard deviation 100.

    a. Find and confirm the missing percentiles.
    b. Explain why the relationship between test score (x) and z-score is linear.

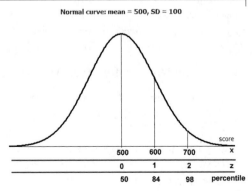

Test score (x)	z	Percentile
500	0	50
600	1	
700	2	

c. Explain why the relationship between test score (*x*) and percentile is not linear.

6. This table shows a detailed match up of *z*-scores and percentile ranks for a normal curve. Suppose that scaled scores on a certain standardized test have mean = 500 and *SD* = 100. Three students retake this test after an intervention. Use the table to complete the adjoining table that shows their scaled scores. For each student calculate their gain in test score, in *z*-score, and in percentile rank.

a. What is the average gain in scaled score?

b. What is the average gain in percentile rank? Why is this average gain not easily meaningful?

z-scores and percentile ranks for a normal curve

z	PR	z	PR
−2	2	0	50
−1.8	4	0.2	58
−1.6	5	0.4	66
−1.5	7	0.5	69
−1.4	8	0.6	73
−1.2	12	0.8	79
−1	16	1	84
−0.8	21	1.2	88
−0.6	27	1.4	92
−0.4	34	1.6	95
−0.2	42	1.8	96
		2	98

Name	Test	Scaled score	z-score	Percentile rank
A	Pre-test	480		
	Post-test	520		
B	Pre-test	660		
	Post-test	700		
C	Pre-test	340		
	Post-test	380		

7. Achievement gaps between groups are often described in terms of standard deviations. The table shows results in 8th grade mathematics for the 2007 NAEP for students in public schools nationally. Assume the NAEP scores are normally distributed.

Grade 8 NAEP scores 2007, mathematics

White		Black	
Average scaled score	Standard deviation	Average scaled score	Standard deviation
291	33	260	33

Source: nces.ed.gov/nationsreportcard/naepdata

a. Using 33 as a common standard deviation show that the mean scores for black and white students differ by about 0.9 standard deviations. This result is also called the *effect size*, or the mean standardized difference.

b. Where would the median black student score among white students? That is, what is the percentile rank for 260 on the normal curve with mean 291 and *SD* = 33?

c. If some intervention could increase the median black score by 1 standard deviation, then where would the median black student score among white students?

Various Scales Associated with Norm-referenced Standardized Tests

Grade Equivalent (GE)

Another reported score on a standardized test may be a grade equivalent score. For instance, if your student gets a GE = 5.6, it means his level of achievement in some category is the level achieved by a typical student in the 6th month of 5th grade. If you have a 3rd grader who gets a GE of 5.6 in a math category it does not mean necessarily that he is ready to do 5th grade work. It may, but it mainly means he is a lot better than the typical 3rd grader in some particular aspect of the curriculum. Test makers such as TerraNova recommend against using GEs as a basis for action.

Normal Curve Equivalent (NCE)

We have seen that equal increments in test scores do not correspond to equal increments in percentile ranks. This makes it unwise to do arithmetic calculations with percentile ranks. Statisticians devised a statistic called the normal curve equivalent to deal with this problem. The NCE was specifically created in 1976 at the request of the federal Department of Education to facilitate measurement of the effectiveness of Chapter 1 (now Title I) Compensatory Education programs.

NCE is a linear rescaling of z-scores defined as follows:

$$NCE = 21.06\ z + 50$$

You can see quickly from the formula that a z-score of 0 becomes an NCE of 50. By design, only NCE values from 1 to 99 are used, but that covers the usual range of z-scores seen in standardized tests.

Because the relationship between scaled scores and z-scores is linear, and also the relationship between z-scores and NCEs is linear, equal jumps in scaled scores produce equal jumps in NCEs.

This makes ordinary arithmetic with NCEs, such as subtraction used to assess change, sensible.

Summing up, NCEs are a linear scale with mean 50, standard deviation about 21, and a range from 1 to 99. NCEs provide a scale that many people find intuitively easier to understand than z-scores. It's more familiar to have scores run from 1 to 99 than from about −2.3 to +2.3.

Exercise on the NCE

1. NCEs can be used to compute a percentile rank for the average performance of a group. Say you have a class of 15 children who take the TerraNova test. They will each get a national percentile rank (NP). To get an average measure of performance for the class, these 15 NPs are converted to NCEs, which can be averaged sensibly. Then this average NCE is converted back to an NP, which is reported as the average NP of your class.

    Here is a small data set on which to see how this works. A class of four students take a norm-referenced national test. Their scores are reported in this table:

Student	NP	NCE
A	16	29
B	50	50
C	84	71
D	98	93

    Using the reasoning above, show that the average percentile rank for the class would be reported as 69, but that this is not the mean of the four given percentile ranks.

Stanines

Certain test results are given in stanines. Stanines (standard ninths) divide the normal curve axis into nine parts as shown in Figure 13.1. They were originally invented in the era of punched card data, when it was useful to have one-digit classification categories.

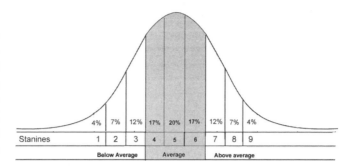

FIGURE 13.1 Stanines

Exercises on Stanines

1. Suppose the scaled scores for a standardized test have a normal distribution with mean 500 and standard deviation 100. Sam scores 600.

    a. Which stanine does his score fall into?
    b. Find some scaled score that is in the fourth stanine.

2. Below we quote first from the abstract of a research article, and then from part of the research itself. In this study the authors used stanine grouping to classify and compare the subjects. Read both excerpts; then decide which of the children shown in the table at the end would be labeled as suffering from "mathematics difficulty"; then complete the table below. (*Source:* Robert L. Russell and Herbert P. Ginsburg, Cognitive Analysis of Children's Mathematics Difficulties, *Cognition and Instruction*, 1984, 1 (2): 217–44.)
    From the abstract:

    > The aim of the study is to investigate the informal and formal mathematical knowledge of children suffering from "mathematics difficulty" (MD). The research involves comparisons among three groups: fourth-grade children performing poorly in mathematics but normal in intelligence; fourth-grade peers matched for intelligence but experiencing no apparent difficulties in mathematics; and a randomly selected group of third graders.

    From the methods section of the paper:

    > The fourth-grade groups were selected on the basis of their performance on the Cognitive Abilities Test (CAT), an intelligence test, and the Iowa Basic Skills Test. "Normal" intelligence was defined as a stanine score of 4 or above on the CAT.
    >
    > . . .
    >
    > Mathematics achievement a year or more below grade level was defined as a stanine score of 3 or below on the Iowa mathematics achievement test.
    >
    > Because a "learning disability" is said to involve a substantial gap between intelligence and achievement, only those children whose mathematics achievement stanine score was two or more stanines below their intelligence test stanine were included in the MD group. Thus, MD children had CAT stanine scores of 4 or above and math stanine scores of 3 or below, which were also at least two stanines below their CAT score.

Child	CAT stanine	Iowa Basic Skills stanine	Mathematics difficulty: yes/no
A	4	3	
B	5	3	
C	3	5	
D	7	5	

Criterion-based Tests

The first issue in creating a criterion- or **standards-based** test is to know what the criteria are. (*Vocabulary note:* "Criterion" is singular and "criteria" is plural.) You must have clearly defined behavioral targets or the test will not give you the information you want. We expect the criteria in educational testing to be directly related to the curriculum of a particular school district or state. For example, "Ohio's Grade 3-8 Achievement Assessments in reading, mathematics, science, social studies and writing are aligned to Ohio's academic content standards" (*source:* Ohio Department of Education website).

It is perhaps obvious that, if the curriculum as it is taught is out of sync with the standards on which the test is built, then the test results will be largely irrelevant to the classroom teacher and of little use in describing what the children are learning.

Once the test is designed then procedures must be put in place to assess the results. For a standardized test the grading must be consistent across graders and specifically sensitive to the skills being evaluated. Rubrics are developed for this purpose, and graders are trained to use the rubrics precisely.

The New England Common Assessment Program (NECAP) as an Illustration of a Criterion-based Test

The NECAP achievement tests are criterion-based tests given in several New England states. The questions on the NECAP, like those on many other standards-based tests, are a combination of multiple choice and open-ended questions. The tests are intended to evaluate student performance in a state's schools based on the state's standards. Finally, a summary scaled score is given to a student for each content area, reading, mathematics, writing, and science. Students who take the NECAP are rated at one of four performance levels: substantially below proficient, partially proficient, proficient, and proficient with distinction. Figure 13.2 shows a sample student report from the NECAP.

Note that the cut scores between achievement levels for reading, mathematics, and writing are not identical, except that 540 is set as the cut between not proficient and proficient. The first digit of the NECAP scaled score indicates the grade level, so the equivalent cut score in third grade is 340.

The categorization of the scores into the four proficiency levels is not done until *after* the test is administered and a significant supply of student responses is available for analysis. The setting of the cut points is primarily done by teams of grade level teachers who receive special training. They make decisions based on criteria such as "Would a third grader be expected to be able to answer this question if he or she had been taught according to the state standards?"

If you look at the band for this student's reading scaled score you see that it reaches about 4 points on either side of the student's score of 548. These 4 points are the **standard error of measurement (SEM)** for the scaled score.

Student	Grade	School	District	State
	5			

Fall 2007 - Beginning of Grade 5 NECAP Test Results

Content Area	Achievement Level	Scaled Score
Reading	Proficient	548

This Student's Achievement Level and Score

Below — Partial — Proficient — Distinction
500 — 530 — 540 — 556 — 580

Content Area	Achievement Level	Scaled Score
Mathematics	Proficient	540

This Student's Achievement Level and Score

Below — Partial — Proficient — Distinction
500 — 533 — 540 — 554 — 580

Content Area	Achievement Level	Scaled Score
Writing	Partially Proficient	535

This Student's Achievement Level and Score

Below — Partial — Proficient — Distinction
500 — 528 — 540 — 555 — 580

Interpretation of Graphic Display

The line (❙) represents the student's score. The bar (⟷) surrounding the score represents the probable range of scores for the student if he or she were to be tested many times. This statistic is called the standard error of measurement. See the reverse side for the achievement level descriptions.

Guide to Using the 2007 NECAP Reports   10

FIGURE 13.2 Sample student report. Used by permission of the New England Common Assessment Program

Each scaled score is reported with a score band that indicates the standard error of measurement surrounding each score. The standard error of measurement indicates how much a student's score could vary if the student was examined repeatedly with the same test (assuming that no learning occurs between test administrations).

(Source: Guide to Using the 2007 NECAP Reports, New England Common Assessment Program, http://reporting.measuredprogress.org/NECAPpublicRI/guides.aspx)

The value of SEM depends on a statistic known as the **reliability coefficient** of the test, which is usually symbolized by α (alpha). The value of alpha is calculated and reported by the test designers, and then SEM is computed as $SEM = SD \sqrt{1-\alpha}$. The maximum value of alpha is 1, for a perfectly reliable test, so you can see that a test with high reliability yields a small SEM. In this context, *SD* is the standard deviation of all the test scores taken by the group of people on whom the test was first developed. In brief, it takes a good bit of technical skill to derive the SEM for a standardized test. As a practical matter for most classroom teachers, we just accept the value provided by the test developers.

For the student whose scores are shown in Figure 13.2, we conclude that the student's true reading ability *probably* has a scaled score somewhere between about 544 and 552. We can be confident in rating this student as proficient in reading. (Because the band was computed by adding *one* SEM it is a 68% confidence interval.) In contrast, we cannot be confident in rating the student in mathematics, because his or her confidence band extends into two adjacent categories.

Notation warning: SEM is a different statistic from the standard error of the mean, even though they may each sometimes be abbreviated to SEM and both are used to find confidence intervals. The standard error of measurement is a measure of the imprecision of the test score for *one* child. The standard error of the mean is a measure of imprecision when we estimate the mean score of a *group* of children.

Exercises for Criterion-referenced Tests

The purpose of these exercises is mainly to familiarize you with the information on reports from a standards-based standardized test.

1. From Figure13.2 above:

    a. How many students are described in this report?

    b. Why is the label "proficient" in reading not a very precise assessment? If two students in this class are both "proficient" in reading, how different could their scaled scores be?

    c. Is the cut-off scaled score between Below and Partial the same in all three content areas? Describe how the cut-off values compare in the three content areas.

    d. Why do you think the Department of Education chose error bars equal to 1*SE* rather than the "usual" 2*SE*?

2. Refer to the sample item analysis report shown below.

    a. Who are the people described in this report? How many are there?

    b. This is an item analysis report. How many items are represented?

    c. How many different content strands are included? What are they? Which strand had the most numbers of items? How might that influence "teaching to the test"?

    d. For the sixth student, Buus, what is the meaning of the "+" under item 1? The "C" under item 2?

e.   How many points did Buus earn in total on these items? What was his scaled score? Why is there a 2 at the end of his row?

f.   Relatively speaking, did this class do better in numbers and operations or functions and algebra?

g.   How did this school compare to the district as a whole?

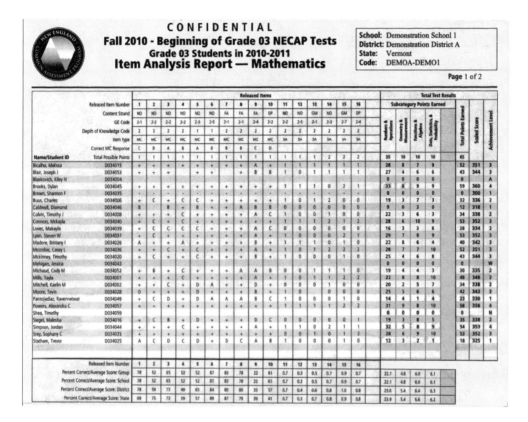

Sample item analysis report. Used by permission of the New England Common Assessment Program

14

DESIGN OF STUDIES

Introductory Inquiry

Teaching Counting

The intervention design: I take some kindergartners who can't count to 25. We practice counting for two weeks, and I give them candy every time they count correctly to 25. Two years later I test them again, and they can all count.

The conclusion: This proves that giving candy is a good way to teach counting.

Exercise: List specific reasons for or against drawing this conclusion.

Introductory Activity

Showing Off

You want to know if putting a document camera in your classroom is a good idea. With a partner design a study to help you come to a data-based decision. Assume that you can borrow a camera at no cost for up to two months. In particular consider these two issues:

1. What does "good idea" mean?
2. What evidence would you want to have? (You can include both evidence that you generate in your class and what you collect by research.)

Design of Studies

Many educational studies turn out to be less conclusive than you would hope because they were not set up properly in the first place. The first rule for designing a research study is to be as clear as possible right from the start about what you want to find out. Once you know what your objective is, then you can design your study to get you the appropriate information. We shall see that this is harder to do in practice than it may first seem.

The various ways that studies are set up are called **designs**. Any study in which the researcher *does something* to the subjects and then looks to see what happened is called an **experiment**. Experiments are designed to evaluate the effect of a known or likely cause. For example, we teach reading by a new method (that's a cause) and we see how much the students' scores change (that's an effect). A more general term for a potential cause is **treatment**. We say, for example, that an experiment that compares a new drug to a placebo has two treatments.

It is useful to contrast experiments with **observational studies**. An observational study is one in which the researcher collects information but does not actively do something to alter the behavior of the subjects. A familiar example is to conduct an opinion survey or give an aptitude test and perhaps collect information such as age and gender from a group of subjects. It is harder to identify causes in observational studies than it is in experiments. For instance, you might collect scores on a standardized test in a town and find that students in one school do better than students in another, but you can't immediately decide they did better just because of the school. You would need to explore other possibilities.

It is often the case in an observational study that the researcher has no influence on who gets which treatment. This opens the possibility that the two treatment groups were very different to begin with, and this in turn makes it harder to explain the results of the study unambiguously. By contrast, in an experiment the researcher may have the opportunity to split a pool of subjects into similar groups before any treatments are given. Generally speaking, particularly if you have a sizeable number of participants, statisticians prefer that subjects be randomly assigned to treatments to minimize any potential bias.

A brief description of some common designs is shown in Figure 14.1. In addition to contrasting experiments and observational studies, the figure also contrasts **comparative** versus non-comparative designs. In this context, "comparative" refers to a comparison between two treatments, not a comparison between a subject's scores before and after a treatment.

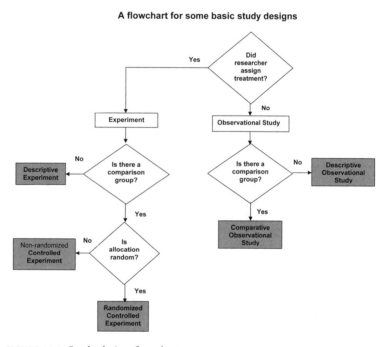

A flowchart for some basic study designs

FIGURE 14.1 Study design flowchart

Exercises in Classifying Studies

1. Identify each study either as observational or as an experiment, and as comparative or non-comparative. If the study is an experiment identify any treatments.

    a. A teacher surveys parents about their attitudes towards mathematics.

    b. A chiropractor measures range of motion in ten patients before and after he tries a new treatment.

    c. A health insurer analyzes hospital costs associated with birthing by checking the records at two similar hospitals, A and B. The number of days each mother stayed in the hospital is recorded to understand how long a typical stay is.

d. A medical researcher randomly gives half the subjects aspirin and half acetaminophen, and then measures time until headache relief.

e. From the *Wall Street Journal*

. . . Over the past two years, Harrah's has quietly conducted thousands of clinical-style trials to determine what gets people to gamble more. Based on its findings, Harrah's has developed closely guarded marketing strategies tailored individually to the millions of low rollers who make up its bread-and-butter business.

. . .

One example – Harrah's chose two similar groups of frequent slot players from Jackson, Miss. Members of the control group were offered a typical casino-marketing package worth $125 – a free room, two steak meals and $30 of free chips at the Tunica casino. Members of the test group were offered $60 in chips. The more modest offer generated far more gambling, suggesting that Harrah's had been wasting money giving customers free rooms. Thereafter, profits from the revamped promotion nearly doubled.

(*Source:* Christina Binkley, Lucky Numbers: A Casino Chain Finds a Lucrative Niche – The Small Spenders, *Wall Street Journal*, May 4, 2000)

2. Invent five studies in educational settings, one each for the five final descriptions shown in Figure 14.1 above. For all five describe each of the following components: a. the purpose of the study; b. the variable or variables you would observe; c. the subjects; and (for experiments) d. the treatment or treatments you would give to the subjects.

Specialized Terminology for Design of Experiments

There is one study design that is considered to be the most efficient for evaluating the effect of some intervention. It is a **controlled, randomized, double-blind experiment**. This design is strongly associated with medical clinical trials. Historically, a **clinical trial** is an experiment that tests a new medical treatment on people in order to compare it to the current treatment. As you will see, it is very rare for a study intended to evaluate an educational intervention to meet the strict criteria of a clinical trial. This failure is one reason that educational research is often controversial.

A classic clinical trial is characterized by three properties. It is "controlled," "randomized," and "double-blind." The effect of an intervention can be specified most clearly when an experiment meets all three criteria.

1. *Controlled experiment:* The researchers begin with subjects who are alike and then split them into as many groups as there are treatments. Often there are two treatments, a new one and an old one. Sometimes there is a new one against a placebo. The group getting the old treatment or the placebo is called the **control group**. An experiment that includes a control group is called a controlled experiment. The group getting the new treatment is called the treatment group or the **experimental group** or the intervention group. Usually the goal of the experiment is to show that the new treatment is superior in some important way to the old treatment. Without a control group in a study you cannot answer the basic question, "compared to what?"

2. *Randomized experiment:* The assignment of the treatment is done randomly *after* the subject qualifies and agrees to be in the study. After the person agrees to be in the study, then he or she is assigned "by the flip of a coin" either to the new treatment or to the old treatment. This

is intended to avoid giving the new treatment to a group that is "special" in some way. In short, it is intended to avoid *bias* in the assignment of treatments.

3. *Double-blind experiment:* During the course of the study, until all the data are collected, neither the subject nor the evaluator of the subject's response knows what treatment the subject had. The subject and the evaluator are both said to be *blind* to the treatment. Often only a statistician and a supervisor assigned to the project are the ones who know.

Exercise on Terminology of Studies

1. Read the following abstract of a study that combines medicine and education and then answer these questions:

    a. Why is it an experiment? How many treatment groups were there? What were the treatments?

    b. What does each of these descriptors mean in this study: randomized; placebo-controlled; double-blind?

    c. The data in this study came from about 600 children. Besides these 600 children, who else do you think these results might apply to? Why do you think so?

    d. How do the authors use confidence intervals to show that "there were no differences in language" prior to the intervention? You will have to read very carefully.

Abstract

A double-blind, placebo-controlled trial of nine months duration was carried out to investigate the impact of malaria and its prevention on the educational attainment of school children in a malaria-endemic area in southern Sri Lanka where both *Plasmodium falciparum* and *P. vivax* infections are prevalent. A total of 587 children attending grades 1–5 in four schools and resident in the area were randomly allocated to chloroquine (n = 295) and placebo (n = 292) arms. Language and mathematics scores of end-of-term school examinations for 1998 and 1999 and number of days absent and reasons for absenteeism during seven months pre-intervention and nine months of the intervention were recorded.

The results indicate that there were no differences in language (95%

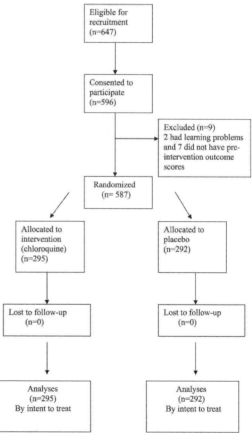

Flowchart of patient recruitment

Eligible for recruitment (n=647)

Consented to participate (n=596)

Excluded (n=9)
2 had learning problems and 7 did not have pre-intervention outcome scores

Randomized (n= 587)

Allocated to intervention (chloroquine) (n=295)

Allocated to placebo (n=292)

Lost to follow-up (n=0)

Lost to follow-up (n=0)

Analyses (n=295)
By intent to treat

Analyses (n=292)
By intent to treat

confidence interval [CI] = 48.44–53.78 in chloroquine group and 50.43–55.81 in placebo group) and mathematics (95% CI = 49.24–54.38 in chloroquine group and 51.12–56.38 in placebo group) scores between the two groups prior to the intervention.

During the intervention, the malaria incidence rate decreased by 55% (95% CI= 49–61%) and school absenteeism due to malaria was reduced by 62.5% (95% CI = 57–68%) in children who received chloroquine compared with the placebo group.

Post-intervention, children who received chloroquine scored approximately 26% higher in both language (95% CI = 21–31%) and mathematics (95% CI = 23–33%) than children who received placebo.

. . . The data suggest that malarial attacks have an adverse impact on the educational attainment of the school child and prevention of these attacks significantly improves educational attainment of children living in malaria-endemic areas.

(*Source:* D. Fernando, D. de Silva, R. Carter, K. N. Mendis, and R. Wickremasinghe,
A Randomized, Double-Blind, Placebo-Controlled, Clinical Trial of the Impact of
Malaria Prevention on the Educational Attainment of School Children,
American Journal of Tropical Medicine and Hygiene, 2006, 74 (3): 386–93)

Controversy in Education Research

Currently there is increasing pressure from funding agencies to design educational research studies like medical studies. This pressure is part of the emphasis now on "research-based" evidence for educational claims. There is support for such studies among some researchers, but there is still considerable resistance. For a taste of this, see the brief excerpt below from an opinion piece by Beth Gamse and Judith Singer that appeared in the *Harvard Education Letter*. What is the nature of the "resistance"? Why would anyone object to the concept of school-based randomized studies?

Over the past few years, the Institute of Education Sciences (IES) at the U.S. Department of Education has funded dozens of school-based randomized trials at the local and national levels.

. . .

Many schools and districts, however, have declined to participate in these trials, and many in the larger education establishment have greeted them with profound ambivalence.

. . .

A particularly vexing issue is the tradeoff between present costs and future benefits, between the short-term consequences for current students and the long-term consequences for those who follow. Decision makers who decline to participate in studies often cite "concern for the children." We share this concern, but we believe that future cohorts are equally important.

. . .

The "new wave of thinking" we advocate will not come easily. And, like any change, it will require education. There is fierce competition for schools' dollars from various publishers, curriculum developers, and professional development providers. Educators need the skills to recognize, and demand, credible evidence about program effectiveness. We believe that all educators – from those standing in front of a roomful of students to those leading state educational agencies – should be able to participate in and use research effectively: to distinguish between random sampling and random assignment, differentiate between credible evidence and anecdotal claims, and apply scientific conclusions for the benefit of their respective "teams."

> (*Source*: Beth C. Gamse and Judith D. Singer, Lessons from the Red Sox Playbook,
> *Harvard Education Letter*, January/February 2005)

Exercise on Randomized Studies in Education

1. The text below is an edited excerpt from a report of a recent educational study focused on reading achievement.

    a. What is the goal of the study?
    b. What is the design? Which aspects of "randomized," "controlled," and "double-blind" apply?
    c. What are the "treatments"?
    d. What variable was used to compare the effects of the treatments?
    e. What conclusion is described?

    ### The Design for Year 1 of the Study

    Intervention: Four reading comprehension curricula (Project CRISS, ReadAbout, Read for Real, and Reading for Knowledge) were selected as interventions for the study based on public submissions and ratings by an expert review panel.

    Participants: 10 districts, 89 schools, 268 teachers, and 6,350 fifth-grade students. Districts were recruited from among those with at least 12 Title I schools, and schools were recruited only if they did not already use any of the four selected curricula. Students in those schools were eligible to participate if they were enrolled in fifth-grade classes when the baseline tests were administered in fall 2006 or if they enrolled after the baseline administration but before January 1, 2007. Students in combined fourth-/fifth- or fifth-/sixth-grade classes were excluded, as were those in special education classes, although special education students mainstreamed in regular fifth-grade classes were eligible to participate.

    Research Design: Within each district, schools were randomly assigned to an intervention group that would use one of the four curricula or a control group that did not have access to any of the four curricula being tested. For example, in a district with 10 schools, 2 schools were assigned to each treatment group and 2 schools were assigned to the control group. Control group teachers could, however, use other supplemental reading programs. The study administered tests to students in intervention and control schools near the beginning and end of the 2006–2007 school year. It also observed classrooms during the school year and collected data from teacher questionnaires, student and school records, and from the intervention developers.

    Outcomes: Impact estimates focused on student reading comprehension test scores.
    . . .

    ### From the Executive Summary

    This report focuses on findings based on the first year of data collected for the study. It presents findings about the impacts of the reading comprehension interventions over one school year (2006–2007) for a first cohort of fifth graders.

The main finding from the first year of the study regarding the basic question of intervention effectiveness is:

- **Reading comprehension test scores in schools randomly assigned to use one of the four reading comprehension curricula were not statistically significantly higher than scores in control schools.**

. . .

The main finding from the first year of the study regarding questions about for whom and under what conditions the interventions may be effective is:

- **Reading comprehension test scores in schools using the selected reading comprehension curricula were statistically significantly lower than scores in control schools for some subgroups defined by student, teacher, and school characteristics.**

(*Source:* Susanne James-Burdumy et al., Effectiveness of Selected Supplemental Reading Comprehension Interventions: Impacts on a First Cohort of Fifth-Grade Students, NCEE 2009–4032, US Department of Education, May 2009, http://www.mathematica-mpr.com/publications/pdfs/education/selectsupplreading.pdf)

Thinking Critically about Studies

All studies have weaknesses. You will need to decide if those weaknesses make the study uninformative for you. There is no general rule for this, but here are some things to check:

- How were the subjects chosen? Could a more appropriate group of subjects have been chosen?
- Who can these subjects legitimately represent?
- Was any important information about the subjects omitted from the study?
- In general, were the data that were collected appropriate to the question the researcher wanted to answer?

Think about the possibility of confounding variables. A **confounding variable** is any influence on the results of your study that was not accounted for in your study. For example, if you are doing a study on the relationship between exposure to gasoline fumes and lung cancer, and you do not get any information about the smoking habits of the subjects, then smoking will be a confounding variable in your study and your results will be less conclusive than they might have been.

Another example: In a pre–post type of study, if a long time passes between the pre- and post-tests, did something not mentioned in the study affect the result?

Exercises on Thinking Critically about Studies

1. A study was done to compare two methods for teaching reading. Method A is used in the Barndoor School and method B is used in the Nofields School, both of which are part of the West Country school district. The comparison was based on the reading ability of 3rd graders. In general, the students in the Barndoor School received higher scores. The district superintendent claimed this proved that method A is a better way to teach reading. Name a possible

confounding variable that could be influencing the reading scores and that would suggest another explanation for the data.

2. A teacher recorded the scores of her students on a pre-test and a post-test after providing some special intervention. She recorded the amount by which each student's score increased. She reported that the mean increase in score was 15 percentage points. Here are her data:

Student ID	Pre-score (% correct)	Post-score (% correct)	Increase
1	50	90	40
2	55	88	33
3	60	90	30
4	90	90	0
5	98	99	1
6	99	100	1
7	100	100	0
Mean	78.9	93.9	15

What might be problematic about evaluating the success of her intervention using only the mean amount of increase?

3. A study shows a high positive correlation between the mean salaries of teachers in school districts in a state and the mean SAT scores of its high school seniors. A teacher claims this shows that raising teachers' salaries in the poorer-performing districts will increase SAT scores there.

   a. Name a possible confounding variable that could be influencing the SAT scores, and that would suggest another explanation of the pattern of SAT scores.

   b. In a scatter plot that illustrates the correlation described above, would each dot represent a student, a school, or a school district?

4. NHANES, the National Health and Nutrition Examination Survey, is a large survey conducted periodically by the United States Department of Health. The table shows some of the NHANES data for heights of men:

Male height data from NHANES, 1999–2002

Age	Number in sample	Mean
20–29 years	724	69.6
30–39 years	717	69.5
40–49 years	784	69.7
50–59 years	601	69.2
60–74 years	1,010	68.6
75 years and over	505	67.4

If you look at the mean height for the age 20–29 group and the mean height for the age 75-plus group, you see that the older group is about 2 inches shorter than the younger one. It is true that most individuals lose some height as they age. But there are other possible reasons that the older people are shorter. Name one such reason.

5. Suppose a study shows that 5% of new 18-year-old drivers who took a driver's education course had an accident in their first year of driving, and that 10% of new 18-year-old drivers who did not take the course had such an accident. Does this finding prove that taking driver's

education reduces a driver's chances of being in an accident in his or her first year of driving? Can you think of another explanation for the disparity?

6. A college vice-president in charge of fund-raising notes that almost all graduates of her college who had studied statistics there are extremely rich ten years after they graduate. She concludes that studying statistics will make you rich after ten years. She might be right. But give some reasons why she might be wrong.

7. The following paragraphs are taken from an article about how ending bilingual education in California affected math and reading scores. What possible confounding variable is mentioned in the article?

> Oceanside, Calif. – Two years after Californians voted to end bilingual education and force a million Spanish speaking students to immerse themselves in English as if it were a cold bath, those students are improving in reading and other subjects at often striking rates, according to standardized test scores released last week.
>
> Many educators had predicted catastrophe if bilingual classes were dismantled in this state, which is home to a tenth of the nation's public school students, many of them native Spanish speakers. But the prophecies have not materialized.
>
> In second grade, for example, the average score in reading for a student classified as limited in English increased 9 percentage points over the last two years, to the 28th percentile from the 19th percentile in national rankings, according to the state. In mathematics, the increase in the average score for the same students was 14 points, to the 41st percentile from the 27th.
>
> . . .
>
> It is too early to know precisely how much the erasure of bilingual education contributed to the rise in scores – class sizes in the second grade have also been reduced over the same period, for example – but the results are remarkable given predictions that scores of Spanish speaking students would plummet.
>
> (*Source:* Jacques Steinberg, Test Scores up since Bilingual Classes Abolished,
> *New York Times*, August 20, 2000)

8. A teacher in an elementary school became convinced that a new way of teaching reading was terrific. She split her class randomly into two groups and taught one group the old way and one group the new way. After two months she asked each student to read to her, and she wrote down her assessment of the student's ability. Her results showed that the new way was better. In terms of this study, what would be meant be "evaluator bias"? What would be a way to reduce this bias?

9. a. You are part of a knee-surgery team. You see that a new type of arthroscopic surgery (débridement – a kind of scraping) for pain relief from osteoarthritis is becoming popular. You would like to know how it compares to the standard surgery (lavage – a kind of washing) and to no surgery at all. How would you design an experiment to help you make an informed comparison of these three treatments? How would you decide who got which treatment? Should the patient know which treatment he or she gets?

   b. Here's what actually happened in the knee-surgery experiment. What do you think about their approach? Is it cool, or what?

   Methods: A total of 180 patients with osteoarthritis of the knee were randomly assigned to receive arthroscopic débridement, arthroscopic lavage, or placebo surgery. Patients in the placebo group received skin incisions and underwent a simulated débridement without insertion of the arthroscope. Patients and assessors of outcome were blinded to the treatment group assignment. Outcomes were assessed at multiple points over a 24-month period with the use of five self-reported scores – three on scales for pain and two on scales for function – and one objective test of walking and stair climbing. A total of 165 patients completed the trial.

Results: At no point did either of the intervention groups report less pain or better function than the placebo group. For example, mean (± SD) scores on the Knee-Specific Pain Scale (range, 0 to 100, with higher scores indicating more severe pain) were similar in the placebo, lavage, and débridement groups: 48.9 ± 21.9,54.8 ± 19.8, and 51.7 ± 22.4, respectively, at one year (P = 0.14 for the comparison between placebo and lavage; P=0.51 for the comparison between placebo and débridement) and 51.6 ± 23.7, 53.7±23.7, and 51.4 ± 23.2, respectively, at two years (P = 0.64 and P = 0.96, respectively). Furthermore, the 95 percent confidence intervals for the differences between the placebo group and the intervention groups exclude any clinically meaningful difference.

Conclusions: In this controlled trial involving patients with osteoarthritis of the knee, the outcomes after arthroscopic lavage or arthroscopic débridement were no better than those after a placebo procedure.

(*Source:* J. Bruce Moseley et al., A Controlled Trial of Arthroscopic Surgery for
Osteoarthritis of the Knee, *New England Journal of Medicine*, July 11, 2002)

A Wrapping Up Activity for Design of Experiments

Note: This can be a time-consuming activity, but the focus should be on understanding the narrow meanings of the categories listed in italics at the end.

Let's Play Pretend!

Do this exercise with one or two other people. Suppose you and a couple of colleagues want to do some action research to show that _____. Or suppose you want to see what would happen if _____.

Chat a bit and discuss how you would set up a study to accomplish your purpose. (Assume for now that it will be possible to do anything necessary for your study.) Imagine that you successfully completed the study, and the results were just what you had hoped for.

Now it is time to describe what you were interested in, what happened, and what you learned, so that the rest of us can benefit from your work.

Write some sentences or draw some graphs or tables in response to each of the following points. Be clear and complete so that at the end of this exercise the reporter of your group can present your responses.

- *Objective:* What did you hope to show or find out?
- *Design:* How did you get your data – or whatever it was that served as evidence?
- *Setting:* Where did you do this action research? What kind of place is that? Why did you do it there? Over what period of time were you engaged in this research?
- *Participants:* Who were the subjects in this study? How many subjects were there?
- *Intervention (if there was one):* What did you do to these subjects?

- *Main outcome measures:* What variables or behavior did you actually observe or record?
- *Results:* What was the result of combining the evidence? Show some (made-up) tables or charts or statistics. (Just do rough sketches.)
- *Conclusions:* What do you make of all this? Do you have any recommendations?
- *Weaknesses:* Is there anything about your study – either in your control or not – that you should mention because it might make your conclusion less certain?

15

HYPOTHESIS TESTS

Introductory Investigation

Yes or No? Are Two Reading Programs Equally Effective?
How Much Evidence Do You Need to Decide?

Two reading programs are being considered for adoption by a large school district with several thousand students. The district has decided to test the programs on two random samples of students before making a final decision. The purpose of this activity is to begin to think about how much data you would need to see before you could be confident you knew whether one of the programs produced a higher average score than the other on a particular standardized test.

We can approach this question through a simulation experiment where we imagine that the scores we would collect in the study are samples of the scores that all the students in the district would have gotten.

Table A.3 in the Appendix contains 2,000 scores that represent the populations of the possible test scores if we had been able to test the programs on all the students. We want to investigate how precisely we can see what is going on by looking only at samples from these two populations.

Rules: Use x and y to represent individual values taken from these two populations. The 2,000 scores are recorded in two separate groups, X and Y. You will need to devise a system for picking numbers at random from X and Y.

1. Pick one value randomly from each population. How different are the two values, x and y, that you picked? Are you confident (without being absolutely positive) at this point that the populations have different means? Why or why not?
2. Start over, but now draw five values from each population. How different are the two sample means, $\bar{x}$ and $\bar{y}$? That is, calculate $\bar{x} - \bar{y}$. Are you confident (without being absolutely positive) that the populations have different means? Why or why not? Make use of the information given by the standard deviations, too, if you think it helps.
3. Start over, but now draw ten values from each. Are you confident now (without being absolutely positive) that the populations have different means?
4. Discuss what it would take to convince you short of seeing all 2,000 values.

An Introduction to Hypothesis Tests

This topic is included primarily to familiarize you with its use in formal research. **Hypothesis tests** are a class of data analysis procedures often used to determine if a finding is statistically significant. There are various specific hypothesis tests to suit different study designs, but they all follow the same logic. It is this logic we want to explore so that as a reader of research you will have a clearer idea of what these tests do and do not accomplish.

At this point it is worth recalling that statistical significance is not the same as practical value or educational importance. Statistical significance is an arbitrary, mathematically based way of describing the degree of confidence we have in the reliability of a study. Generally speaking, reliability increases when sample size increases. In classroom-based action research where samples may be small the achievement of statistical significance may not be a primary goal. Failure to reach statistical significance does not necessarily imply that an intervention was worthless. It may mean only that there is not enough evidence yet to assess its reliability very well and that further study is needed.

Statistical significance is not the same as educational significance.

The whole issue of statistical significance makes sense only in the context of inference. It is a label used to indicate that we are confident a finding from a study is likely to hold beyond the subjects that were in the study. Figure 15.1 illustrates this relationship.

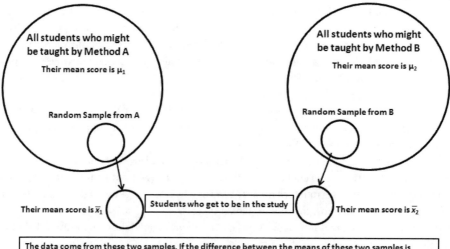

Question: Do students do equally well on these two methods of teaching reading?

All students who might be taught by Method A

Their mean score is μ_1

Random Sample from A

All students who might be taught by Method B

Their mean score is μ_2

Random Sample from B

Their mean score is $\bar{x}_1$

Students who get to be in the study

Their mean score is $\bar{x}_2$

The data come from these two samples. If the difference between the means of these two samples is statistically significant, we conclude that almost certainly there is some difference between the means of the two populations the samples came from.

FIGURE 15.1 Logic of statistical inference in a comparative study

Statistical Significance and *p*-Values

In the context of hypothesis testing, statistical significance is associated with a particular number called a *p*-value. When you understand what a *p*-value represents you can interpret the conclusions of a study more precisely.

In a published report you may see a phrase like "The observed difference was statistically significant, $p = .032$." The value of *p* is intended to convey the degree of confidence that the difference observed in a study reflects a similar difference in the populations being compared.

The letter *p* is chosen because the number is a *probability*. As a measure of probability, therefore, *p* is always between 0 and 1. Perhaps unintuitively, the closer *p* is to zero the *more* confidence you can have that an effect found in a study is "real." A small value of *p* means there is only a small probability you are *wrong* when you decide that an intervention that was successful with a sample of subjects will still work in a larger population.

We will say more about how *p* is calculated and its precise meaning in the section below on statistical hypotheses. For now, let us just see how it appears in published research in connection with the announcement of statistical significance. By custom, a result is called statistically significant when the corresponding *p*-value is less than .05. The choice of .05 produces conclusions about statistical significance that agree with a 95% confidence interval.

A small *p*-value (less than 5%) is associated with statistical significance.

Box 15.1

History of p = .05 in statistical inference

Our concept of statistical significance derives from earlier attempts to answer the question "How high does a probability have to be before we can be sure that a finding is not accidental?" James Bernoulli in the late 1600s called this high degree of confidence "moral certainty." We might say "virtual certainty" today. His illustrations were equivalent to using a *p*-value of .01 or .001. In the following Bernoulli quote, you can see that he was advocating for someone in power to make an official rule.

> Because it is still rarely possible to obtain total certainty, necessity and use desire that what is merely morally certain be regarded as absolutely certain. Hence, it would be useful if, by the authority of the magistracy, limits were set up and fixed concerning moral certainty. I mean, if it were fixed whether 99/100 certainty would suffice for producing moral certainty, or whether 999/1000 certainty would be required. Note that then a Judge could not be biased, but he would have a guideline which he would continually observe in passing judgment.
>
> (*Source:* Bernoulli quote, in A. Hald, *A History of Probability and Statistics and Their Applications before 1750*, 2003, John Wiley)

The current use of *p* = .05 was heavily influenced by the work of Ronald Fisher, the preeminent statistician of the early 1900s.

Exercises on Interpreting *p*-Values in Published Research

For each of the following excerpts from published studies a different statistic was computed appropriate to the study design. In each example comment on the following questions:

a. What *p*-value was reported?
b. What statistic received that *p*-value?
c. Why did the authors give the *p*-value? Did the author's use just the word "significant" or the entire phrase "statistically significant"? Did they report that any findings were not statistically significant?

1. Developing teacher's mathematics knowledge

    One goal of the WTMSMP is to develop middle-level mathematics teachers' knowledge for teaching. In the first year, middle school mathematics teachers enrolled in a graduate level summer mathematics course with emphasis on deep conceptual understanding of the algebraic structure of the rational number field. The course was developed by a senior level mathematician and taught by a team of mathematicians across four university sites in West Texas.

    . . .

    Claim(s) or hypothesis(es) examined in the work . . .

    The WTMSMP activities will significantly increase teachers' deep conceptual knowledge of elementary mathematics. (This hypothesis was partially supported by initial findings)

    . . .

    Initial analyses of within-subject differences revealed the following:

    Overall, participants performed slightly better on the number concepts and algebra MKT tests, although these improvements were not statistically significant to suggest the change was beyond what would be expected by chance. Because participants received WTMSMP at four different locations and times through the summer of 2009, paired-sample *t*-tests were also conducted for each participant group. That is, pre- and post-test comparisons were separately calculated for participants attending the Texas Tech (TTU), Angelo State (ASU), Sul Ross (SRS), and University of Texas at the Permian Basin (UTPB) locations. Evidence was present for the significant growth in only the Sul Ross participants on one measure, the MKT Algebra test ($t(6) = -2.54$, $p = .04$). Two groups, those attending the SRS and UTPB, locations, showed growth, although not significant, across all MKT measures. Participants attending the ASU location also showed growth on the Number Concepts and Algebra measures. TTU participants, however, scored lower, although not significantly lower, on all MKT measures at the posttest in comparison to their pretest scores.

    (*Source:* Tara Stevens and Gary Harris, West Texas Middle School Math Partnership, Developing Teachers' Mathematics Knowledge for Teaching: Challenges in the Implementation and Sustainability of a New MSP, http://hub.mspnet.org/index.cfm/msp_conf_2010_call)

2. Effect of teacher math anxiety

    People's fear and anxiety about doing math—over and above actual math ability—can be an impediment to their math achievement. We show that when the math-anxious individuals are female elementary school teachers, their math anxiety carries negative consequences for the math achievement of their female students. . . .

Results

As expected, at the beginning of the school year, there was no significant relation between teachers' math anxiety and students' math achievement (girls: $r = -0.13$, $P = 0.31$; boys: $r = 0.12$, $P = 0.40$). However, by the end of the school year, the higher a teacher's math anxiety, the lower was the girls' ($r = -0.28$, $P = 0.022$) but not the boys' ($r = -0.04$, $P = 0.81$) math achievement.

(*Source:* Sian L. Beilock, Elizabeth A. Gunderson, Gerardo Ramirez, and Susan C. Levine, Female Teachers' Math Anxiety Affects Girls' Math Achievement, *Proceedings of the National Academy of Sciences*, www.pnas.org/cgi/doi/10.1073/pnas.0910967107)

3. Hospital and cognitive decline

MedPage Today Action Points

Explain to interested patients that this study showed an association between hospitalization of older patients and cognitive decline. But as an observational study, it could not prove a causal relationship.

Review

Among older patients, hospitalization for any reason is associated with reduced cognitive function, researchers found.

Patients hospitalized for both noncritical and critical illness had lower cognition scores ($P \leq 0.047$ for both) than those who were not hospitalized, according to William Ehlenbach, MD, of the University of Washington in Seattle, and colleagues.

However, the magnitude of the differences (-1.01 and -2.14 points on a scale of 100, respectively) has unclear clinical relevance, they reported in the Feb. 24 issue of the *Journal of the American Medical Association*.

(*Source:* Todd Neale, Hospitalization Linked to Impaired Cognition, *MedPage Today*, February 23, 2010, www.medpagetoday.com/Geriatrics/Dementia/18642)

The Structure and Logic of a Hypothesis Test

In a hypothesis test we make assumptions about populations and test them by analyzing samples of data from these populations. Here is a brief outline of a comparative study followed by a flowchart to show the hypothesis testing process schematically.

The Study

- *Research question:* Do children learn to read better by Method A or by Method B? We define "better" as scoring higher on a reading assessment.
- *Design:* Start with two similar groups of children and teach one by each method. Then administer the test to both groups.
- *Result:* Suppose the mean score on A is 80 and the mean score on B is 70. The primary statistic used to summarize the comparison is the difference between these two means.
- *Statistical question:* Is the difference between the means statistically significant?

The Hypothesis Test

Every hypothesis test starts with an assumption called the **null hypothesis (H_0)**. Then the data are used to test it. In a typical comparison study the null hypothesis assumes that the two treatments are "equally good." In this illustration this boils down to the assumption that the *mean* scores on a reading test are equal in the populations being compared. The logical flow of the testing procedure is shown in Figure 15.2.

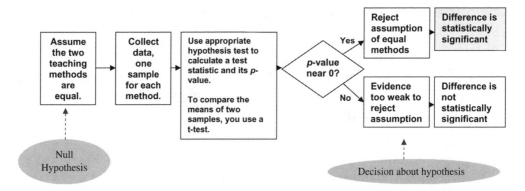

FIGURE 15.2 Flowchart for the logic of a hypothesis test

The Relationship Between Null Hypotheses and p-Values

In this section we will see that a *p*-value can be pictured as a tail area of a curve that is determined by the null hypothesis.

The null hypothesis is a claim that two *population* means are equal. If two *populations* have the same mean, then if we pick a random *sample* from each population we would expect these two sample means to be pretty close to one another. Put another way, we would expect the *difference* between them to be pretty close to zero. We expect the difference between the means of two such randomly picked samples usually to be near zero and only rarely far from zero. We can imagine the distribution of all possible observed differences under the null hypothesis. It would consist of many differences that were near zero and fewer differences that were far from zero.

It might be evident to you that this null distribution is mound shaped and centered at zero. Its shape is similar to a normal curve but it does not precisely fit the normal curve equation. It is called a ***t*-distribution** and it shows the chances of getting various sized *sample* differences from two *populations* that have equal means. Under many conditions, especially when the two samples are large, its shape is extremely close to a normal curve.

The first person to work out the precise shape of this distribution was William Gosset, who published it in 1908 under the pen name Student. Historians credit Gosset f̲ ̲e of the letter *t* for it. Sometimes the distribution is called "Student's *t*-distribution."

The *p*-value for a particular statistic tells you how far into the tails of the null distribution that statistic is located. For example, if your study produces an observed difference, *d*, between two sample means, the *p*-value for that *d* is the percentage of all the possible values of *d* that are more extreme than that one. See Figures 15.3 and 15.4. A large value of *d* will be located in the

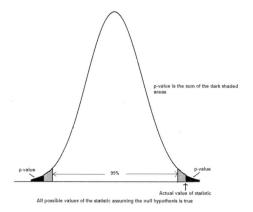

FIGURE 15.3 Illustration of *p*-value in a hypothesis test. In this image the value of *p* is less than .05. We would decide that the weight of the evidence was against the null hypothesis. The statistic is statistically significant

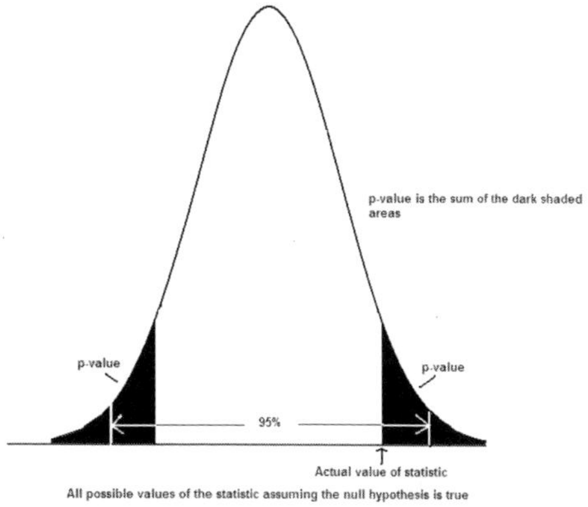

FIGURE 15.4 Illustration of *p*-value in a hypothesis test. In this image the value of *p* is greater than .05. We would decide that the weight of the evidence was insufficient to reject the null hypothesis. The statistic is not statistically significant

Note: The dark areas represent outcomes that are more extreme then the outcome observed in the study. If the study produces a result far in the tail it is unlikely that the null hypothesis is true.

tail and will therefore have a small *p*-value. The smaller the *p*-value is, the less likely it is that the null hypothesis is true.

By common practice, values of *p* that are less than .05 correspond to a finding of statistical significance. That is why one paper may simply report $p < .05$ while another may say something like $p = .031$. Both authors are telling you their statistic was statistically significant. The second author is indicating more precisely how far the sample statistic fell in the tail of the distribution.

A Bit More on the Meaning of the p-Value

In each of the following three sets of data the two groups differ in exactly the same way, but only in the last case, with the largest samples, is the difference statistically significant. Only in that case is the evidence strong enough to reject the hypothesis that the two populations from which the samples were taken have the same mean. Note that the difference in the sample means has not changed, just the amount of data that show it. *The p-value reflects the degree of certainty in rejecting the null hypothesis.*

The assumption is that these data represent random samples from two populations. In each case the mean of Group 2 was five points higher than the mean of Group 1. If these data were from a study where Group 2 received some intervention, it would be wrong to say that the intervention *failed* in the first two cases. Lack of statistical significance does not necessarily mean an intervention was worthless.

Group 1	Group 2		Group 1	Group 2	Difference
		t-test: two-sample assuming equal variances (Excel)			
50	55	Mean	57.50	62.50	−5
55	60	Variance (SD^2)	41.67	41.67	
60	65	Observations	4	4	
65	70	*t* statistic	−1.10		
		p-value	**0.32**		

Group 1	Group 2		Group 1	Group 2	Difference
50	55	Mean	57.50	62.50	−5
50	55	Variance	35.71	35.71	
55	60	Observations	8	8	
55	60	*t* statistic	−1.67		
60	65	**p-value**	**0.12**		
60	65				
65	70				
65	70				

Group 1	Group 2		Group 1	Group 2	Difference
50	55	Mean	57.50	62.50	−5
50	55	Variance	33.33	33.33	
50	55	Observations	16	16	$p < .05$
50	55	*t* statistic	−2.45		
55	60	**p-value**	**0.02** ←		
55	60				
55	60				
55	60				
60	65				
60	65				
60	65				
60	65				
65	70				
65	70				
65	70				
65	70				

> With this much data (16 people in each group) we can be almost certain that the two populations from which these data came have different means. It is very unlikely that these data came from two populations whose means are equal.

Note: Variances were calculated using *n*–1 as the divisor. The story would make the same point if *n* had been used. But in all three cases the variance would be 31.25.

Exercises Finding *p*-Values

As sample sizes increase, the *t*-curve becomes more and more like a normal curve. So when we have large enough samples we can refer to a normal curve table to find tail areas. For simplicity, assume that is the case in these exercises and you may want to refer to the given normal curve table. For more precise results you need to use a *t*-table.

1. A study compared the number of times a 2nd grader could do a repetitive motion in one minute versus how many times a 1st grader could do it. Fifty students in each grade were the subjects. Use the table of data below to find the *p*-value for the last row of the table. Make a shaded sketch to show the corresponding area in the tails of a normal curve. Decide if the observed difference is statistically significant.

Repetitions in one minute			
	Group 1 (2nd grade)	Group 2 (1st grade)	Difference
Mean number of times	25.5	23.0	2.5
SD	6	6	
n	50	50	
Summary statistic (t)	$t = \dfrac{\bar{x}_1 - \bar{x}_2}{\sqrt{\dfrac{s_1^2}{n_1} + \dfrac{s_2^2}{n_2}}} = \dfrac{25.5 - 23.0}{\sqrt{\dfrac{6^2}{50} + \dfrac{6^2}{50}}} = \dfrac{2.5}{\sqrt{\dfrac{72}{50}}} = 2.1$		
p-value	p = tail area outside of $t = \pm 2.1 = $ _____ Because the ns are large we can use a normal curve to find the tail areas.		

2. Redo Exercise 1, but this time change both *SDs* to 12. What does this change say about the resulting student scores? Should this change make the evidence against the null hypothesis weaker or stronger than it was in Exercise 1? Is the resulting *p*-value larger or smaller than the value in Exercise 1?

3. Redo Exercise 1, but this time change both *ns* to 25. Should this change make the evidence against the null hypothesis weaker or stronger than it was in Exercise 1? Is the resulting *p*-value larger or smaller than the value in Exercise 1?

Statistical Hypotheses

In order to use a hypothesis test you need to be able to cast your research question into a pair of opposing statements about a population parameter. These statements are called **statistical hypotheses**. Often these hypotheses are not explicitly stated in a published study, but they provide the underlying justification for the data analysis.

Usually, one of the two hypotheses is the one the researcher hopes is the correct one. This one is called the **motivated** or **alternative hypothesis (H_a)**. The opposing one is called the **null hypothesis (H_0)**. As we have seen, the logic of a hypothesis test says that the researcher can claim she has strong evidence for her motivated hypothesis only if the analysis leads to a small p-value. When this happens, she may say that the data allow her to "reject the null hypothesis."

Example 1: H_a: My new teaching idea will raise student performance.
H_0: My new teaching idea will not raise student performance.

Example 2: H_a: Birth order affects IQ.
H_0: Birth order does not affect IQ.

A hypothesis test is always set up to ask "Do the data allow us to rule out the null hypothesis?" If they do then your result is called statistically significant.

In Example 1, because H_a specifically says the new method will *raise* performance it is called a **one-sided hypothesis**. In Example 2, because H_a does not say *how* birth order affects IQ it is called a **two-sided hypothesis**. Throughout these notes we will generally stick with two-sided hypotheses for symmetry with confidence interval approaches. You may see examples of one-sided hypotheses in published research.

Exercises on Identifying Statistical Hypotheses in Published Studies

Based on the given excerpts, answer the following three questions for the study in each of these exercises:

a.   What was the purpose of the study? Who were the subjects?
b.   What was the null hypothesis?
c.   What was the conclusion?

1.   These back-to-back histograms are from the article "Are Women Really More Talkative than Men?" by M. R. Mehl et al.

> The data suggest that women spoke on average 16,215 (*SD* = 7301) words and men 15,669 (*SD* = 8633) words over an assumed period of on average, 17 waking hours. . . . The difference does not meet conventional thresholds for statistical significance (*p* = 0.248, one sided test).
>
>   Thus the data fail to reveal a reliable sex difference in daily word use. Women and men both use on average about 16,000 words per day, with very large individual differences around this mean. A potential limitation of our analysis is that all participants were university students. The resulting homogeneity in the samples with regard to socio-demographic characteristics may have affected our estimates of daily word usage. However, none of the

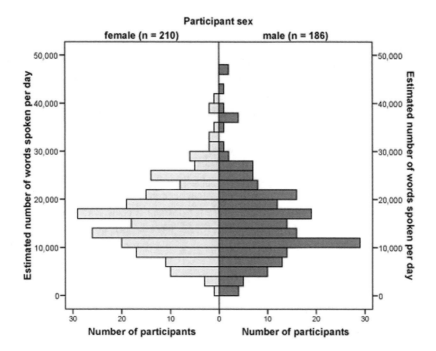

samples provided support for the idea that women have substantially larger lexical budgets than men. Further, to the extent that sex differences in daily word use are assumed to be biologically based, evolved adaptations, they should be detectable among university students as much as in more diverse samples. We therefore conclude, on the basis of available empirical evidence, that the widespread and highly publicized stereotype about female talkativeness is unfounded.

> (*Source:* M. R. Mehl, S. Vazire, N. Ramírez-Esparza, R. B. Slatcher and J. W. Pennebaker, Are Women Really More Talkative than Men?, *Science*, July 6, 2007)

2. Mentoring program

In the summer of 2005, data were gathered on 57 students from the Indian River School District. Most of the mentored students attended North Georgetown Elementary, Sussex Central Middle School, or Selbyville Middle School.

. . . Results show that in math, 36% of the mentored students showed improvement in their grades between the first quarter and second quarter marking periods and 43% of the mentored students showed improvement in their grades between the third and fourth quarter marking periods. Although there was a slight increase in the percentage of students that showed improvement in their math grades, this difference is not statistically significant. A chi-square test of independence was conducted to determine if the mentored students' improvement in math was significantly different from first semester to the second semester.

No significant relationship was found (χ^2 (1) = .30, p > .05).

> (*Source:* B. A. Shepperson, with K. Scollon, M. Kedzior, and X. Uribe-Zarain, *Mentor Delaware, Year One, Annual Evaluation Results*, Delaware Education Research and Development Center, September 2005)

Note: Mentor Delaware is a statewide mentoring program in Delaware.

3. Behavior and achievement

The authors examined a new assessment of behavioral regulation and contributions to achievement and teacher-rated classroom functioning in a sample ($N = 343$) of kindergarteners from 2 geographical sites in the United States. Behavioral regulation was measured with the Head-Toes-Knees-Shoulders (HTKS) task, a structured observation requiring children to perform the opposite of a dominant response to 4 different oral commands. Results revealed considerable variability in HTKS scores. Evidence for construct validity was found in positive correlations with parent ratings of attentional focusing and inhibitory control and teacher ratings of classroom behavioral regulation. Hierarchical linear modeling indicated that higher levels of behavioral regulation in the fall predicted stronger levels of achievement in the spring and better teacher-rated classroom self-regulation (all $ps <$ .01) but not interpersonal skills. Evidence for domain specificity emerged, in which gains in behavioral regulation predicted gains in mathematics but not in language and literacy over the kindergarten year ($p < .01$) after site, child gender, and other background variables were controlled.

Discussion focuses on the importance of behavioral regulation for successful adjustment to the demands of kindergarten.

(*Source:* C. C. Ponitz , M. M. McClelland, J. S. Matthews and F. J. Morrison, Abstract: A Structured Observation of Behavioral Self-Regulation and Its Contribution to Kindergarten Outcomes, *Developmental Psychology*, 2009, 45 (3), 605–19)

4. Computer games and snack choice

Objective To examine how advergames, which are online computer games developed to market a product, affect consumption of healthier and less healthy snacks by low-income African American children.

Design Cross-sectional, between-subjects examination of an advergame in which children were rewarded for having their computer character consume healthier or less healthy foods and beverages. Children were randomly assigned to 1 of the following 3 conditions: (1) the healthier advergame condition, (2) the less healthy advergame condition, or (3) the control condition.

Setting Urban public elementary schools.

Participants Thirty low-income, African American children aged 9 to 10 years.

Main Exposure Children in the treatment conditions played a less healthy or a healthier version of an advergame 2 times before choosing and eating a snack and completing the experimental measures. Children in the control group chose and ate a snack before playing the game and completing the measures.

Main Outcome Measures The number of healthier snack items children selected and ate and how much children liked the game.

Results Children who played the healthier version of the advergame selected and ate significantly more healthy snacks than did those who played the less healthy version. Children reported liking the advergame.

Conclusions Findings suggest that concerns about online advergames that market unhealthy foods are justified. However, advergames may also be used to promote healthier foods and beverages. This kind of social marketing approach could tip the scales toward the selection of higher-quality snacks, thereby helping to curb the obesity epidemic.

(*Source:* T. A. Pempek and S. L. Calvert, Abstract: Tipping the Balance: Use of Advergames to Promote Consumption of Nutritious Foods and Beverages by Low-Income African American Children, *Archives of Pediatric and Adolescent Medicine*, 2009, 163 (7): 633–7)

Hypothesis Test Calculations

This section shows in some detail two basic hypothesis tests, a *t*-test for comparing two means, and a chi-square test for comparing two percentages. The detail is intended to help you understand published results more fully. At this level of expertise you should ask for assistance if you intend to do your own research. It takes a while to appreciate important subtleties.

A t-Test to Compare Two Means

We illustrate the *t*-test procedure using fictional data for a reading comprehension comparison.

The question: Is there a statistically significant difference in mean reading comprehension between students who learn by Method A and those who learn by Method B?

1.   *State the two hypotheses:*

(Informal) In words: Null hypotheses: Method A and Method B are equally effective.
                         Alternative hypothesis: The two methods are not equally effective.
(Formal) In symbols: $H_0: \mu_A = \mu_B$ (The two population means are equal.)
                         $H_a: \mu_A \neq \mu_B$ (The two population means are *not* equal.)

Note that, even though informally we talk about the "effectiveness" of the methods, the *t*-test specifically deals only with the equality of *means*. You have to decide for yourself on a case by case basis if a mean score is the best way to summarize effectiveness.

2.   *Collect the data:*

Test scores for 20 students who were taught by Method A:

71	88	81	87	71
59	78	83	69	83
84	92	82	92	75
83	88	97	67	76

Test scores for 16 similar students who were taught by Method B:

63	85	66	47
66	77	75	82
58	78	77	73
50	79	64	71

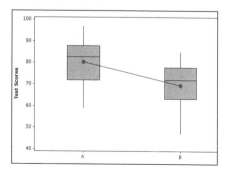

Look at the box plots, just to see if anything weird is going on.

3. *Process the data:* The information shown is what Microsoft Excel produces when you ask it to do a *t*-test.

t-test: two–sample assuming unequal variances

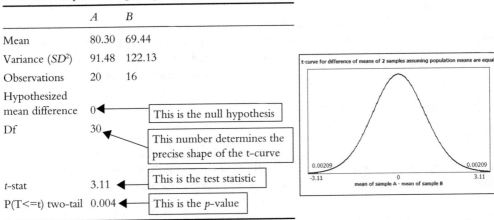

	A	B
Mean	80.30	69.44
Variance (SD^2)	91.48	122.13
Observations	20	16
Hypothesized mean difference	0	This is the null hypothesis
Df	30	This number determines the precise shape of the t-curve
t-stat	3.11	This is the test statistic
P(T<=t) two-tail	0.004	This is the *p*-value

4. *Make the decision:* Because *p* is less than .05, the difference between the mean scores for Methods A and B is statistically significant. We conclude that, on average, students like these will score better in reading comprehension if they have been taught by Method A.

Further Details about the Components of a Hypothesis Test

The Test Statistic

A *t*-statistic is a standardized score similar to a *z*-score. Its value is based on a value computed from sample data divided by a standard deviation. In this illustration we are evaluating the difference in the two means: $d = 80.30 - 69.40 = 10.90$. The standard deviation for this difference is based on the two sample standard deviations:

$$SD \text{ for a difference} = SD_d = \sqrt{\frac{s_1^2}{n_1} + \frac{s_2^2}{n_2}} = \sqrt{\frac{91.48}{20} + \frac{122.13}{16}} = 3.5$$

The test statistic is $t = \frac{sample\ difference}{SD\ of\ difference} = \frac{d}{SD_d} = \frac{10.90}{3.5} = 3.11$

The *t*-Curve

The *t*-curve shows the sampling distribution of the difference of means statistic when the null hypothesis is true. The precise formula for this *t*-curve is derived by probability theory. The formula for a *t*-curve includes a constant called **degrees of freedom (*df*)** that depends on the sample sizes, so you get a slightly different *t*-curve for each combination of sample sizes. This is all taken care of automatically by software. As sample sizes increase so does *df*, and then the *t*-curve comes closer to a normal curve. The graphs in Figure 15.5 show how the *t*-curve approaches the normal as *df* increases.

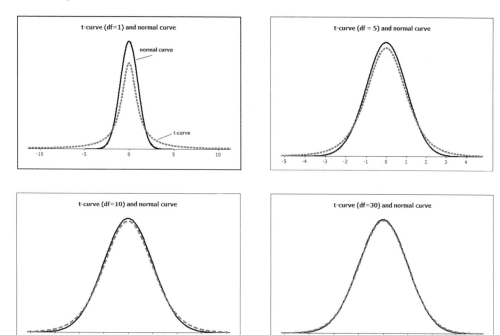

FIGURE 15.5 Comparison of t-curve and normal curve

Exercises for *t*-Test Calculations

It is easiest if you use an automatic calculator or computer software. If you decide to do a problem by hand then you will need to know the degrees of freedom for each exercise. You can use $df \approx n1 + n2 - 2$ as a reasonable approximation. Your software will have a more acurate value. For example, it will get $df = 29$ instead of 30 for Exercise 1 and 19 instead of 22 for Exercise 2.

1. Here are two sets of sample values. Make up a story that could have produced such data. Analyze the data by a *t*-test, giving the null hypothesis, and a conclusion.

Sample 1	Sample 2
79 79 76 80	82 72 85 79
65 69 76 64	81 73 93 80
76 79 72 67	74 75 69 74
70 74 75 66	75 74 88 76

2. Here are two sets of sample values. Make up a story that could have produced such data. Analyze the data by a *t*-test, giving the null hypothesis, and a conclusion.

Sample 1	Sample 2
141 150 179 132 126 176	132 163 176 139 156 146
95 164 153 150 165 131	134 153 152 122 147 123

Comparison of confidence intervals and hypothesis tests: inference based on comparing two sample means

Logic of confidence interval	Logic of hypothesis test
1. Collect the data.	1. As an opening hypothesis, assume for the sake of argument there is no difference. Hold to this hypothesis unless contrary evidence from the samples is strong enough to make its truth seem *very unlikely*.
2. Compute the difference, *d*, between the means of the samples.	2. Decide what "very unlikely" means. Commonly this is taken to mean that the probability is 5% or less, which corresponds to constructing a 95% confidence interval.
3. Attach a margin of error to *d* to get a confidence interval (usually a 95% confidence interval).	3. Collect the data and compute the difference, *d*, between the sample means.
4. If the confidence interval does not include zero, *d* is called statistically significant. The interval itself gives you a range of values that probably contain the true population difference. According to step 3, there is at most a 5% chance the interval does not include the true difference.	4. If *d* meets the requirements you set in step 2, it is called statistically significant. The *p*-value for *d* shows just how unlikely it is to have occurred if the original assumption were true. This implies that *p*-values less than 5% correspond to concluding that a difference is statistically significant.

A Chi-square Test to Compare Two Proportions

When you prepare to do a hypothesis test, it is important to identify the data you want to analyze as either numerical or categorical, because different tests apply. As we have seen, the *t*-test is used to compare the means of two sets of numerical data, such as test scores.

By contrast, the chi-square test is used when you are investigating the association between two **categorical variables**, where the responses are simply counted in various categories. Sometimes it is convenient to convert quantitative variables into categories. For instance, you can categorize heights into three groups (short, average, tall) or test scores into two groups (met the standards, did not meet the standards).

Because the calculations for the chi-square test are among the easier to grasp, we will show them in detail next. You may still prefer to have a machine do the calculations for you, but at least you'll have a good idea of what it is doing.

A table that shows the counts in the various categories is called a **contingency table**. Table 15.1 below is a 2×2 contingency table; each variable, gender and performance, has been split into two categories. The counts from the data in a study are called the *observed* values.

Let us assume that these data were collected from samples of boys and girls who represent larger populations. The question is: Does performance depend on gender, not just for these 120 people, but in general for the people they represent?

- *Data:*

TABLE 15.1 A 2×2 contingency table: gender versus performance

Observed values		Gender		
		Boys	Girls	Total
Performance	Passed	25	65	**90**
	Failed	15	15	**30**
	Total	**40**	**80**	**120**

- *Null hypothesis:* There is no statistical association between the two variables, gender and test performance. Performance does not depend on gender. Boys and girls do equally well. (Mathematically, this means the *proportion* who pass is the same in both groups.)
- *Alternative hypothesis:* Performance depends on gender. People of one gender are more likely to pass than the other. The proportions who pass differ according to gender.
- *Name of hypothesis test:* Chi-square test.
- *What does it do?* The chi-square test compares the four observed cell counts to four theoretical cell values that would be expected if girls and boys had the *same* pass rates. (That, after all, is what the null hypothesis states.)
- *Expected values:* What values can be placed in the four interior cells to show that boys and girls are exactly equally capable? *You must keep the same row and column totals. You still need 40 boys and 90 total passes, for example.* The numbers that are in the totals places are called *marginal* values. Chi-square tests assume that the marginal relationships are the same in the observed and expected tables.

Expected values		Gender		
		Boys	Girls	Total
Performance	Passed	30	60	**90**
	Failed	10	20	**30**
	Total	**40**	**80**	**120**

You find the expected values by first getting the overall pass rate in the observed table (90/120 = .75) and then imposing that rate on each gender group in the expected table. So 75% of 40 = 30, and 75% of 80 = 60.

Note 1: If you get decimal values for the expected cells, keep a reasonable amount of decimal places. The expected values do not need to be whole numbers.

Note 2: Notice that, as soon as you determine that the first interior cell value is 30, all the others are determined because of the totals in the margins. A 2×2 table is therefore said to have *1* degree of freedom, abbreviated as $df = 1$).

- *Compute the test statistic:* $\chi^2 = \text{sum of} \left(\dfrac{(\text{observed} - \text{expected})^2}{\text{expected}} \right) = \sum \dfrac{(O-E)^2}{E}$ over all four

interior cells, where the observed values are what you actually got in your study, and the expected values are what "should" have been there if ability is the same in both gender groups. Because this is a sum it does not matter what order you do the addition in.

$$\chi^2 = \frac{(25-30)^2}{30} + \frac{(65-60)^2}{60} + \frac{(15-10)^2}{10} + \frac{(15-20)^2}{20}$$

$$= \frac{25}{30} + \frac{25}{60} + \frac{25}{10} + \frac{25}{20} = 5.00$$

- *Find the p-value:* We refer to a chi-square probability table, graph, or calculator function for $df = 1$. For example, Excel gives chidist $(5,1) = .0253$. Figure 15.6 shows the graph of the chi-square function with the tail area beyond 5 equal to .0253.

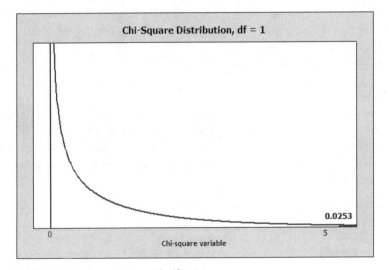

FIGURE 15.6 Graph of chi-square curve with $df = 1$

Therefore the test statistic is statistically significant. The *p*-value still represents a tail area, but this sampling distribution is not mound shaped. Because we will reject the null hypothesis only if the chi-square statistic is large, we consider only the right-hand tail area.

- *Conclusion:* Because the *p*-value is less than .05, we reject the null hypothesis. We have good evidence that boys and girls do *not* perform equally well. Girls perform better. In the study the pass rate for girls was $65/80 = 81.25\%$ and for boys $25/40 = 62.5\%$.

Degrees of Freedom for Contingency Tables

A contingency table may have any number of rows and columns. We saw that a 2×2 table has 1 degree of freedom. In general, a table with r rows and c columns has $df = (r-1)(c-1)$.

Confirm that $df = 2$ for this 2×3 table with given marginal totals by showing that you are free to put any reasonable numbers in the first two cells of row 1, but then all the rest are determined by the totals in the margins. Two of the six cells are "free."

	Democrat	Republican	Independent	Total
Male				80
Female				70
Total	50	60	40	150

Exercises for Chi-Square Hypothesis Test

1. After an action research intervention Pat compared her experimental and control groups. Her results are shown.

    a. Name the two variables and name the categories within the variables.
    b. What is the null hypothesis?
    c. Use a chi-square test to determine if her results are statistically significant.

		Variable 1	
		Experimental group	Control group
Variable 2	Scored at least 90% on test	12	8
	Scored less than 90% on test	6	10

2. Imagine that this is your data sheet from a study of students under stress:

Simulated data

ID	Sought advice	Gender		ID	Sought advice	Gender
1	Y	F		16	N	F
2	Y	F		17	N	F
3	Y	F		18	N	F
4	Y	F		19	N	F
5	Y	F		20	N	F
6	Y	F		21	N	F
7	Y	F		22	N	F
8	Y	F		23	N	M
9	Y	F		24	N	M
10	Y	M		25	N	M
11	Y	M		26	N	M
12	Y	M		27	N	M
13	Y	M		28	N	M
14	Y	M		29	N	M
15	Y	M		30	N	M

    a. Condense the data into a contingency table.
    b. Name the variables and name the categories within the variables.
    c. Does there seem to be a relationship between the two variables?
    d. Show one or more graphs or tables to support your impressions.
    e. Conduct a chi-square test and interpret the results.

3. Use the data in this excerpt of a review of a medical study to construct a contingency table for the data and compute the chi-square statistic. If possible, confirm the given *p*-value.

    MedPage Today Action Points
    Explain to interested patients that in this trial of symptomatic patients, endarterectomy was associated with a lower rate of procedural stroke, MI, or death than carotid artery stenting. Note that the choice of treatment—surgery or stenting—depends upon a number of factors that require individual assessment by a physician.

    Review
    In patients with symptomatic carotid stenosis, stenting was associated with a higher rate of stroke, death, or procedural myocardial infarction than endarterectomy, results of a randomized trial showed.

    In the 1,700-patient International Carotid Stenting Study (ICSS), the incidence of stroke, death, or procedural MI was 5.2% among patients randomized to endarterectomy versus 8.5% in the stenting group (44 versus 72 events $P=0.006$).

    (*Source:* Peggy Peck, Excess Stroke, MI, and Death Seen with Carotid Stenting, *Med-Page Today*, February 25, 2010, www.medpagetoday.com/Neurology/Strokes/18682)

4. Examine the relationship between writing effectiveness and number of books read per year. The data are for 8th graders in one state. What is going on? (*Source:* Vermont Department of Education, 1999 NSRE English Language Arts, Grade 8.)

No. of books read per year	Number of students (n)	Percentage who met or exceeded standards
0–5	1,270	42.4
6–10	1,256	58.0
11–15	1,042	66.1
16–20	1,024	67.9
21–25	852	71.2
>25	1,300	74.5
Total	6,744	

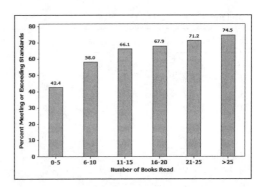

Recast the information into the contingency table below. Analyze the data by a chi-square test to confirm that there is a statistically significant association between number of books read and NSRE score.

What is the null hypothesis? The table of expected values should conform to the null hypothesis, but the marginal totals must be the same in both tables. *Hint:* If there were no association all the bars in the graph would be the same height.

Data Worksheet for Practising Hypothesis Tests

Imagine that this is your data sheet.

Observed values

No. of books read per year	Number of students who met or exceeded standards	Number of students who did not meet or exceed standards	Total
0–5			1,270
6–10			1,256
11–15			1,042
16–20			1,024
21–25			852
>25			1,300
Total	4,226	2,518	6,744

- What impressions do you have from looking at the data?
- Formulate some informal hypotheses and support them by offering statistics from these data.
- Show one or more graphs or tables to support your impressions.
- Conduct one or more hypothesis tests to see if any of the patterns you see are statistically significant.

Simulated data sheet 2

ID	Classroom	Gender	Pre-test score	Post-test score
1	1	F	10	20
2	1	F	9	18
3	1	F	11	22
4	1	F	10	20
5	1	F	9	18
6	1	F	11	22
7	1	F	10	20
8	1	F	9	18
9	1	F	11	22
10	1	M	5	10
11	1	M	6	12
12	1	M	4	8
13	1	M	5	10
14	1	M	6	12
15	1	M	4	8
16	2	F	10	27
17	2	F	9	26
18	2	F	11	28
19	2	F	10	27
20	2	F	9	26
21	2	F	11	28
22	2	F	10	27
23	2	M	5	25
24	2	M	6	26
25	2	M	4	24
26	2	M	5	25
27	2	M	6	26
28	2	M	4	24
29	2	M	5	25
30	2	M	5	26

16

REGRESSION

Introductory Investigation

Wealth and Achievement

What is the relationship between economic status and student achievement as shown in this scatter plot?

The data are for all public schools in New York State, 7th grade, 2009. Proficiency refers to achievement in English Language Arts (ELA). FRPL means free and reduced price lunch. Each dot represents one school.

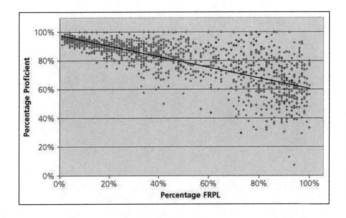

Source: Analysis by Uncommon Schools from New York State Department of Education data, reprinted with author's permission from *Teach Like a Champion*, published by Jossey-Bass Teacher, Doug Lemov, 2010, page 22.

Describe the general impression made by the graph. What does each dot represent? Be specific about what is being measured on each axis. Why are the dots all so close to the trend line on the left end but not on the right end?

Introduction to Regression Analysis

Cause and Effect

Things happen and we want to know why. Why do some kids do well in school and some do poorly? Why do some schools outperform others? If we knew we could take steps to fix the problem.

In some areas of research it is relatively straightforward to establish the cause of a particular phenomenon. Figure 16.1 shows the data from a physics experiment in which an investigator stretched a rubber band to a certain length and then recorded the resulting force on an attached gauge. The experiment was repeated five times at each distance. You can see that there was some variability in the resulting force at each distance, but it is still clear that greater stretching results in greater force. You can use this scatter plot to determine how far you need to stretch the band to achieve a desired force. For instance, if you want to produce a force of about 30 newtons you can tell that you need an elongation of about 18 centimeters.

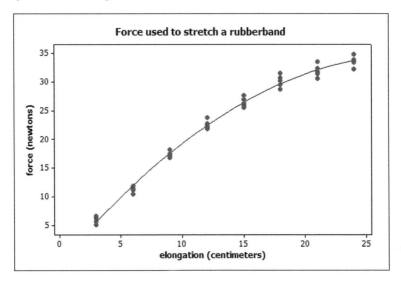

FIGURE 16.1   Physics experiment

Source: Chris R. Brown, Unpublished data, 2009.

There are some limits to our ability to get precisely the force we want. There is some vertical spread of the dots at each given elongation value. The physicist says there is some "noise" in the data, some random variation that is out of our control, but it is small and is likely not going to make any practical difference. It is reasonable to conclude that stretching the rubber band is the main factor in determining the force shown on the gauge.

(By the way, there is no evidence in this data for what would happen outside the elongation limits tested. It would be very risky to bet that the pattern will continue.)

But what a difference when we try to understand what determines student performance. Not only are there a great many conceivable influences on performance, but the children in a class are not nearly as alike as one rubber band is to another, and the measurement tool (typically a test) is not nearly as reliable as the force gauge. We are more likely to get results like the ones in Figure 16.2. In this study a teacher wanted to see if she could improve her students' ability to calculate with fractions if she increased the use of visual models. This scatter plot has considerably more noise than Figure 16.1. At every value on the horizontal axis there is a good bit of spread in the vertical scores. This scatter makes it harder to quantify the effect of the intervention. It may still seem reasonable to say that her intervention raised scores, but there is a whole lot of other stuff going on. There is much more noise in the system.

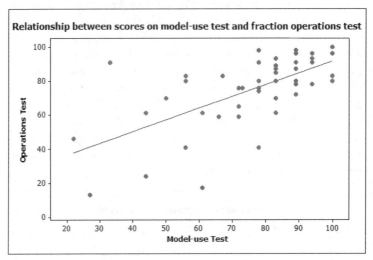

FIGURE 16.2   Classroom data from an action research study

Source: Melissa Rice, Unpublished paper, May 2009.

Generally speaking, in educational research, because it is so hard to nail down direct causes of outcomes, we first hope to discover and shed light on key variables that are associated with particular outcomes. We try to decide which of these variables have more influence than others. We talk about *association* rather than cause. We make statements such as "Parental level of education is strongly associated with success in school" or "Lifetime earnings are strongly associated with years of education."

An investigation that looks into the relationships among two or more variables is called a **correlational study**. *Such studies are never absolutely conclusive about cause*, but they are a necessary step towards understanding how one variable might influence another. Any outcome is subject to many influences, not all of which can be evaluated in any one study, and there will always be influences we remain unaware of.

One basic statistical approach for investigating relationships among variables is **regression analysis**. A regression analysis involves finding a suggestion of an underlying pattern in the data and measuring how well the data fit that pattern. In Figure 16.1 the pattern is slightly curved and it fits the dots very closely. In Figure 16.2, the pattern is a straight line and it does not fit the dots very closely. Identifying a pattern means finding a curve defined by a mathematical function that does a good job of coming close to the points. That function, or that curve, is called the **regression model** for the analysis. When the curve fits the dots very well we say that the model "explains" the relationship. Information about one of the variables translates well into information about the other. The stretch of the rubber band explains the force on the gauge.

Basics of Regression Analysis

In virtually every study, the researcher is first interested in some outcome variable, such as success in school, or good health, or profit. Then the researcher tries to see what "input" variables, or predictors, influence or account for the outcome. In short, she tries to identify predictors that are statistically significant. Finding a model that relates statistically significant predictor variables to an output is the purpose of regression analysis.

The simplest version of regression relates *one* input variable to *one* output variable by a *linear model*. Such an analysis is called **simple linear regression**, and the line that indicates the underlying pattern is called the **regression line** or **the line of best fit**. If you add more input variables, then the analysis is called *multiple* linear regression. You can construct more mathematically complex non-linear models, but in this text we'll concentrate on linear models to stress basic concepts.

Example of a Simple Linear Regression Analysis (One Predictor)

Refer to Figure 16.2. The researcher investigated the linear relationship between scores on a model-use test and scores on a test about numerical operations. She anticipated a positive relationship: higher scores on one should be associated in a consistent way with higher scores on the other. She was hoping to find evidence that moving children higher on the use of models would consequently move them up in operations skills.

The specific placement and slant of the line shown in Figure 16.2 were determined by a regression analysis algorithm carried out by computer software. The equation of the line is given in the output from that algorithm.

For the data in Figure 16.2 the computer output reads:

The regression equation is
Operations Score = 22.8 + 0.69 Model-use Score

This equation has the general form $y = b + mx$, so that it is straightforward to interpret the slope and intercept.

The positive slope, 0.69, and the intercept, 22.8, were determined by the computer algorithm. Those two numbers are the basic output of the regression algorithm. Together, they are called the **regression coefficients** for the model. No other combination of slope and intercept can do a better job of describing the underlying linear pattern in the scatter plot. The equation implies that *on average* an increase of 1 point on the model-use test is associated with an increase of about 0.69 points on the operations test. But keep in mind that because of all the noise in the scatter plot this average increase has a substantial margin of error and so it is not possible to state very precisely and with high confidence what would happen to a specific class or student if you could raise their mean score on the model-use test by a certain number of points.

The intercept of the line implies that zero on the model-use test is associated with about 23 points on the operations test, but this value likely has no useful meaning. (In the whole data set no one got a score at or near zero.)

Example of a Multiple Regression Analysis (Two Predictors)

Suppose you are looking into student performance on a certain standardized test given in 5th grade. You suspect that scores on this test (T) are predicted fairly well by a student's 4th grade math achievement score (M) and gender (G). M and G are therefore the predictor (or input) variables, and T is the outcome variable. You wish to determine a linear model (or equation) that relates T to M and G.

The general form of a linear model with two predictor variables is:

Outcome = $a + b$ (predictor 1) + c (predictor 2)

In this example we have:

$$T = a + bM + cG$$

As in the one-predictor case, we use a regression analysis computer program to find the specific values for the three regression coefficients, a, b, and c.

We demonstrate on a small data set how you might go about using technology to do the work:

1. You collect data from a sample of students for each of whom you already have all three numbers, M, G, and T. Maybe you get something like Table 16.1. *Note:* In this table we have used $G = 0$ to represent male and $G = 1$ to represent female. That is an arbitrary choice. Any two different numbers would work, but this choice allows for an easier interpretation of the regression statistics.

TABLE 16.1 Data for regression analysis

Child	M	G	T
A	65	0	344
B	75	1	394
C	62	0	346
D	74	1	385
E	61	0	352
F	74	1	389
G	42	0	280
H	68	0	366
I	46	0	294
J	23	1	226

Note: Male = 0, female = 1.

2. You process the data with regression analysis software. The program determines the particular function that does the best job of describing the underlying linear relationship between the predictors and the output variable.

Note: You still need to exercise judgment to decide if a linear model with a given set of predictors makes sense in the first place. The software is thoughtless and will crank away on any data set.

For the data in Table 16.1, regression software will give you the linear model:

$$T = 148 + 3.18\,M + 4.90\,G$$

These coefficients (148, 3.18, and 4.90) determine the particular linear model that fits the observed data best.

In summary, a linear regression analysis takes your data and produces a set of coefficients for an equation.

Interpreting the Model

1. *Interpreting the coefficients*

   From the form of the equation, $T = a + bM + cG$, you can see that a is like the y-intercept of a line, while b and c are like the slope.

   The regression calculations yielded $a = 148$, $b = 3.18$, and $c = 4.90$. The coefficient 3.18 implies that (on average) a 1-point increase on the 4th grade math achievement score is associated with about a 3-point increase on the 5th grade standardized test. Similarly, a 1-point increase in gender is associated with about a 5-point increase on the 5th grade standardized test. By the coding scheme in Table 16.1, a "1-point increase in gender" means being female rather than male. All else being equal, on average, girls score about 5 points more than boys.

   The 148 represents a baseline score where both M and G are zero. As in the case of any y-intercept, this number may or may not have a practical interpretation.

2. *Making predictions based on the model*

   To get a predicted score for a new student you substitute his or her math achievement score for M and gender code for G.

   For instance, this model says that, for a female student whose math score is 70, her score on the standardized test "should be" $T = 148 + 3.18(70) + 4.90(1) = 148 + 222.6 + 4.90 = 375.5$ or about 376. You can think of 376 as an estimate of the *average* score on the standardized test for all female students whose math score is 70.

   You should not assume that the predictions of this regression equation are extremely precise for any one student, largely because the regression equation has no way to account for influences other than gender and average 4th grade math score. A regression model cannot account for the influence of confounding variables that are not present in the list of predictors to begin with.

   The values that the regression analysis produces for a, b, and c are *statistics* because they are calculated from the data in the study. And, because they are statistics, we can think of them as estimates of a set of "true" coefficients. If we knew the true coefficients we could say exactly how T "really" depends on M and G. Because we have only limited data we can't do that, so the best course of action is to attach a margin of error to each of these estimates to establish confidence intervals for their true values.

Confidence Intervals, p-Values, and Statistical Significance for Regression Coefficients

Imagine that instead of 4.90 the true value of the coefficient for G, gender, is 0. Then, no matter what a student's gender, its contribution to the predicted 5th grade achievement score would be 0. The model would not make any distinction between male and female students. Gender would not be a factor in determining student performance on the 5th grade standardized test. Gender would not be statistically significant.

Because we are working with sample data we can never determine the true population value of any regression coefficient. We can't know for certain if the true value is zero. A good approach is to see if the confidence interval for the coefficient *includes* zero as a possible true value. If it does not, we can at least be confident that the predictor has *some* association with the outcome. This is useful information, because we are trying to identify variables that *may* affect the outcome.

If the confidence interval for a regression coefficient does *not* include zero, then the predictor is statistically significant. If the confidence interval for the 4th grade math coefficient is say 2 to 4, then 4th grade math score is a statistically significant predictor of performance on the 5th grade standardized test. We would decide that 4th grade math achievement matters, not just for these ten children but also for larger populations of similar students.

In every regression analysis there are buried hypothesis tests, where the null hypothesis for each regression coefficient is that its true value is zero. A *p*-value less than .05 for a regression coefficient says it is statistically significant.

Caution: You need to be particularly careful when you report the influence of a predictor in a regression analysis with more than one predictor, because the value of its coefficient was calculated when all the other predictors were also included in the model. For example, the value 3.18 we got for the influence of the 4th grade math score represents its influence *given that* we simultaneously evaluated the influence of gender. A report might say that the 4th grade test influences the results even after gender has been accounted for. If you did a different analysis, just using the single predictor 4th grade math scores – and omitted any information about gender – you would get a different value for the coefficient. It takes a good bit of practice with regression to build and interpret sensible models.

Example of Computer Output from a Regression Analysis with Two Predictors

The data for the ten children from Table 16.1 were submitted to the Excel regression algorithm. Table 16.2 shows the relevant part of the output. Note that the *t*-statistic is a standardized version of the original coefficient found by dividing the coefficient by its standard error.

TABLE 16.2 Output for linear regression of 5th grade standardized test scores against 4th grade math scores and gender

	Coefficients	Standard error	t-stat	p-value	Lower 95%	Upper 95%
Intercept	147.77	7.05	20.96	0.00	131.10	164.45
M	3.18	0.12	27.52	0.00	2.91	3.46
G	4.90	3.80	1.29	0.24	−4.09	13.89

We would conclude from this that the math test scores are statistically significant, but that gender is not. You can see this by looking at either the *p*-values or the 95% confidence intervals.

Historical note: The statistical use of the term "regression" was first used by the English scientist Sir Francis Galton around 1877. It was used to describe relationships between children and their parents. Galton found it remarkable that the children of exceptional individuals tend on average to be *less exceptional* than their parents and more like their more distant ancestors. Galton's method of analysis was made mathematically precise by his mathematician colleague Karl Pearson, who coined the phrase "multiple regression." Galton's first regression data were weights of "parent" and "child" sweet peas, but he later investigated human characteristics.

Exercises for Interpreting Regression Output

1. This analysis looks at the relationship between years of education and hourly wage among American adults. The data are from 1995. The data were collected for a national survey called the Current Population Survey (CPS). Several thousand people were asked their wage and their years of education. In developing this model we are considering only one input (years of education) and one output variable (hourly wage).

Computer output from regression program: linear regression of hourly wages against years of education

Wage	Coefficient	Standard error	t	p-value	95% confidence interval	
Educ	1.47	0.10	14.36	0.00	1.27	1.67
Cons	−4.96	1.40	−3.54	0.00	−7.70	−2.21

Source: Adapted from www.math.dartmouth.edu/~matc/eBookshelf/statistics/CPS/cps4.pdf.

Note: Outcome variable: hourly wage (Wage); Predictor variable: years of education (Educ); Intercept: constant (Cons).

a. Confirm that according to this output the regression model is: $y = -4.96 + 1.47x$ where x = years of education and y = hourly wage.

b. Is the predictor, years of education, statistically significant? How can you tell from the computer output?

c. What does the value 1.47 tell you?

d. Does the regression equation represent a linear function? Graph it. How will you label the two axes?

e. What does the value −4.96 tell you? Explain why it has no sensible interpretation in the context of this analysis.

f. What average hourly wage does the model predict for people with 12 years of education?

2. A regression analysis was done with data collected for the 50 US states (2007 school year). Two input variables were chosen: average annual teacher salary (both primary and secondary public schools); and average pupil/teacher ratio. The output variable was mean SAT score in mathematics.

Computer output from regression analysis

SAT	Coefficients	Standard error	95% CI
Constant	642.964	48.307	(545.836, 740.091)
Pupil/teacher ratio	0.227	2.083	(−3.961, 4.414)
Average salary	−0.002	0.001	(−0.004, −0.001)

a. Is this an illustration of simple or multiple linear regression? Why?

b. Is either one of the predictors statistically significant? How can you tell from the computer output?

c. Write the equation for the model determined by this analysis.

d. What average math score on the SAT does the model predict for students from states where the average teacher salary is $46,000 and the pupil/teacher ratio is 15?

e. What does the value 642.964 tell you?

f. What does the value −0.002 tell you? Does this value make sense to you?

g. Would you conclude from this analysis that you could raise SAT scores by cutting teacher salaries?

3. Here is a totally abstract regression analysis based on the six points shown:

	Coefficients	Standard error	Lower 95%	Upper 95%
Intercept	1.60	0.98	−1.12	4.32
X	1.10	0.22	0.49	1.72

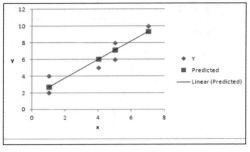

a. From the table write down the equation of the regression line.
b. Is the predictor, X, statistically significant? How can you tell from the computer output?
c. What does the value 1.10 tell you?
d. What does the value 1.60 tell you?
e. What value of Y does the model predict for $X = 7$?

4. Here are two scatter plots and the corresponding regression analysis results. Each dot represents one person.

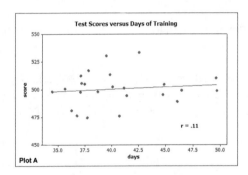

Plot A

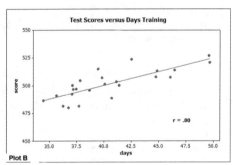

Plot B

Output A	Coefficients		95% confidence interval		Output B	Coefficients		95% confidence interval	
	B	Standard error	Lower bound	Upper bound		B	Standard error	Lower bound	Upper bound
Constant	484.648	29.905	422.628	546.667	Constant	402.648	16.079	369.304	435.993
Days	.394	.734	−1.128	1.915	Days	2.439	.395	1.621	3.257

a. In which plot would you expect the relationship between days spent training and test results to be statistically significant? Why?
b. How can you see in the output tables whether or not Days is a statistically significant predictor of test score?
c. Write out and compare the regression equations for both analyses. Explain the meaning of the slope and the intercept in each equation.

5. A regression line is shown in this scatter plot. The graph plots deaths from heart disease (in deaths per 100,000 people) against wine consumption (in liters of alcohol from wine per person per year) for 19 developed nations.

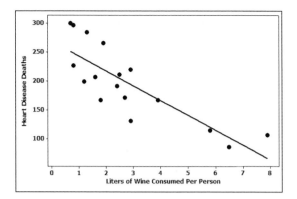

Source: Scatter plot adapted from Renze, John and Weisstein, Eric W. "Scatter Diagram." From *MathWorld*--A Wolfram Web Resource.
http://mathworld.wolfram.com/ScatterDiagram.html. The data are from Moore, D. S. and McCabe G. P. *Introduction to the Practice of Statistics*. New York: W. H. Freeman,1999.

a. By looking at the graph, estimate the slope of the line, and using the units given above explain what the slope tells you.

b. True or false? These data indicate that countries with greater per-capita wine consumption tend to have lower rates of heart disease.

c. True or false? These data indicate that drinking more wine lowers a person's risk of heart disease.

Evaluating a Regression Model: The R^2 Statistic

We have seen how to use a regression analysis to identify predictors that are statistically significant. In this context statistical significance means that the predictor has *some* association with the outcome. But a regression analysis can also tell us in an overall sense how well the model fits the data points or, in other words, how well the predictors account for the outcome. This evaluation is done by a statistic called the **coefficient of determination**, usually denoted as R^2.

R^2 can be defined for any linear model no matter how many predictors it has. But we give as a first example the simplest case of one predictor because it is easiest to draw.

Consider Table 16.3 and its scatter plot. Assume that X is the only predictor variable and Y is the outcome variable.

TABLE 16.3 Data for regression analysis

Person	X	Y
A	2	5
B	5	4
C	8	6
D	12	14
E	15	17

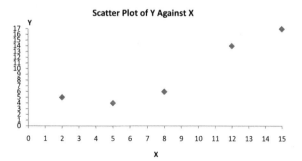

The results of a regression analysis for these data are shown in Table 16.4.

TABLE 16.4 Output of regression analysis

	Coefficients	Standard error	t-stat	p-value	Lower 95%	Upper 95%
Intercept	0.38	2.29	0.17	0.88	−6.89	7.66
X	1.05	0.24	4.41	0.02	0.29	1.81

This gives us the equation $y = 0.38 + 1.05x$ as the equation for the line that comes closest overall to the five dots. Let's see how that line looks (Table 16.5 and its scatter plot). We use the model to get the new "predicted" values of Y; then we draw that line.

TABLE 16.5 Regression data with predicted Y-values

Person	X	Y	Predicted Y
A	2	5	2.48
B	5	4	5.63
C	8	6	8.78
D	12	14	12.98
E	15	17	16.13
Mean	8.4	9.2	9.2
SD* (s)	5.22	5.89	5.49
var (s²)	27.30	34.69	30.14

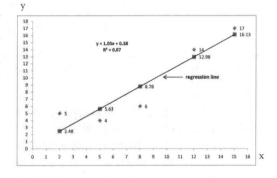

Note: * SD can be calculated with n or $n-1$. R^2 will be the same. The value shown here is based on $n-1$.

The diamonds indicate the original data points. The squares are the corresponding points on the regression line.

One way to measure how well the model fits the data is to compare the variability of the predicted y-values to the variability of the original y-values. The standard way to do this is to look at the ratio of their variances. The ratio of the variances is one way to define R^2.

$$R^2 = \frac{variance\ of\ predicted\ y\text{-}values}{variance\ of\ original\ y\text{-}values} = \frac{SD^2_{y\text{-}predicted}}{SD^2_{y\text{-}original}}$$

If the model fits perfectly then the predicted y-values will be the same as the original y-values, so they will have the same variance and the ratio will be 1. Otherwise the numerator will be smaller than the denominator and R^2 will be less than 1.

When the model does not fit the data perfectly, there is "extra" variability in the original y-values that is not in the variability of the predicted y-scores. We say that the linear relationship does not account for this extra variability. Something that we have not included in the model is making the points not fall on the line given by the model. The output, y, is not completely explained by the input, x.

For the data in Table 16.5 we get:

$$R^2 = \frac{5.49^2}{5.89^2} = \frac{30.14}{34.69} = 0.87$$

On the basis of R^2, we say that the predictor X accounts for 87% *of the variance* of Y. It is often disappointing in a regression study to find that, even though some predictors are statistically significant, the whole model accounts for only a very small fraction of the variance of the outcome variable. In short, real life is often more complex than the model that was chosen to describe it.

> This kind of statement – "Blah blah accounts for some percentage of the variance of bleh bleh" – is very common in the announcement of the results of correlational studies.

The R^2 statistic is used to evaluate the fit of many kinds of regression models, not just the simple linear model. It is the most common way of expressing how well a model accounts for the behavior of some outcome variable. The statistic $1-R^2$ gives the proportion of variance *not* accounted for by the model.

Exercises about Strength of Regression

1. The regression lines for these two scatter plots are almost identical. For which plot will R^2 be larger? Why?

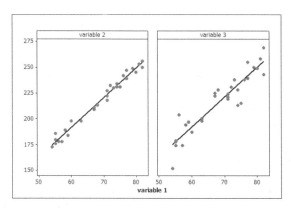

2. Here is computer output from a regression analysis that analyzed the relationship between education and income. Poke around in all those statistics and find what you need to determine the percentage of the variance in wages that is accounted for by years of education. What percentage of the variance in wages is *not* accounted for by years of education?

Linear regression of hourly wages against years of education

Number of obs = 1003
F(1, 1001) = 206.20
Prob > F = 0.0000

Source	SS	df	MS	
Model	14666.8401	1	14666.8401	R-squared = 0.1708
Residual	71201.2121	1001	71.130082	Adj R-squared = 0.1700
Total	85868.0522	1002	85.6966589	Root MSE = 8.4339

Wage	Coefficient	Standard error	t	P>|t|	95% confidence interval	
Educ	1.466404	.1021203	14.360	0.000	1.26601	1.666799
Cons	−4.956578	1.399311	−3.542	0.000	−7.702497	−2.210659

Source: www.math.dartmouth.edu/~matc/eBookshelf/statistics/CPS/cps4.pdf.

Note: Outcome variable: hourly wage (Wage); Predictor variable: years of education (Educ); Intercept: constant (Cons).

3. In this study, the authors used 13 predictor variables! With all of them in the model, the model yielded $R^2 = .607$. Read the abstract and determine how much of the variance in contributions was accounted for by just the one predictor, attendance at home football games.

This study created a model to predict annual fund raising contributions to NCAA Division I-A athletic programs using 13 explanatory variables, re-examining an area of the literature unstudied in two decades. A statistically significant model was developed, explaining 60.7% of the variance in contributions. Football home attendance ($r = .721$) and conference affiliation ($r = -.621$) were identified as the variables most closely related to annual athletic contributions.

(*Source:* Chad McEvoy, Abstract: Predicting Fund Raising Revenues in NCAA Division I-A Intercollegiate Athletics, *Sport Journal*, 2005, 8 [1])

Comment: Note that the sum of the two values of R^2 for attendance and conference affiliation is more than .607, which was the percentage of variation accounted for by all 13 predictors. This implies that these two predictors are not acting independently. The problem of untangling the influences of several predictors is one of the main concerns of multiple regression.

4. Based on this report, how well does number of fires "explain" temperature change? How can you tell there are other influences besides number of fires?

Global warming may be largely to blame for the increasingly destructive wildfires in the Western United States in the last two decades, new research suggests.

Longer and fiercer wildfire seasons since 1986 are closely associated with warmer summer temperatures, earlier arrival of spring, and earlier snowmelts in the West, scientists reported yesterday in the online edition of the journal Science.

. . .

Scientists had previously believed that increased wildfire activity resulted from changes in land use practices. In particular, tactics to suppress fires had allowed dead and dry vegetation to build up in Western forests, providing more fuel for fires.

But the new study shows that most of the increase in wildfires has occurred in the Northern Rocky Mountains, where few land-use changes have occurred. Also, the scientists found that 66 percent of the yearly variation in forest fires could be explained by temperature changes alone, with hotter years producing more fires.

(*Source:* Naila Moreira, Study Links Increase in Wildfires to Global Warming, *Boston Globe*, July 7, 2006)

5. For these data the line of best fit is given by $y = 8.09 + 2.36x$.

Person	x	y
A	3	20
B	8	25
C	2	15
D	9	30
E	0	0
F	−4	1
Mean	3	15.2
SD	4.5	11.3

a.   Use the formula slope $= r\dfrac{SD_y}{SD_x}$ to determine the correlation coefficient, r.

b.   What percentage of y's variance is determined by x?

6.   Here is another reference to variance accounted for in a medical article about Alzheimer's disease. What were the predictor variables? What were the dependent variables that the model was trying to predict? Why would Dr. Irizarry say the plasma markers were not "sufficiently predictive"?

"These plasma markers contributed about five per cent to 12 per cent of the variance accounted for on the Blessed Dementia Scale and Activities of Daily Living Scale," the investigators report.

   Dr. Irizarry, now at GlaxoSmithKline Research and Development, Research Triangle Park, North Carolina, said: "The individual blood tests are not sufficiently predictive to be useful clinically, and the findings require further careful validation. However, the study supports incorporating blood tests with cerebrospinal, genetic, imaging, and neuropsychological measures to develop biomarker profiles that could predict clinical course and responses to treatments."

(*Source:* http://www.medicexchange.com/Neuro/news.
aspx/14353/Plasma-amyloid-beta-protein--CRP-influence-Alzheimer-s-progression)

Regression Analysis and "Value-Added" Evaluation of Schools and Teachers

Most systems for determining the contribution of a school or teacher to student achievement depend at some point on a multiple regression model. These models are more complex than any we have illustrated in this book. In particular, they have many more input variables, and the models are not necessarily linear in structure.

   Here, for example, is a model used by the Chicago schools to determine the impact of a particular *school* on student test scores. The formula is very scary looking, but you can probably see that it has the basic format of the multiple regression models we have already examined: a function of input variables is used to predict an outcome variable.

$$y_{1i} = \lambda y_{0i} + \beta X_i + \alpha S_i + \varepsilon_i$$

where Posttest is y_{1i}, Pretest is y_{0i}, School Effects = Value Added by School is αS_i, Student Characteristics is βX_i, and Unobserved Factors is ε_i.

The capital letter S in this style of notation represents a whole set of schools. The output of the analysis includes a corresponding set of regression coefficients for the schools. Each school will get its own value, which represents the influence of that school on student test grades.

   As a second example, the District of Columbia uses the next model for the value added by a *teacher*. Here the letter T represents the whole set of teachers. The regression analysis will determine a regression coefficient for each teacher.

$$Y_{ig} = \lambda_{2g} Y_{i(g-1)} + \omega_{2g} Z_{i(g-1)} + \alpha'_2 \mathbf{X}_i + \eta' \mathbf{T}_{ig} + \varepsilon_{2ig}$$

where the labeled terms are: Post test (Y_{ig}), Pre test ($Y_{i(g-1)}$), Pre test in another subject ($Z_{i(g-1)}$), Student Characteristics ($\mathbf{X}_i$), Teacher Effects = Value Added by Teacher ($\mathbf{T}_{ig}$), and Unobserved Factors (ε_{2ig}).

The issues of statistical significance and goodness of fit of the model in these complex models are the same as in the simpler cases we have seen:

- Is the model measuring "the right stuff"? Have you left out important influences on student achievement? Constructing the model takes careful deliberation.
- Does statistical significance represent educational importance?
- How much confidence can you have in the precision of any estimates based on these models? They all have associated margins of error.
- Most importantly, what will you do with the results of the analysis? What role should these statistical calculations play in educational policy in the first place?

Here is one take on the situation as given by LynNell Hancock in a comprehensive piece about value-added testing:

> But here is perhaps the most telling observation: nearly every economist who weighed in agreed that districts should not use these indicators to make high-stakes decisions, like whether to fire teachers or add bonuses to paychecks. The numbers, they said, can't carry that kind of weight. By last summer, it should be noted, Michelle Rhee had already fired twenty-six DC teachers based in large part on low value-added scores. And New York City wants principals to use them immediately for tenure decisions.
>
> (*Source*: L. Hancock, Tested: Covering Schools in the Age of Micro-Measurements, Columbia Journalism Review, March/April 2011)

APPENDIX

TABLE A.1 Cumulative normal distribution (percentile ranks)

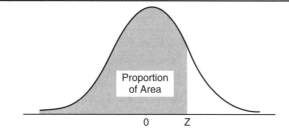

Proportion of Area

z	Area	z	Area
0	0.500	1.5	0.933
0.1	0.540	1.6	0.945
0.2	0.579	1.645	0.950
0.3	0.618	1.7	0.955
0.4	0.655	1.8	0.964
0.5	0.691	1.9	0.971
0.524	0.700	1.96	0.975
0.6	0.726	2.0	0.977
0.674	0.750	2.1	0.982
0.7	0.758	2.2	0.986
0.8	0.788	2.3	0.989
0.842	0.800	2.33	0.990
0.9	0.816	2.4	0.992
1.0	0.841	2.5	0.994
1.02	0.846	2.6	0.995
1.036	0.850	2.7	0.997
1.1	0.864	2.8	0.997
1.2	0.885	2.9	0.998
1.28	0.900	3.0	0.999
1.3	0.903		
1.4	0.919		

TABLE A.2 Multiplier for 95% confidence interval: t-statistic

n	Multiplier
2	12.7
3	4.3
4	3.2
5	2.8
6	2.6
7	2.4
8	2.4
9	2.3
10	2.3
11	2.2
12	2.2
13	2.2
14	2.2
15	2.1
16	2.1
17	2.1
18	2.1
19	2.1
20	2.1
21	2.1
22	2.1
23	2.1
24	2.1
25	2.1
26	2.1
27	2.1
28	2.1
29	2.0
30	2.0

TABLE A.3 Data for "yes or no" worksheet

Population X

66	54	52	76	70	59	70	64	60	53	62	33	77
71	72	69	61	54	75	44	54	41	85	57	76	74
68	48	55	53	70	64	67	67	56	54	72	64	49
70	50	58	53	75	48	47	70	65	43	70	66	66
47	76	57	49	56	56	85	58	60	53	46	57	62
74	54	62	51	66	63	55	76	60	62	70	51	64
65	49	54	63	58	80	58	63	65	45	63	60	73
80	81	65	59	70	62	55	58	82	92	65	65	59
53	76	61	55	64	70	62	65	57	59	63	60	64
65	65	72	69	62	47	60	54	56	73	56	71	57
46	36	67	56	60	64	59	54	70	53	59	57	66
38	76	60	71	49	61	58	53	76	58	58	80	67
62	56	41	60	61	63	67	44	60	58	51	60	47
71	53	51	82	65	52	59	57	53	44	65	75	60
50	63	54	54	67	54	64	57	61	74	56	61	53
59	66	46	62	59	63	48	69	58	64	70	69	74
49	56	72	64	54	70	71	56	66	61	77	39	62
45	70	75	63	70	76	75	75	58	64	65	51	65
47	66	52	52	54	54	69	72	58	70	45	58	56
71	68	52	59	61	49	72	40	63	52	58	64	51
59	52	61	58	82	65	55	60	72	38	69	55	58
56	48	75	49	34	48	71	54	66	53	53	58	48
64	62	82	78	72	66	51	51	76	69	55	55	65
50	58	68	61	52	60	20	56	62	55	62	64	32
57	52	75	49	68	52	60	46	51	55	65	39	42
47	58	68	48	61	59	55	61	52	67	74	62	71
74	50	71	67	46	60	54	74	47	71	63	43	69
58	63	51	50	79	81	73	63	50	59	56	48	68
64	42	38	84	63	54	52	50	64	79	57	70	57
51	55	47	48	54	48	65	63	57	61	48	69	46
49	57	51	56	40	54	44	50	65	67	67	64	68
56	75	54	62	56	59	63	61	68	57	59	69	57
71	61	46	56	52	68	61	66	69	64	58	65	60
61	59	51	50	57	71	55	83	75	65	69	66	64
68	55	60	64	63	50	67	55	59	61	69	51	62
69	49	68	61	58	52	63	63	37	36	76	42	47
69	65	62	57	66	66	71	60	79	56	58	53	73
53	65	43	57	57	56	58	72	63	49	79	70	45
54	57	49	55	46	66	64	64	71	76	74	80	51
59	57	66	53	68	56	68	64	31	60	55	51	70
72	47	53	43	62	58	66	70	56	59	45	56	60
43	57	55	63	62	57	51	61	68	66	46	66	59
64	73	61	66	64	59	73	72	58	36	60	58	44
66	74	58	75	42	62	53	71	57	64	43	59	45
55	59	45	46	66	53	61	57	62	62	44	58	65
76	39	67	59	67	56	63	68	50	55	58	60	58
40	57	51	42	47	59	59	74	60	67	68	65	63
54	59	68	64	56	45	46	64	50	71	61	53	56
69	63	35	81	56	52	91	56	57	61	70	63	54
62	68	70	56	56	52	57	53	62	51	65	47	57
43	66	58	54	60	54	66	58	55	76	53	67	66

56	45	52	61	70	46	60	70	58	44	53	53	71
60	55	65	59	65	65	59	71	62	69	63	63	58
61	44	72	58	57	54	59	57	57	68	57	70	74
58	41	60	29	63	49	73	66	58	64	65	58	72
57	50	61	58	61	47	55	67	71	57	82	73	69
78	63	58	62	37	43	55	38	72	60	36	55	60
60	70	75	61	59	72	61	54	58	71	44	59	72
66	49	66	66	67	61	54	43	66	79	54	70	60
50	69	68	69	75	52	78	73	83	42	67	55	54
36	72	53	53	44	68	49	48	45	61	62	72	46
68	59	61	46	64	74	53	71	37	79	81	66	53
49	47	63	67	69	74	62	47	68	70	65	58	51
55	63	62	67	63	47	68	58	69	59	68	62	54
66	60	61	56	44	64	60	78	62	58	61	60	59
62	66	41	47	56	63	61	44	71	62	68	60	55
86	65	53	59	39	48	49	58	73	59	60	66	68
59	63	76	49	31	68	75	63	45	48	46	69	38
57	46	56	70	77	62	50	60	69	58	79	63	83
48	48	72	62	59	56	53	38	70	59	44	47	63
43	63	52	32	65	68	60	53	63	63	67	56	53
62	52	56	68	59	74	48	59	61	64	61	63	53
65	72	48	61	62	54	55	50	57	62	63	51	71
79	64	69	78	41	73	64	63	67	62	50	69	57
53	58	53	70	77	41	66	60	58	48	58	46	70
72	56	64	72	64	61	50	71	53	57	42	69	54
64	65	69	40	53	56	54	56	57	67	65	55	

Population Y

57	82	81	70	64	81	82	59	76	65	66	72	60
77	59	66	55	80	77	57	71	61	81	70	54	86
53	51	58	80	78	75	69	74	57	55	58	58	54
60	78	77	64	51	78	72	61	75	65	72	57	68
69	62	63	68	65	62	62	62	82	53	73	69	72
74	82	82	77	73	80	70	74	63	68	71	65	51
65	58	74	71	71	74	76	63	67	74	74	56	67
63	40	39	76	66	57	57	61	57	64	58	64	85
57	61	70	55	75	71	66	59	61	87	60	53	75
53	68	75	58	58	55	73	60	75	78	66	52	73
68	61	70	85	76	61	74	70	89	56	62	50	66
45	61	67	67	66	46	76	61	73	66	48	61	60
78	65	68	63	68	67	58	63	60	72	51	59	63
66	56	57	69	49	56	61	65	68	74	71	65	64
73	60	70	60	59	69	59	53	66	48	63	79	51
74	62	76	41	56	50	64	66	82	68	63	31	82
54	95	54	77	62	59	59	62	75	64	70	81	67
55	81	80	59	57	70	69	71	72	68	60	57	65
66	84	68	37	65	71	54	90	62	65	71	68	80
69	64	70	69	69	43	72	81	54	64	61	68	77
68	62	70	51	80	80	55	64	52	67	68	66	74
60	64	65	81	51	65	55	68	55	45	75	68	70
65	60	45	66	66	60	65	71	57	73	66	65	44
73	69	59	72	71	76	62	57	56	66	61	65	70
63	59	85	68	51	47	59	52	60	67	67	63	64
62	68	73	68	69	49	74	69	75	72	68	71	84

52	45	68	85	71	75	58	71	76	66	56	59	82
62	67	58	70	48	65	58	73	69	80	66	64	59
72	67	62	77	56	51	61	56	71	53	70	66	67
87	60	68	65	87	57	66	59	46	56	70	62	54
51	67	64	70	53	75	50	79	60	60	55	65	70
60	64	62	58	67	58	57	63	68	58	63	66	50
43	55	72	52	74	70	64	55	78	54	67	63	53
84	49	80	59	77	65	77	66	61	56	63	58	65
59	50	50	80	66	78	76	77	61	68	64	68	40
61	66	63	74	59	52	64	77	63	62	62	52	65
60	76	76	71	64	61	67	68	74	58	59	71	59
68	65	54	73	63	64	43	59	70	57	67	57	67
65	86	79	69	62	66	50	77	70	61	65	74	77
77	75	73	65	62	53	77	46	67	60	62	76	95
77	48	57	76	50	67	40	65	71	68	66	72	65
65	55	84	75	71	74	39	57	62	52	77	81	61
64	55	73	71	84	62	59	47	73	70	75	61	37
55	57	58	55	71	71	59	55	88	72	56	69	83
69	63	62	67	61	61	59	73	68	58	42	66	57
62	60	73	51	53	66	67	72	70	64	68	64	55
68	70	70	57	62	62	67	74	72	57	65	52	61
76	60	62	75	51	73	72	49	78	49	58	56	81
79	58	64	65	51	66	67	61	82	55	72	65	52
59	59	84	55	93	61	71	59	50	50	73	51	49
63	56	73	78	58	79	55	80	74	70	53	47	70
68	71	63	69	69	71	56	54	57	73	79	51	59
57	48	62	69	50	65	60	69	62	57	56	60	65
71	53	75	54	72	76	68	67	68	64	61	78	57
71	60	69	65	63	50	55	63	58	68	65	72	64
57	68	61	43	56	61	84	67	54	66	85	73	79
44	71	54	48	60	51	72	79	57	57	68	55	56
57	78	56	49	65	54	63	65	66	49	58	57	51
61	69	63	64	52	59	57	61	60	50	76	80	48
66	75	71	76	72	57	90	64	60	63	65	68	64
54	71	53	74	67	68	61	60	53	62	57	79	79
76	61	83	67	56	58	50	58	63	67	73	74	73
76	73	82	52	52	63	47	68	62	60	69	73	56
82	58	66	49	60	74	64	62	75	47	60	52	62
69	53	59	68	69	61	60	58	61	70	71	60	69
68	75	69	68	63	59	64	65	73	72	54	77	97
70	65	69	65	69	54	70	61	71	61	79	42	65
73	55	68	67	65	68	65	80	64	65	58	65	60
57	69	73	67	73	61	59	48	52	74	74	65	49
50	69	64	71	64	68	59	80	65	76	81	72	59
74	76	60	62	66	87	65	79	77	46	60	39	58
61	66	65	50	73	63	75	63	78	73	68	54	68
58	73	95	70	87	47	54	67	63	75	64	56	71
63	72	55	83	68	69	50	68	72	72	58	82	62
76	72	75	89	60	75	83	71	72	63	62	61	68
60	49	74	59	51	67	62	52	84	73	50	61	63
74	49	68	62	72	37	59	86	77	72	65	70	

TABLE A.4 200 instances of 16 coin tosses

1	H T H H H T T T H H H H T T H T
2	H H H T H T H T T H T H H T H T
3	T H H H H T T H H H T T H T T H
4	H H H T T H H T T T T T H T H H
5	H T T T H T H T T H H H H T T T
6	H T T H T T T T H H T H T T H
7	H H T T H H H H H T H T T T H H
8	T T T T H T H H T H T H T H T T
9	T H H H H H T H T T H H T H T H
10	T T T T H T H H H T H T H T H T
11	T H H H H H T H H T H T T H T T
12	H H H H H H T T T H T H H H T H
13	T T H T T H T H T H H H T T T T
14	T H H H H T H T H H T T T H H T
15	T T H T T T T H H H H T T T H
16	H H H T T T H H H H T H T T T H
17	T H H T H H H T H H T H T T H T
18	H H H H T T H H T H T T T T T T
19	T H H T T H T T T H T H H H H H
20	T H T H H H H H T H T T H T H H
21	H H T H T H H H T T T H H T H H
22	T H H H H H H H T T H H T H T T
23	H T T H T T H H T T H H T H H T
24	T T H T T H T T T H T H T T T T
25	H T T H H T H T H H T T T H H T
26	T T H H T T H H H H H T T T H H
27	H T T T T H T T T T H T H H T T
28	T T H H H H H H H T H T H H T H
29	H T T H T T T T T T H T T T H T
30	H T H T T H T T T T H T H H H H
31	T T H T H T H H H T T T T T T T
32	T H H T H H H H H H H T H H H H H
33	H T T T T T H T H T T H H H H H
34	T H T T H H H H T H H H T T H T
35	T H H T H T H H T T T H T H H
36	H H H H H H H T T T T H H T T H
37	H H T H T H T T H T T T T H T T
38	T H H T T H T H T H T H T T T T
39	T T H H T H T T T H T H T H H T
40	H H H T H H H H H T H H H H T H
41	H H H H T H T T H H T T H T T T
42	T T H T T T T T H H H T T T H H
43	H H H H H H H H T H H T H H H T
44	H T T T H T H H T T H H H H T H
45	T T H H T H T T H T H H T T T T
46	H T T H T T H T H H H T H H T T
47	H T H H H T H H H T H H H T H T
48	H T H H H H T T H H T H H T T H
49	H H T T H T H T H T T T H T T T
50	H H T H T T T H T T T T T T H T
51	H H T H H T T T H T H T T H H H T
52	T H H T T H T H H T T T H T H H
53	H T T H T T T H H T T H H H H T
54	H H T T H T H T T T T T H T H H H
55	T T T H T T H T H T H T H T T H T H
56	H H T H H T H H H H H T T T H H
57	H H H H T H H H H T T H H H H T
58	T T T H H T T H T H T T H H H H
59	T T H H H H H T H T H H H H H H
60	H T H T H H H H H H T T H T H T
61	H H T T T T H H H H T T T H T T
62	H H H T H H H H H H T T T H T H T
63	H T T T H T T H T T T T H H T T
64	T T H H H T T H H H H T T H H H T
65	T H H T T T T T H H T T H H H H T
66	T T T T T H H T H H T T T T H
67	T T T T H T T T T H T H H H T H T
68	H H H H T T T T T H H H H T T T T
69	H T H T H H T T T H H T T T H T
70	T H T H T H H T H H T H T H T H
71	H T H T H H T H T T H T T T T H H
72	T T H H H H T H T H T H T H T T T T
73	H H T H H T T H H T T T H H H T
74	T T H T T T H T H H H H T H T T H
75	T H H H H H T H H H H T H H T T H
76	T H H H H T H H H H T H H H H T T
77	H T T T H T H H T T T T T T T T
78	T T T T H H H T H H H H T T H H H
79	H T T T H T H H T T H T H T T T T
80	T H H H T T H T H T T T T T T T T
81	T H T H T H H H H T H T T T H T
82	H T T T T T H T T H T H T T T T H
83	T H T T H H H T H T T H T T T T T
84	T T H T H T T H H T T T H H H H T
85	T T H T H H T T T T T H T H H H
86	T H T T H H H H H H T T T T T H H
87	T T T T H H T H H T T H T T T T
88	H H T H H T H T T T H H H H H T
89	T T T T T T T H H H H T H T H
90	T T T T T H T H H H T H H T H H H
91	T H T T T T H T T H T H H H H H
92	H H H T H H T T T H H H H H H T T
93	H T T H T H T H T T H H H H H H
94	T T H H T H H T T H H H T H T H
95	H T H T T H T H T H T H T H H T H
96	T T T H H H T H T T T H H T T H
97	T T H T H H T T H T H T H T T H H T
98	T T H T T T H H H T T T T T H H
99	H T T T T H T H H H H H H T T H T
100	H T H H H H T H H H H T T T H H
101	H T H T H T H H T T T H T H T T
102	H H T T T T T T T H H H T T H H
103	H T H H T H H H T H H H H T H H T
104	H H H H H H T H H H T T T H H H
105	H H H H H H H H H H T H H T T H H
106	T T H H H T H H H T T T T T H T

107 T H H H T H H H T H H T T H T H	154 T T T T H T H T T T H T T T H
108 T T T H H H T H T T T H T H H	155 T T H T T H T T H H H H H H T H
109 H H T T H H T H T H T T T H T T	156 H H T H H T T H H H T H T T H H
110 T T T H H T T H T T T H H H T H T	157 H T H H T H T H T H T H T H H T
111 T T H H H H H H H H H T T H T T H	158 H H H H H H T H H T H H H T T T
112 T T T H T T H H H H T H H T H T	159 H H H H T H T H T H T T H H T
113 H H T T T T T T H T H T H T T T H	160 H H T H T T H H H H T H H H T T
114 T T H T T T H H T H H T T H H T	161 H H H T T H H T T H T H T T T T
115 H T H H H T T T T T H T T T H H	162 H T H T T H H T T H T H H H H T
116 T T H T T H T T T H H T T T T T	163 T H H H H H T T H T H T H H H T T H
117 H H H H T T T H T T T H H H T H T	164 H T H H H H T H T H H H H H T T H
118 H H H H H T T H T T T T T T H T T	165 H T H H H H T H T H H H H H T T T
119 T H T T H T T H T H H H T H H T T	166 T H T H T H H H H T H T T T H T
120 T T H T T H T T H I I I I H H H T H	167 T H H T H H T T T T T T T T H T
121 T H T H H H T H T T H T H H H T H	168 H T H H H T T H H T T T T H T T
122 H H H H H H T H H T H H H H H H	169 H T H H T H T H H H H T T H T T T
123 T H H H H H H T T H H H H T H H T	170 T H T T H T H T T T H T T T T H
124 H T T T T H H T H H H H H H H T T	171 H H T T H T H H H H T T H T H H H
125 T H T H T T H H T T H T T T T H T	172 H T H T H T T T H T H H T T H T
126 H T T T T H T T H T T H H H T T	173 T H H T H H H T H H T H T H T H
127 H T H T H H T T H H T H T H T T T	174 T T T H T T T T T H H T H H H H
128 T H H T H H T T T T H T H T H T	175 H H H T H T T T T T T H H H H H
129 H T H H T T T H T T T H H H T T	176 H H T T T H H H T H H H H H H T H
130 T T T H H H H H T T T H H H T T	177 H T H T H H H H H H H H H H T H H
131 H T H H H H T H H T T T H H T T	178 T T T T H H T H T H H H H T T T T
132 H T H T H T T H H T T H T H H T	179 T T H H T H T H T H T T H H H H T
133 H T H H H T T T H T T H T H H H	180 H T T T H T T T H H T H H H H T H
134 H T H H T T T H T T T T T H H T	181 H H T H T H H T H T T H T T H H
135 H T T T H H T T T H H T H H T T	182 H H H H H H H T H T T T H T T H
136 H T T H T H T H H T T T H H H T	183 H H H T T T T T T H H T T H T T
137 H H H H T T T T H T H T H H T T H T	184 H H H H T T H H T T T T H H T T
138 T T T T H T H H H H H H H T H H	185 H T T H H H T T T H H H H H T T H
139 H T T H H H H T T H H T H T H T	186 T H H H T H H T H H T H H H H T T
140 T H T H H T T H H H H T H H H T T	187 H H T H H H T H T H T H T H H T H H
141 T T T H T T T T H H H T T H H T	188 T T H H T T H T T T T T H H T H
142 H T T H T T H H H H T H T T T T H	189 H H T H T H T T T T T T H H T T
143 H T H T H H H H H H H H H T H H H	190 H T H H T T H T H T H T H H T T T
144 H T T H H T T T H T T H H H H H	191 H H H H T T H H T H T H H T H H H H
145 T H T T T T H H T H H T T T T H	192 T H H T T H H T H H T H T H T T
146 T H H T H T T H H T H H H H H H	193 T T H T T H T H H T T T T T H T
147 T T T H T H H H T H T H H H T H T	194 H H H H T T T T T H T T T H T H
148 T T T T T H T T H T H T T H H H	195 H H T T T H H H T H T T H H T H
149 H H T H T T T H T T H T T T T H	196 H T T T T H H H H T H H T H T H
150 H T T T H H H T H T T T H H T H	197 H H T T T H T H H H H H H H T H H
151 T H H T T T T H H H H H H T T T	198 T H T H H H H T H T H H H H T T H T
152 T H T T T H T T H H T H H H T H H	199 T T T T H T H T H T T H T T H T
153 T H H T T H T H H T T H H H H T	200 H T T H T H H H T H T T H H T H T

Note: H = heads and T = tails.

INDEX